A PASTOR'S STORY

A PASTOR'S STORY

Where Does This Find You?

Pastor Dave

Library of Congress Control Number: 2016901154

(Softcover): 978-1-970617-28-3

(eBook): 978-1-970617-29-0

Dear Readers,

This book was written as God inspired me. It elated and thrilled my heart the way the Holy Ghost gave me the words and message to write. However, this book is not, nor should it ever be, taken as the Word of God, for you see, there is only one true Word of God.

The Holy Bible . . . It is the only book that was blessed and inspired by God to contain His Holy Word because the Bible was written by holy men, as God led them. It is the living Word of God and will stand throughout the ages of time. God will take care and protect His Word. Man should hold the will and Word in the highest regards, for in the Word of God, we find man's only means of salvation. AMEN.

This book was written by man, one who through the preaching of God's Word was called to CHRIST by the Holy Spirit, one who has been saved by the blood of JESUS CHRIST our Lord, a born-again Christian and child of God. But still just a man and must be taken as such, a mere man who loves God and is trying to live by His Word through the guidance of the Holy Ghost.

This book's intention is not to add to or take away from the Holy Word of God. It is not the purpose of this book to deceive or lead astray, nor do I want this book to cause any hard feelings or resentment toward myself or those mentioned herein. My only intention is to teach you and show you the will and ways of Almighty God. I will try to do this by the blessed Word, through and by the inspiration of the Holy Spirit. Jesus loves you. He died for you and now calls you to repentance!

Should you be offended or disagree with words of teaching in his book, please take it to the Lord in prayer, for I love you and want you to become a child of God. I would never want to hurt anyone, but by faith, I am steadfast. I stand strong on the words and promises of the Almighty God, for in them lies the redemption of mankind. I do hope that while you read this book, you receive a blessing from God and/or a call unto salvation from the Lord Jesus Christ, our Savior, for it is He who was sent from God the Father, His only begotten Son. It is He who shed His blood on Mt. Calvary so that through Him, we might be saved. It was by His inspiration and guidance that I was led to write this book. Praise be to God!

In this book, I will tell you different parts of my life. I will tell you the time before I met Christ and after I met and accepted Christ as my personal Savior. In this book, I will mention people and events that I encountered while serving the Lord. I will touch strongly on the Word of God, using it to tell you of the gospel of Christ, for this is the foundation of our salvation. I will try to do so as I am led by the Holy Spirit, for He leads and inspires me and all mankind of the ways of our Lord. So, as you read, keep an open mind. Let your heart also be open to the warm, soft touch of God's hand. For in His hands is found sweet peace for your soul. Amen.

Keep this in mind: schools and colleges were made by man and for man so you and I can learn of man's knowledge. This is very important for our life here on earth, even though it is a short life. Do not get me wrong. By no means am I knocking anyone getting a good education. I got my bachelor's degree in Divinity and Bible Studies. I also completed a two-year doctrinal study. A good education is very important. It is the only means we can prepare ourselves and better ourselves for this life.

But as I said, this life is short and will end. However, the life to come is neither short nor will it end. That is why it is so much more important to make the same preparation for it. How, you ask? Through the teaching of Christ. By letting the Holy Ghost lead, you, by educating yourself in the Word of God, just as it is recorded in the books of the Bible, which are the only teachings given under the direct guidance of God. Who, better than the master, created all and will end all to get our information?

Man's schools are a must. God's school, church (His church), is more of a must! Man's schools give us a paper of degrees, a diploma that enables us to advance in the workplace in our life. However, God gives us so much more, f or learning of His Word comes faith. By following His teachings, He, through Christ Jesus, gives hope and peace for this life, which enables you to deal and overcome the pain and woes of this life. It also lets you enjoy it to its fullest. Through His Word and promises in this life, you are also prepared to advance in your workplace and in your home life. Not so much advancement in money or title but in the richness of fulfillment to God's plan for man. By relying upon Him and teaching others of His ways, you will live a blessed life, one full of joy and peace.

Sure, trouble and even death will come. However, you have a friend, a heavenly friend, one who will lift you, enwrap you with love, take away your troubles, dry your tears, and give you a life worth living.

Yet it does not stop there. The benefit of a Godly life goes beyond just this life. It goes even beyond the grave. It sees you through the next life. Can man's knowledge do that? I think not. Man's way will just try to trick you into believing a lie, like there is no God or many Gods.

Please look into God's Word and read these stories.

Look and see what God is trying to show you. God hates man's deceiving ways. He will put a stop to it. He is fed up with man trusting man instead of Christ. He turns His face from those who deny His Word. He will unleash His anger and wrath upon those who disbelieve. Make your peace now or face whatever comes.

The final reward for learning and obeying God's Word is the eternal Kingdom of God, a glorious place prepared by Christ, a place set up where your soul lives and lives forever, a place much greater than here, where nothing of man or sin dwells within. Remember, only God's plan can allow you to live therein.

I am sure you will get something out of reading this book, even if it is just entertaining. However, because this book was written by a man who wants to please and serve God, I trust in Him that it will serve a much greater purpose. I know God can use it for His glory and edification. Then it will help someone in his or her Christian life. God will use it to strengthen their spirit or inspire their faith.

He can and will use it to show someone his or her need to seek Christ as his or her Savior. Maybe it will cause you to read in God's Word, which will allow Him to speak to your soul. However He uses it, the angels in heaven will rejoice. Praise God! You can put a smile on Jesus's face as you reach out for His nail- scarred hands. You can defeat Satan and accept salvation, which is what God wants for you!

I will be so happy just to know after all God has done for me, I was able to do something for Him. No way could any man or I repay Him for His love and mercies. We just do very little thing we can. We need to show Him we are truly thankful for His loving grace.

Remember I am a man. I am not famous or rich or very educated in the wisdom of man. Nor do I want to be. I am only interested in pleasing my Lord. I want to preach the gospel I was called to preach. I want to lead people to Christ. I want to cause you to find truth, the Word of God. I want you to see the need for man to turn from his ways to the teaching of the cross. The upbuilding of God's Kingdom is the true purpose of my book, thoughts, preaching, and very existence.

So, if any good comes from this book besides the good it has already done for me, then join me in giving God all the praise. At the same token, if for some reason nothing good comes from this book, do not lay it on God. Put the blame on me; only man can make a mistake.

For only those things that are good cometh from God. All things, which have no good in them, come from Satan or the foolish wisdom of man.

This book is dedicated to God, the keeper of our souls who is also the Father of the living Savior of our souls. It is dedicated to the only begotten Son, Christ Jesus our Lord, the Son whom God sent and allowed to die for our sins, the Holy One who loved us enough to shed His precious blood and give His life that through Him we might be saved, and the One who arose from the grave and sits by the throne of God. He is the only mediator between God and man. It was Him who brought us the gospel of salvation. He is the Son of God who prayed unto the Father to send us the guidance and comfort of His Holy Ghost. Amen.

This book is also dedicated to the born-again, Bible-believing, called-of-God preachers. Those who know of His mercy and grace, those men of God who also fear the power of His wrath, those men of God who hold to and preach on God's Holy Word, those whose doctrine is that of the bloodshed salvation of the Lord Jesus Christ, our precious Savior and the Lamb of God. I truly thank God for those whose aim and goal is to preach to and win the souls of those who are lost. Blessed is those who are called of God and strive to please God instead of man.

One such preacher is Reverend Evans whom I have a lot of respect for, not because he is any better than any other man of God. Reverend Evans stands out to me for one reason; he is the first to ever preach the bloodshed salvation to my soul (Romans 10:14). For that, I thank and praise the holy name of God, for I have found peace and joy to my soul all through the power of the

Word and the salvation of Christ the Lord. Now I want to shout and sing praises unto God forever. I want the whole world to know of His great love, mercy, and grace. He deserves our praise and service.

Yes, I am thankful for Brother Evans and all others like him. I pray and thank God every day for those whose lives are dedicated to preaching the holy doctrine of Christ. It is the only means to redeem the souls of those who are lost. There is no other name given among men or in heaven whereby we shall be saved. We need more preachers, churches, and Christians who stand on the gospel. We need more who will hold up the banner of Christ, for He is the Lord of Lords, King of Kings; Christ is the Lamb of God. Let no man, regardless of title, cause you to believe in or on any other. Christ is the One who died for our souls and paved the way for our sins to be forgiven. He is the blessed redeemer. Amen.

After I had been a Christian for some time, reading and studying God's Word, and after a lot of soul-searching and prayer, I was called of God to preach His Holy Word. It took some time for me to accept God's call. I am not a well-educated man; I did not possess a degree. I could not imagine why God would pick me to be called into ministry. I felt very unworthy that such a great cause should be laid upon me. I was scared to no end of the fact that God was entrusting the preaching of His Word to me. The call did come, and I answered. That is a blessing and honor of the highest degree, one that is held deep and to my heart. I am humbled but proud of such a precious call, and by His grace, I plan to do the His will.

You could say this is my written testimony and sermon, just as it is given to me by God through His Holy Spirit. It is written for the public and, I hope, read by many. Some of the names of people have been changed, and the events mentioned are told so that the impact of the point could be better illustrated. This had to be done in order to comply with the rights of those persons involved. Nothing else is changed!—This you can be sure of. I did not change the Word of God to fit my needs. I would never add to or try to take anything away from or out of the divine Word of Almighty God. I would not do a thing like that for any reason! "For I love the Lord with my every breath. I want nothing more than for Him to be pleased with me. I cherish His will, and I want to serve Him well. I want the Lord to use me for His glory. I am not interested in pleasing man, for by man, sin and death were brought into this world. I am not interested in the thoughts of man for man; not being born again knows nothing of the will of or ways of God Almighty. It is foolishness to those not of God.

Because I want to serve the Lord and was called to preach His Word, it is my love, honor, and duty to preach the Word of God as it is written, NOT the words, thoughts, ideas, or theories of man! I will not teach or preach any of my own thoughts or ideas. Man does not hold the keys to death, hell, and grave. Man cannot save his own soul. It takes the Word of God being preached under the power of the Holy Ghost to save the souls of man. So, the true Word of God is what I will preach and stand on.

In the contents of this book, you will find many references to God's Word. I will give you book, chapter, and verse. I ask you to please read it for yourself. Do not just read my reference verses. Read the whole contents of the chapter that deals with the thought I am trying to make. I would not and I did not take a verse out of context to verify or justify my thoughts or ideas. This is a betrayal of the call to preach. Have your Bible open while you read my book. If you do not agree or you do not understand, if you cannot let go of family or church tradition, please read the gospel of Christ for yourself and ask God to give you the knowledge you lack.

Because it was Almighty God who called me to preach, it is to Him that I must answer. God himself will hold me responsible for any and all things I do or say. I will be held accountable for any souls that I have deceived or led astray (1 Corinthians 9:16). This one thing is for sure; God holds the key to my eternal resting place; it is either His way or the way of the lost. My soul's desire and my obedience are to God. Being in the center of His will is far more important to me than life itself. There is nothing I could hope to gain from man. There is nothing this world could offer me; no way would I want to do anything unpleasing to God!

There is nothing to gain. You will lose your soul if you deceive or lead someone away from the true Word of God. Amen.

What I hope to gain for serving and doing the will of God is not of this world. My gain is in the life to come. I want to spend my eternity in the sweet presence of God the Father.

I am truly thankful for all the preachers and Christians whom through the Spirit I have come to know. They have been a wonderful blessing to my soul. They have inspired and helped me in my Christian life. They mean so much to me, for they are my Christian family. They are the ones (along with the saints of God) I will spend eternity with. "We, being born again" (John 3:3--7). We are the children of God. "For ye are all the children of God by faith in Christ Jesus" (Galatians 3:26). We are brothers and sisters through Christ Jesus. We have the same Father---God. We are born of the spirit of Christ, and we are protected, led, and directed by that same spirit. Look what Jesus says to us in John 14:23--27.

It is wonderful, isn't it? Just to know that you are now of God, and He will take care of you. It is an assuring blessing, isn't it? Just to know you have made peace with the Father. "Just like your earthly father punishes you for not obeying so much more will our heavenly Father punish the ungodly" (John 3:18--36). It is peaceful, is it not? Knowing the mighty wrath (punishment) of Almighty

God is not facing you in eternity. It is a joy, isn't it? Knowing that while obeying Him, you are rewarded both in this life and in the eternal one to come. What a wonderful thought. Praise His holy name!

God's people are a great people to be with, for they are blessed and led by Him. They are full of His spirit and His precious love. Along with them, I too want you and all to have and enjoy the many blessings of our Lord. We want you to have all the love, mercy, and grace that are intended for those of God. We want you to experience the sweetness and joy in our hearts while being with God's people. You can feel His presence in their lives and testimonies. Oh, the stories they tell! The stories of how God has used them, about His love and grace, and how the Father heard and answered their prayers. They are truly a chosen people, for they are of the family of God.

I thank and praise the Lamb of God for the many souls I have seen saved. Oh, how it fills my heart with joy just to see or hear of ones who have found their salvation through God's Son. Just think of the joy it puts in Him who came and died for us, not to be denied by you.

I thank Him for people like Pastor James Stevens and the Heaven Bound Singers, the Young Adult Choir at the church I attended. They have helped and uplifted me in so many ways. I thank Him for all who work and live for the glory of His name; the preachers preaching His Holy Word and the Christian singers singing the beautiful songs of Zion are such a joyful blessing and a strengthening of my spirit. Yes, I am very thankful for all who do service unto the Lord and teach of His ways. We need more who will stand up for this gospel. Why? Because Christ holds the key to the eternal Kingdom of God (1 Peter 3:22) and also because we owe our existence to Him.

At this time, let me also thank Brother Tim and Brandy (Brenda) Young and Bonetta Hutson. I am very grateful for their help and long hours. Tim and Brandy were the first ones to have a peek at my book. I asked them for their help in the first edition of the book, and Brandy worked very hard on typing the draft from my very scribbly pages, which I know was very hard and time-consuming. I waited a long time before letting someone help me. I did this so I would be sure that whoever it was would have the same aim and goal as me. I wanted them to also be led of God. Years later, Bonetta Hutson came along and retyped this for submission for publishing.

I am glad to have known the people I mentioned in this book. I know they all love God. I know I speak for them when I say we want to teach you and show you the words and ways of God. We want to enlighten you to the many joys and goodness of serving the Lord Jesus Christ. We want to share with you the blessings, peace, mercy, and grace of our Lord. We want you to have the promises made (and kept) to His people. Yes, I am glad and treasure my physical family and my spiritual family. I look forward to seeing them and you as we step inside heaven's golden gates. We look forward to meeting you and beholding the glorious Kingdom of God.

However, I love and thank our most heavenly Father because He loves us so much (John 3:16). "No greater love is there than that of Him, who left His home in Glory. Having all power given to Him by the Father, being hated and denied by man, still laid Himself on the cross there to be the supreme sacrifice for the sins of all mankind" (John 15:13).

Yes, Christ is my blessed Savior and my dearest friend. He will always be with me even through the end. He will never forsake me. He will be there for my needs, in times of joy, and in times of sorrow; and whether I am rich or poor, my friend, Jesus, will always be by my side (Hebrews 13:5). He will pick me up when I fall; He will lead the way when I am not sure. He bestows on me joy that is unspeakable and full of glory. Yes! I am His, and He is mine. What a friend we have in Jesus. I love and praise Him with all that I am.

I am so glad that God sees to our every need. He knew that man alone could not overcome the temptations of sin and lust. Even though He showed man His love, power, and grace, He knew the devil would not allow man to believe in the will and words of

Him. Adam and Eve showed Him that. The people in the days of Noah proved unrighteous. The people He led out of bondage after He had performed many miracles and wonders of power turned away. Even though He would have spared the cities of Sodom and Gomorrah if one righteous man could be found, the cities were destroyed.

Even though Abraham, Moses, David, and others spoke to God and through His power showed many wonders, man turned away. Why? Because man is just man, made in the image of God but just a man. No man can overcome the powers of the immortal Satan. This is a battle that started in man's beginning and still is fought and lost today. But Praise His holy name, we can now claim VICTORY through Christ Jesus, for He holds all power, and after paying for our sins, He went back to the Father and now sits on God's right hand and is the mediator for all the sins of man (Romans 8:34). This was done in order for the spirit of Him; the Holy Ghost could come and dwell in us, thus giving us the power over him that is in the world, which we could overcome.

The Holy Ghost is the spirit that comes into your heart. When you fully accept Christ as your Savior, He leads you in the way you should go. He inspires you to the will of God. He fills you with joy and peace that cannot be found anywhere else. All the joys and excitement of this world cannot match just one touch from God through His Holy Spirit.

Nothing or no one can love you, bless you, or save your soul from God's wrath. We must fear it, for it is His judgment we must face. In addition, it is His spirit that will make you victorious. The same spirit will also make you heirs to

His throne and give you a home in His Glory Land (Romans 8:16--17).

It is through the Holy Ghost whereby my soul has been led and inspired. It now has called me to preach and given me the honor of writing this book, which I did and do so to praise and glorify God the Father from which the spirit comes. For without God, I am nothing, but through Jesus, I am now a child of God. Glory,

glory to Him in the highest, for He is the Savior and keeper of my soul!

God has been so good to me. I want to tell the whole world of His precious love and grace. I want everyone to know just how He spoke sweet peace to my soul. I want to do all I can for my Lord. That is the least I can do for all He has done for me.

What He has already done for me is nothing compared to what is to come. He has promised me an eternal home in glory, where there will be everlasting peace and joy, a land of no sickness or death. No reason for tears or sorrow there, just an endless age of bliss for you and me to share. Praise God!

My aim and goal for this book are to edify my Lord and His plan of salvation. I want my book to lead someone to Christ. As I said, I want it to serve as my written testimony of all the love and praise I have for He who saved me. I want to do whatever I can to enrich and enlighten mankind the world over. I want to teach you your need for the love and mercies of God.

I want this book to open your eyes to the darkness of this world. I want you to know and understand the wrath is going to come. It will come to all those who have not accepted Christ as their Savior (Romans 1:18). I want this book to thrill your heart to the many wonders of serving Him. I want you to know there is a reward for being a child of the King.

This world is in bad shape. Just look around you . . . Where have our morals gone? I know where they are coming from. It sure is not God, is it? With all the knowledge of man, why do we revert to the ways of sin? How in the world can we believe the world is getting better? How can we allow ourselves to think we are on the right track when the track leads us away from God's love and teaching? We are just like the different generations in the Bible who turned away from God. They followed their manly knowledge and lusts. Yes, they followed their ways right to the wrath of God. Will we? Will you? Remember, there is a way that seems right unto man, but the end thereof is the ways of death (Proverbs 14:12).

Why would you ignore God when He has so much to offer? There are peace, joy, and blessings in serving our Lord. His path leads to a home in glory. He is pleading with your soul. Choose me. I am good. I love you. I want to save you from my wrath and judgment because my punishment is forever. My glorious Kingdom is for eternity. I have given you, my Son. I give you His spirit to guide and protect you. You will die. That is a fact. You will face hell or heaven after your body dies. That is also a fact. Which do you choose?

This world is lost. It has no future, just destruction. It will be destroyed by God's mighty hand. The only hope is for you. You have a chance to make peace with God. You have a chance to bring your family to God. The only hope that is left is to tell all our friends, family, and neighbors to get on the right path. Please open you heart and mind. Open your Bible to Luke 16:2--31. I am not going to write it for you. Read it for yourself. Think about it. Let God speak to you.

My book cannot save you. God's book can and will if you will let it. Close your mind for just a moment to the ways of this world. Shut out the knowledge of man. Do not listen to Satan. Do it anyway. You know he does not want you to, and if you do not, you serve him instead of God! Forget all else and try to feel the touch of Him who loves you.

Why doesn't the world listen to God's Word? Why won't you?

Why is there something always drawing you back from the truth? Who or what are you letting keep you from the hearing of God's call?

We need to turn to and trust God today. Praise His holy name! We need Him to instill in us and empower us with the Holy Ghost! It will guide us and protect us all the way to the hills of glory, there to be forever with the Lord, a place Christ has prepared for us where our soul will live forever, a place where we will bask in the many pleasures of God's glorious Kingdom.

That is the climax of our salvation. However, you do not have to wait until you are in heaven. The love, mercies, and promises to

God's children are here for you to have today. He wants to show you His grace, love, and kindness. It is yours, just for the asking. Do not be shorted and do not be denied. The price you will pay is much too high!

When this book is finished, my part will be done. It will then be in the hands of God Almighty, for I give it unto Him for His use. I want Him to get any praise or gain from this book. I want my sweet loving Savior to use any and all things I do or achieve for His glory. Yes, all that I do I do for the upbuilding of His Kingdom.

The words of my preaching or testimony, the words of this book, are just those . . . words. Man's words are mere words until God empowers them through the Holy Spirit. Then and only then can they do service unto the Lord. Remember what I wrote earlier; do not let yourself be misled or be led astray because of man. Man is man. Jesus Christ is Lord of Lords. Whom do you trust with your soul? Whom SHOULD you trust?

My service both as a Christian and as a preacher is to praise and glorify the Lord, to spread His gospel, and to teach the world about the salvation of Jesus Christ, the Son of God. My service is to worship Him in spirit and in truth. My duty is to serve Him by reaching out to those who are lost.

As I was led to write this book, I asked the Lord to take it and use it for His glory. Please, let it be a means of leading someone to Christ. Use it to enlighten some lost soul to the love and mercies of you, my Savior. I want this and my life to serve as a witness to the bloodshed salvation of my Lord. Everyone deserves and owes it to themselves to receive and enjoy the blessings in this life and also to the eternal life to come, which is prepared for all those who love and follow God's only Son.

In this book, you will find no mention of denominations. Denominations are a farce. God did not divide the church into denominations. Christ set up one church, and He is coming back for that church (Ephesians 4:4--14). To be a member of the church, you must be born again. You must also live according to God's Word, for only His plan can save you and keep you until that day.

That day, you will be delivered from this world to His precious Holy Kingdom.

Man can never accept anything as it is. He always thinks he can improve it. He always has to find a way to do it his way. That is why we are in the shape we are in. The world is in bad shape. The United States is falling into destruction. The families and morals of America are in jeopardy. The churches are in turmoil. Man's soul is facing God's wrath, and he is trying to change or ignore that fact.

The knowledge of man will lead us straight to hell; that is a fact. Man, alone cannot save his own soul, yet he listens to anything that comes along. Man must leave the Word of God to God. Man must let the spirit of Christ lead the church. Man's thoughts and theories are too influenced by evil spirits, lust, greed, and pride of life. Love not the world, neither the things that are in the world. If any man loves the world, the love of the Father is not in him (1 John 2:15--17; James 1:13--16).

Because man split up the church and because man put names on them, I make no mention of them, for there is nothing in a name. You can call yourself anything. If you do not fit into God's plan, you are lost. Even though I do not mention different names of churches, I do discuss the different beliefs and traditions that are going around.

I do this only to show the importance of reading God's Word for yourself. This is a must. You cannot live for God without His Word (2 Timothy 2:15). You need the inspiration of the spirit to lead you through it. Remember, man alone cannot stand against the power of Satan.

Please do not underestimate the power of the one who wants to rob you of your soul. He is good at what he does (1 Peter 5:8). He will use any means to lead you to him. He wants no one to know God. His spirit is what keeps man on this Godless pathway. He has tempted mankind since the beginning, and he is winning the battle. Because we let him, he has become the little god of this world. Satan will let you think you are doing right just to keep you from the truth. If you think he has no power in your thoughts or beliefs, if you have not accepted the plan of salvation through Christ Jesus, then he has led you to believe a lie.

If you do not have the power and inspiration of the Holy Spirit, it is so easy to be misled and deceived. If you have not accepted Christ as your Savior, you have no choice; you are a disciple of Satan. Fact: You do serve a master. Who is yours? (Matthew 6:24; John 3:17--18).

This is a fact you cannot ignore. There are about one hundred different types of doctrines and beliefs. Thousands of people are being led astray each day. Why? Need you ask? Man has tried to change God's Words and plan of salvation to suit himself. All through the history of time, man is led to believe he can do all things his way. Man tries to justify his thinking and acts by any means.

Look, you will acknowledge that Jesus is the Son of God and has sent here as our Savior. He was raised from the dead that his spirit could come to us for guidance (Romans 14:11; 6:15--16). When will you accept Christ? I hope it is not when you cry out for death!

Now some of the doctrines only differ in the way they worship. Some differ in the way their service is run. Some do not like music, while some are laid back in personality. Others are emotional. That is just the difference in man's personal taste. As long as they do not condemn each other or think we are better than others, as long as they read, teach, preach, and practice the whole Word of God, what does it matter?

What does matter are those who offer alternatives to God's Word, those being misled into believing a lie. There are some who believe your good works will please God. Others reject the power and salvation of Christ. Some believe that water washes away sin. False!

There are some who bow and pray to someone other than Jesus. Some doctrines are based totally on the Old Testament, while others are accepting tradition as gospel. Some even denounce that there is a God. Some say God is a woman. Some doctrines teach that the church or a man of so-called God can save you. Some even believe in abortions and homosexuality. These, along with many other doctrines, are all false doctrines. A lot of them are set up and run by the Antichrist.

I do not have to mention any names. If the shoe fits, you know it. If you are in or a part of a false doctrine, get out! (Romans 16:17--18; Ephesians 6:10--18; Revelation 22:14--21).

Do not let Satan use you. Do not be denied. Read God's Word for yourself and see where you stand according to His Word. Remember, without His spirit, you cannot please or serve Him.

You cannot put your faith in the name of a church or doctrine. You cannot and must not entrust your soul to the wisdom or ways of man (Acts 4:12; 1 Timothy 2:5; 1 Corinthians 1:25).

By doing so, you are a subject and an open target for the deceiving tactics of Satan himself. Remember when this world is destroyed by God's power, all things of man and flesh, sin and death, will be no more. We will all answer to God. So, in whom should you rely? Surely, not man?

Look, it is simple to decide in whom you should entrust your soul. If God's Words and ways are not the way, you simply live a good life here. In the next life, you will go or be whatever your mind now allows you to believe. However, because the Word of God is true, you will face His wrath in hellfire. Don't you at least owe it to yourself to discover the truth? If God's plan was or is wrong (which it is not), why do man and Satan steer you away from it?

People must be warned. Man must be awakened to this horrible fact: Satan, because of man, has churches and religious cults and doctrines that will rob your very soul from the presence of God. You will be led to the fiery pits of hell all because you trusted man.

I know this is a touchy subject, but it must be covered. These groups teach you their doctrine or tradition. They do not want you to read God's Word for yourself. They want to tell you what it means. Why? Why not let God lead you Himself? After all, it is His Word. It is empowered by His spirit. It is His Son who died to save us. It is He who created heaven and hell (whether you believe it or not). It will be Him who judges your soul. No matter what we think or believe, we cannot alter the will or ways of God. Why would you let anything keep you from accepting the pure simple plan of salvation? By doing this, you allow yourself to be used, misled, and denied the joys of heaven. Then Satan used our thoughts and ideas to lead others to their fiery graves.

Please read Matthew 27:11--26. See how that Pilate wanted nothing to do with crucifying Christ. See how his wife warned him not to harm Jesus. Pilate knew this was a just man. His wife as warned in a dream about killing Jesus. Pilate could have spared the life of Jesus instead of Barabbas. Yet he listened to man. Please listen to God instead of man. The men he listened to were religious leaders; they were not of God.

Do not let yourself be deceived like so many others, for it is written in God's Word. "And except those days should be shortened, there should no flesh be saved: but for the elect's sake those days shall be shortened. Then if any man shall say unto you, Lo, here is Christ, or there; believe it not. For there shall arise false Christ's, and false prophets, and shall shew great signs and wonders; insomuch that, if it were possible, they shall deceive the very elect" (Matthew 24:22--24). Matthew 11:22 is just one of the many subjects I will use the Word of God to cover also.

In the following chapters, I will try to show you the many joys and blessings in serving the Lord Jesus Christ, for you see, it is only then that life truly begins. Man's life is merely just existing until you are born into the family of God. You have no heavenly Father unless you become a child of God. Being born in the flesh is not being born into God's family. You have no one to help you overcome perilous times. You have no one to answer your prayers. You have no one who can speak sweet peace and joy to your soul. You have no one to lead you to the glorious Kingdom. I will attempt to show you the nearest of the day for Christ to come and redeem those which are His. I want you to understand because the day of our Lord is so near, that Christ loves you more than you love yourself. He also needs you as much as you need Him, for He wants no man (or woman) to perish. He wants and all to repentance (2 Peter 3:9).

The time is near; the time of the coming of Christ is at hand. Your call of death might be at hand. A friend or loved one might be called out of this world yet today. That is why there is such a desperate need for those who will serve and work for the will and ways of God.

There is a lot to be done. There are a lot of people we need to reach. There is a hell to shun and a heaven to gain. What better life is there? Let God use you for His glory. What better thing can you do for yourself or a loved one than keeping a lost soul from the danger of hellfire?

That is why we must be about our father's work (Romans 12:11; Luke 2:49). He needs you. He needs us all. We need to reach out and teach all those that we can. The devil and his deceiving ways are winning the battle. However, the war is not over. It does not matter what man thinks. It does not matter what the devil causes you to believe. It does not matter what false religion or doctrine you accept. It does not matter what tradition you have been taught. God will be victorious!

Another subject that needs to be dealt with is the confusion of both the world and the (so-called) churches of the world. By churches of the world, I mean those not preaching and/or not teaching the gospel of Christ as it is written, not proclaiming His bloodshed salvation as man's only means of redemption.

Being any of which based their faith on tradition or what science has taught them. Then there are those who have changed their way just to fit the lifestyle and morals of society, being those who have adapted their ways according to the knowledge of man, which in all cases is unbecoming to God. They also denounce the power of the Holy Ghost.

I will also try to enlighten you to the signs of the time as depicted in the Holy Word of God. You see there are signs and warnings at the end of time. No matter whether you believe it or not or what you think, it will come to pass. God's will and His Word will prevail. You can accept it now or later. However, you will accept it.

I want you to see what you can expect as told to us by Christ Himself. Please take time right now and read Matthew chapters

24 through 26; see for yourself. Listen to what the Word is telling you. Block out all else. Just you and the Lord, looking into His Word. Find the truth. Do not settle for anything less. You are important to God. He loves you. He wants to save you.

There are many subjects to cover; however, the most important thing is to show the need for Christ in your life. I want to plead to every lost soul. Please open your heart to the love and mercy of God. Accept Jesus Christ, the Son of God, as your personal Savior. Prepare yourself and be at peace, knowing you are ready to meet thy God. Allow yourself to be welcomed into His heavenly Kingdom.

You do not want to face God unprepared. You will not enjoy His mighty wrath. Do not, I beg of you, cause your soul to have to face and endure the fiery pits of hell, a hell that was prepared for all who do not accept the salvation of Christ. It does not matter to God what you think or do not think about His Word. His Word will judge you. You have nothing to say about it. But you do have time to do something about it.

Through the words, teachings, and prayers of this book, it will enable the gospel of Christ to reach many. I hope to open the hearts and minds of man to the divine love of God. I want to bring you glad tidings of His Word and wondrous blessings. I want to introduce you to the loving Savior, the Lord Jesus Christ.

I sincerely hope you get a blessing or are uplifted while reading this book. If you do not know Jesus, I hope you at least see your need for Him in your life. I pray the soft holy hand of God will touch your soul. I hope you get a message concerning the signs of God's time. I truly want and ask God to speak to you while you read through the pages just as He spoke to and blessed me while writing them. I wish all of you could read from the original pages on which I wrote, then all would be able to see the many stains on them---stains caused by tears as they rolled from my eyes, falling down my cheeks and onto the pages as I wrote.

Oh, what a glorious feeling it is to be touched by the hand of Almighty God. That is one feeling that cannot be achieved by any other means known to man regardless of what you do. No matter what you dream up in your mind, you can use all the tools and pleasures Satan has to offer, and you will still fall way short.

For eye has not seen, ear has not heard, man's mind cannot even imagine . . . Your wildest dreams cannot compare to the wonders of our Lord (1 Corinthians 2:9--14).

Yes, you can do or dream anything you want. You can drink, smoke, or get high. You can use anything and/or everything you want. You will never come nowhere close to just one touch from God the Father. If you doubt God, try Him! Try the spirits to see for yourself (1 John 4:1--6).

One or all, the joys of this world is a product of man through sin. They cannot begin to measure up to the many blessings received when being a child a God. I ask you, who or what can outdo our Lord?

As I wrote and was touched, I knew God was pleased with my effort. He blessed me in many different ways. At times I would have to lay my pen aside and just rejoice, giving praise to His glory, because His hand ever so softly touched my heart. Then there were times my heart was so burdened for the lost souls of man, family, and friends I would just lay back sobbing and crying out to God for their salvation.

Sometimes I would just sit back, resting in pure and total peace, as I felt the nearest of God to my soul. Well, praise His Holy Sweet Name! Then there were times when my hand would ache from writing the words as they came ever so easy to me, for you see, it is not His will for any man to perish. He does not want you or anybody to miss out to the joy and sweet peace to your soul just knowing our Lord.

I ask and beg of you to do these few things while reading this book. Please stop and just think. Take time to think about what you have read. Think of the pros and the cons of your disbelief. Think of the promises God made to you and all mankind. Keep this one thought in mind: if the Word of God is true, and it is, what is in store for you? Think about the inspiration and reward God has for our soul. Remember (just for the sake of asking you this question), if His Word is true, and you reject it, how will you face His judgment and angry wrath? Just what will you do or say?

If, for some reason, you cannot accept something I have written, do not ask the opinion of man. Look into God's Word on the subject. If you cannot find it, ask a preacher where to find it. Call any pastor. Ask for help in finding a subject that you have doubt about. Do not look anywhere else; turn to God's Word for therein is truth and means of salvation for your soul. Plus, unlike man or tradition, God will not mislead you.

If something does not strike you as right, go to the Bible and see what it has to say. Then you will see and know firsthand. His Word will teach you the need to accept Christ or face the torment of His wrath, for He is the One who gives life. His Word will show you how He loves us more than we love ourselves. It will show how He gave His only begotten Son for our redemption. You will see how He holds your life and soul's destiny in His hands. Amen.

Do not read this book to find fault in it or in me. That would be too easy, for I am just a man, saved by His Grace, but still just a man. I have faults like you and all mankind. Only God and those things that are His are perfect. Yes, perfect in every way. So do not dwell on my faults. Dwell instead on the teaching of Christ. Dwell on how and where you fit in God's plan. At least read this book and see how God blesses and leads His people. See what God has in store for you as a child of His. Then go into His Word and understand the truth of life.

Let me take time to explain just briefly the New Testament writings. The first four books are the gospel of Christ: the birth, the teachings, the death, and the resurrection of Jesus Christ. Also, the fulfillment of the prophecies, the beginning of salvation, the promise of heaven and hell, His powers and miracles, the setting up of the apostles, and the setting up of the church through His salvation.

The next book is Acts. This is the delivery and power of the Holy Ghost. The work travels and powers of the apostles, preaching and teaching man's need of the bloodshed salvation of Christ. Their trials and hardships of bringing man into the change: the change from the law of old into the faith of new.

The next books are the letters written to the early churches. These are letters of instructions to get the people back on the right track. Some of those early churches had drifted away from Christ's teachings; they had fallen prey to the whims of man. This could be called the big I and little your syndrome. Just like today!

Some of the churches today proclaimed to be more holy; others claim to be apostles saved through Paul and Silas, while some churches took their blood birth as having special rights. Just like some churches today, man has not changed. He WANTS to be better. Man cannot leave well enough alone. Yet man's way is not of God; it is the way of sin. Man will deceive himself rather than trust God. Why?

There was division among the early churches as well as division among the members. Each of which believed that their way was right. See how history repeats itself? See how man has not changed? Well, God and His Word has not changed, no matter how or what man has tried to do. That is why God had these letters to the churches written.

They were written by the holiest of men, inspired and led of God to teach them again the ways and the gospel of Christ, to put the churches back into ONE faith---the faith of being born again saved of the Son of God. The letters turned them away from the thoughts, theories, and pride of man. They returned them to the teaching of the One who brought them salvation by grace through faith.

Today no book could contain all the letters to the churches that have drifted away, away from the true Word of God. There are too, too many. Remember that God set up His church; it was set up through the redemption of Christ, and the church is maintained by His teaching. It is powered through the Holy Ghost. The church will be redeemed when Christ comes for it and those who are members thereof.

The final book is Revelation, a book of prophetic nature. This book deals with the past, present, and future tenses of God's plan and Words; it deals in symbolic, spiritual, and literal meanings. One must have a good general knowledge of the whole Bible and be inspired by the knowledge of God to discern the whole of this book (if that is possible). There are some things in this book man may not know until revealed by God.

That is a very brief summary of the New Testament, a very brief summary. However, it does give you a general idea. Read it for yourself. You will see in the letters the same is going on today although on a much larger scale because there are millions of more people, which leads to thousands more in thoughts and theories. Yet there is still one God and only one true Word of God. Do not mislead.

God did not let the early church go astray without writing to them, warning them of their deceiving ways. He will not allow you to be misled if you trust in His Holy Word; His true Word will bring you and all mankind back to the foundation of Christ and His teachings.

You can read the letters and pick out the same false doctrines then as now. You can read the old laws and rituals of the days of Moses, Jacob, and David. There you will see the traditional teaching of some churches today even though Christ brought us from that law into the law of faith and grace. See just as the Jews of old who would not accept the change and crucified our Lord. Man, today still does not want to accept Christ's teaching.

Before going on, there is something you must know. I am not rewriting or rewording the Word of God; I am only using His Word, using it to show you the redeeming plan of and the power therein. Man, still has to and needs to be taught of the salvation and gospel of Christ Jesus, the One who did not destroy the prophecies or the law but came that both might be fulfilled (Matthew 5:17; Romans 10:3--4; Romans 8:2--8; Galatians

3:10--11).

Nor am I trying to translate the Bible to you; this cannot be done by any man. The Bible contains the *LIVING* Word of God. God will give you the understanding that you need to know, and He will give it to you when you need it. You will understand more and more as you grow in grace. We grow in knowledge of God's Word just like the schools of man. You cannot teach a first grader ninth-grade math. We must grow into it. God will help you grow in His Word as you need to.

Know ye this: no one, and I do mean no one, can read and study the Bible and even attempt to give the full meaning therein. If man could do this, you could read and master the Bible and then just toss it aside as you would any other book. However, it is not so with God's Word, for you see, it is a never-ending Book of Life that brings us unto salvation and leads us in this life. It also prepares us for the endless ages of eternity and also to the face that His judgment lies within His Word.

That is why His book had to be written by these holiest of His saints, not by their knowledge or the wisdom of man but by the divine power of the Holy Ghost (2 Peter 2:21). That is why it lives on and on. That is why when all else is destroyed, and time is no more, the Word of God will still stand. That is also why you need His spirit to rightly divide the word of truth (1 Corinthians 2:14). But because man relies on man, because he trusts his own knowledge, that allows Satan and his deceiving way to have a field day. Satan uses man to deceive man, and he uses man to denounce and mock God. This explains why there are so many false doctrines, prophets, and teachings (1 Corinthians 2:5--14). In other words, a person who has not been of God and filled with

His Holy Spirit cannot discern God's Holy Word.

Just as you and all Christians must grow daily in God's Word, so must I, for when we are saved, we become a child of God, a babe in Christ, a new creature needing to be taught the milk of His

Word. Before trying to digest the meat of His Word, please read these scriptures: 1 Peter 2:2 and 2 Corinthians 5:17. Let God enlighten you, for your worldly knowledge has nothing to do with the wisdom that lies in God's Word.

The longer you serve Christ, the closer you get to Him. The more you let Him use you through the spirit, the more you will understand of His Word. It is because of this: you can read over and over from the Bible knowing that each and every time, you will get more and more from it, not just in the knowledge and understanding of God's Word, but you will also be blessed as you study. The Word will give you strength and bring comfort to your soul. Remember, faith comes by hearing God's Word.

His Word will give you peace in troubled times. It will lift away your worldly burdens. It gives hope when all else fails. In His Word, you find direction and faith. You learn of the promises God makes (and keeps) to his family, like how He hears and answers your prayer (1 Peter 3:12), how to worship Him (Psalm 100; John 4:23). It teaches you . . . WHO? (Romans 3:23). WHAT (John 3:3--7; Acts 2:38). WHEN (Matthew 3:2; 2

Corinthians 6:2). WHERE? (1 Timothy 2:5; Revelation 21:16--27; John 14:6). WHY? (John 3:18). Then it shows you the destiny of our choice---heaven or hell? Nothing or no one lays it all out for you as the Lord does. Why not?

Nothing or no one has the love, mercy, joy, peace, and eternal Kingdom to offer. That is why you should be ever so eager to read and study His Word. You know for every action; there is a reaction. God just wants you to know what those reactions are. The clear picture is before you.

It works like this: The closer you get to God, the closer He gets to you. The closer He is to you, the more joy, blessings, and understanding you will receive. The more of these that you receive, the closer you get to the Lord. The closer you get to Him, the more He uses you, strengthens you. and inspires you through the Holy Spirit. The more of this, the closer you get to God and so on and so on it goes. All through the power and truth of His divine Word. Amen.

However, no matter how much you read, study, and follow His Word, you will never know it all. You will never get to a point (in this life) where you master it all, for man's mind is not capable to comprehend all the meanings and wonders of His Word. All the knowledge and wisdom of man together is nothing when compared to Almighty God!

I have said all those things to say this: IF God is almighty; if He holds the key to death, hell, and grave; if he wants man to love and follow His teachings; if He gave His only begotten Son as a sacrifice for our sins; if He gives unto us the Holy Spirit to guide, lead, and comfort us, then it is in Him we should trust, not man!

The following are all kinds of teachings in God's Word to show us:

1. Man's ways may seem right, but the end thereof is sin.
2. True wisdom is the fear of God.
3. There is more than one spirit, one of which is of Satan.
4. Satan, whether you believe it or not, can and does use anything he can to serve his purposes.
5. The only truth is in the Word of God.
6. All things of this world and in this world will pass away.
7. Only the things of God will stand throughout eternity.
8. There is a hell to shun, and there is a heaven to gain.
9. There are a plan and a path we must travel, and only you can decide on what path you want to follow.
10. And most important, when all is said and done, when all the time on God's clock stops, you will know the truth in God's Word, and you will see Jesus Christ the Lord in all His glory!

My prayer is that the path you choose will make this a joyful time, not a time of awakening and agony. Do not let the memory of "I should have listened" burn in your mind throughout the endless ages of hellfire. Do not think just because you do not believe it will alter God's plan. Do not think you can make your own way. Do not deny the power, anger, and wrath of God. You will pay!

Here are a few facts you need to be assured of:

1. The Word of God does not cause confusion. It does not contradict itself. Man causes that.

2. No one, and I do mean no one, can teach you the meaning of every Word of God. Beware of those who think they can.

3. There is no one who can even guess the time of the end. The angels in heaven do not even know this.

4. Man cannot use his knowledge to master God's.

5. God will not let you be deceived or misled if you trust in His Word.

6. The different denominations and different doctrines are not of God or in His Word. This is man trying to do what he thinks is Godly.

7. God's Word is His Word; God's church is His church. He does not need man to improve on it.

8. It is because of man that the Son of God came to save our souls.

Man, and his so-called knowledge killed the Son of God and denies Him daily.

9. God loves you and wants to save your soul.

I do not mean to step on any toes. I do not want to tell you that your religion is in vain. I do want you to know if you are not following God's plan, you will face His angry wrath. Look at these facts:

1. You can only pray to God through Jesus our Lord.

2. You are not to bow before any image of anyone.

3. You and you alone must pray for your forgiveness.

4. You must be born again through faith by grace. It is a gift God, a gift that cannot be earned by deeds or merits.

5. You must love and fear God.

6. You must use the gifts of the Holy Spirit for God's glory, not for your gain.

7. Do not try to be something you are not. You are just a sinner saved by the blood of Christ trying to do the will of God.

8. You cannot serve God by the deeds and traditions of the Old Testament. Christ brought us from that to grace. That is WHY He came.

9. You must humble yourself before God yet stand strong against the false teaching of man.

10.Jesus stands ready to save you. Your gift of money to the "whatever's," your rites and ceremonies, your good works or deeds, your Hail Mary's and tenets, your tongue-speaking, your candle lighting---these are all for nothing. Only JESUS can put your name in the Lamb's Book of Life. Amen.

Do not let anyone tell you different. I do not care what they show you or tell you; they are a liar. Do you hear me? A liar! They will cause you to lose your soul. If you seek the truth, seek God. If you want to find the true church, find Jesus. Let His spirit shows you the church. After all, it is His, and He will come and take His church to glory. All others will have to face God's almighty wrath.

Dear Readers, I love you. I love you as much as myself. But most important, God loves you. I stand before you as a witness of His love and mercy. But most important, I stand before God as my witness, for God Himself will judge me for the things I tell you. As God is my judge, I know that what I have to say unto you is of God.

I retract nothing. I have written as God has led. Therefore, I am at peace, for I have done all I can do to please and glorify God. I want you to know that I know I am saved. I know without a shadow of doubt that I am on my way to heaven. Not because of anything except that Jesus died for my sins as He died for yours. I truly hope and expect to meet you in glory. Amen.

Since the death of our Lord, this world, now being in its two thousand and some odd years of existence, has become a melting pot. The morals of mankind have bottomed out. The sins of the world are at their peak. All mankind is in a troublesome state. We have caused hurt and pain upon our God, for we have drifted so far from the teaching and the salvation of Christ.

God (and there is a God) hates sin. He is hurt and angry, for man has turned away from His holy goodness. How much more will God put up with? How much longer will He allow man to deny His power and teachings? How much longer will He allow you to ignore His precious Son? When will He put an end to man's mockery of His divine being? How many more days will He give you to prepare for the judgment? Time is running out, sayeth the Lord, yet we do not listen. We just drift further and further down the path of sin and disobedience.

We ignore His Holy Word. We do not heed to His warnings. We listen to the things of this world to prepare us for the next. Why? This life is short; eternity is everlasting. Prepare to meet thy God because your eternity lies in His hand. It does not matter what you think; it does not matter what you believe in or how you believe. When death calls, you will answer.

Think about it. Man, in all his so-called wisdom and knowledge, is unable to stop death. Now put this in the back of your mind. Man can do nothing to stop the will of God. His WILL will be done on earth as it is in heaven. We can do and say anything we want. That is our choice. However, when it comes to dying and facing God, we have no choice! Do not be misled!

Man has always mingled in things where he had no business. He has always taken to his own way of thinking there was a better way. Man, today has butchered our Constitution. Our forefathers did not intend to be second-guessed; they wrote our laws and developed the government for the people. Look what man has done.

Crime has been dealt with by punishment---harsh and hard. Criminals had no rights. Now they have more rights than we do. They get room and board, medical and dental care, education, etc., while our senior citizens who have worked all their lives exist on social security. Our elder generation does not have the same types of luxuries as those incarcerated; in fact, some cannot even afford their medication.

We had free speech written in. Man, today says that "free speech" allows us to speak out against our country or to form groups to defy our nation's policies. We have made our schools a mockery to education. This country was founded on "In God We Trust." Yet now we, as this same nation, are not allowed to teach, display, and in most cases even mention God. We have really come a long way. But which way have we come?

The government used to be for the people. Now those in office are in it for themselves. They pass laws that benefit themselves. They only listen to those special interest groups that will pad their pockets, such as doctors, lawyers, bankers, and the ACLU. These groups have run and ruined our country. This is NOT what our forefathers had in mind.

We cannot even accept the laws and governing of our founders without changing it to suit certain groups or ourselves. We (man) could not call "black" black or white without saying it could be gray. Mankind thinks he is always smarter than the next guy. PRIDE. Man, always wants what he is not supposed to have, by any means. LUST OF THE EYE. Man, always wants what feels good or makes him think it feels good. ADULTERY, HOMOSEXUALITY, DRUGS, POWER, LUST OF THE FLESH . . . all of which is sin.

See, man is the same as he was in the beginning. He has not come up with something better or new. He has fallen into the oldest trap of the devil. These are the same sins that tempted Adam and Eve. These are the same sins that caused those two to turn from God in the garden. These are the same sins that caused God to destroy the earth by the flood. These caused God to rain fire and brimstone from heaven on Sodom and Gomorrah. These are the three items Satan used to tempt Christ after he had fasted forty days. Nothing has changed.

Man, just calls it a new name. God tells us man will be drawn away from Him by his own lust of the flesh, pride of life, and lust of the eye. He warns us of this. He tells us Satan uses these three weaknesses of man to deceive, mislead, and bound their souls to hell.

Yet we ignore and go on following the ways of sin and destruction. Now we call it knowledge, improvement, and advancement. It is simply self-righteous of the foolish mind. By nature, and sin, man will believe in his own know-it-all ways than in the laws and governing of the Almighty God. How smart are we?

Just like everything else, man has added to and taken away from the laws and Words of God. Man cannot accept the Word as it is written. He must put his two cents in it. We cannot accept the fact that God Himself (Almighty God) laid His hand and spirit on holy men to write His Words. Yet we think that these men did not write it as God spoke it. I guess we believe God has all power; however, He cannot take care of His Word. He needs us to tell Him what He meant. Are you insane? Why believe in God at all if He cannot take care of His own matters?

Then again, we might believe we are more holy than the men God picked to write His Words. That is why we read things between the lines and change them to suit us. Or we are just like man from the beginning; we allow Satan to put these stupid thoughts into our minds and hearts, just as they did when they killed our Lord. Think about it. Whose side would you have been on?

Just think. Those righteous and so-called religious people killed the Son of God, the very One who came to save them. They were the same as man today. They did what was right to them, but the ways thereof were sin. We make or allow ourselves to think we are doing right, but our ways are of sin. Nothing has changed, only gotten worse. Things will not get better, only worse, as we drift further and further back into the ways of sin.

I guess we think we can change the Word and ways of God and make Him accept them. I guess we think we can destroy God's Holy plan, destroy the salvation and teachings of His only Son, and destroy or deny the power of the Holy Ghost. Yet we allow ourselves to think that God Himself cannot and will not destroy our (man's) teachings, ideas, and ways. Boy, are we in for a rude awakening!

Man has no knowledge of true wisdom. Man is blinded by sin and cannot see the light. Man does not know the truth until he finds God. Man has no way of saving his own soul until he finds Christ. Man cannot overcome the deceiving and misleading of Satan until he receives the power of the Holy Ghost. Why will we not accept that we cannot change those things that we do not have power over? Who of us has power over death, hell, and grave?

Who of us is holier than those holy men picked of God Himself? Who of us are prophesied about in the Word of God? Just who of us is more righteous than the Lord Jesus Christ? Finally, who is causing us to believe we can change or alter the Holy Word of God?

Who set up the church? Christ. Why did Paul write letters to the early churches? To put them back in tune with the gospel. They had started to drift away from the teaching of Christ the same way churches are doing today. If Paul would have allowed the early churches to go their way, they would have been just like the so-called churches of today, out of tune with God, set up by man for man, unpleasing to God yet worldly accepted.

You see, some may want to do right, but they want to find favor in the world. This cannot be. God's way is holy, loving, merciful, and without sin. The world's way is greed, lust, pride, and doing whatever and however. There is the way of God, and there is the way of man. There is a path of righteous, and there is a path of sin. God loves one and hates the other. God does not mix the two. He will have no part of our ideas or theories. Yet we go on trying to instill what we want instead of what God wants.

We have churches that have changed just to fit the lifestyles of man today. We have others who still live in the past and live and teach by the Old Testament. They have not accepted the teaching of Christ. Yet Christ is the One who is coming after His church. Will your church be called up by Christ? Will your church be left behind with all other worldly things of man? One thing is for certain; you will do one or the other: be called up with Christ to a wondrous home in glory or be left behind to hell and the wrath of God. There is no middle ground; either you are on the rock, which is the foundation of Christ, or you are sinking in the waters of sin and destruction.

We have others who have set themselves in high order, being holier than thou. We have churches proclaiming to have powers to do all kinds of things. I acknowledge the power and gifts of the Holy Ghost. I also acknowledge God's Word on the power and gifts. I also accept His teachings on how, when, and where these gifts are to be used.

Some people believe there is only one sign of the Holy Ghost. That is fine for them; however, it is against God's Word to teach you must have this one gift. Read 1 Corinthians 12: 4--10. Some teach that water baptism or penance is remission of sin, while others teach as the act of water baptism is found in Acts 2:38. What I am trying to show you is this: man has instilled his views and opinions into the teaching and preaching of the Word of God just as he has done to everything else. He has screwed it up.

Look, some churches send men to school to become preachers, and that is fine. A well-educated preacher is an honor to God, if at first, he was called of God, which can only happen after he has been born again through the bloodshed salvation of Christ. After he has received the Holy Ghost, he receives his calling. This is also one of the gifts of the Holy Ghost given to man by God through Christ, of the spirit. This honor is not decided upon by you or your church or by anyone else.

There are no great secrets, deeds, acts, or works in salvation. It is free; it is gift of God, bought and paid for by Christ. It is yours for the asking. We need to just accept it by faith and then confess to man by our mouth. That is why man cannot leave it alone; it is simply too easy.

There is no secret in serving or worshipping God, just read His Word and let His spirit lead you. If you read a verse and do not understand it, that is all right. When you are ready for the understanding, God will give it to you. But the "how-to" be saved, the "way" you are saved, and "who" saves you, it is plan for all to understand. God loves you, and He wants you to be saved. He does not want to punish you for your disobedience or disbelief. That is your choice.

After you are saved, read God's Word. Let His spirit gives you true understanding. Find and attend a church that believes not just in words but also the whole Word of God. Listen to the preaching of a man called of God to deliver His Word, full of the Holy Ghost. The same spirit dwells in you because you are both of the same true God. Your spirit will bear witness with His spirit. If not, then move on. Do not let man mislead you. Remember Satan will use what seems right and cause you to do wrong. Trust in God, for in Him is the truth.

While some churches have turned a deaf ear to God's Word, others have gone and split apart. They have written their own books on how to worship and serve God. They simply refuse to accept the holy doctrine of Christ. This is done for bigger memberships and more money and for bigger and prettier buildings. The display of gold, silver, and bronze is for God's glory . . . or for the favor of man and worldly acceptance.

Some churches have big bank accounts; some have holdings in stocks and bonds. Some churches invest more money in the things of this world than in the work of God. Yet God tells us not to lay up treasures in this world. How can this be? Please be careful, for this is a crazy, mixed-up world, knowing not which way to turn.

There is a song written called "It's a Man's Man's World." Do not take part in it. Become a new creature. Let the thoughts and theories of man pass away. Grab a hold and partake in the Holy Greatness and mercy of God. Let Him touch your life and grant unto you the redemption of your soul. Amen.

I do not know why man allows himself to think that he is better than God, that he can actually alter the plan of God. What are we coming to? I cannot believe we think we are smarter than God. First, He is the One who gave us life. Second, He is the One who gives eternal life. What are we coming to? I know . . . an end! That is right! God is getting sick and tired of our sinful ways. He has given all that He can that we might be saved. He is hurt because we deny His only Son. He is angry and jealous because we listen to, follow, and worship other gods and forms of religion. He will put a stop to it, and it will be sooner rather than later.

Yes, the end is fast approaching. The tracks of our lives are swiftly leading us into eternal destruction, unless we heed to the warning. The next stop is hell. Switch tracks! Go the other way---the way of truth, love, and goodness of God.

You know, I cannot help to wonder, even as I write this book, that this might well be the year that brings forth the great day of our Lord. Then too this could very well be the day of the second coming of Christ. I could say, even as you read from this book, this very minute or the next second in time could bring God's book to an end.

This could be the last second to tick on God's big clock, meaning that time, as we know it, has run out. Our life and this world are now about to change. It may be time for Christ to fulfill the final promise of God's plan, that being that all things of man have come to an end.

This world and all that is on it and of it shall be destroyed. Christ will come back for His people. Those who accepted his bloodshed salvation will be led of Him to God's glorious Kingdom as God's angry wrath is poured out upon all who choose to reject the teaching and doctrine of Christ.

Yes, judgment and wrath are to all those who did not believe in the Word of God as it is written, seeing now the Word of God in its fulfillment. Regardless of your thoughts or theories, you are being judged by the very words you use, for whatever reason.

Just think, even though you did not believe in it, even though you thought somehow God would not bring this kind of judgment on mankind or the church you belonged to; you now are seeing every word in detail coming to pass, knowing now that nothing or no one can change, slow down, or stop the plan of God.

Christ will come for His people, just as He said He would. Who can say when that time will be? No one except the Almighty Himself. You know that time might be closer than you think. That is why we do not want to think about it. That is why we try to change it to suit us. That is why we ignore the warnings. Yes, our time is but for a season, and like the seasons, it will change.

That is what Satan wants to keep from you---the truth. That is why he misleads and deceives. He does not want you to know what lies ahead. How can you say "I'm knowledgeable of my path" when you know not where it leads? If you had any wisdom, you would let God's Word speak to you. You would see the start and end of your life's path. Unlike Satan or the ways of man, God tells it all---the good and the bad. You want wisdom . . . fear God. Satan, nor man, does not want you to know where you stand in God's plan. Yet remember this: no one is excluded from the plan of God. No one is left out. Every soul of every man, woman, and child has a place in God's plan. Yes, everyone who has ever lived, everyone who now lives, everyone who will ever live will take his place according to the Word of God. God has a place for you. It does not matter whether you want it or not, God will put you in our place.

The ways and teachings of man, meaning being led by the deceiving ways of Satan, do not want you to know your place. Nor do they want you to know you CAN change your place in God's plan. That does not and will not change the fact that God has a place.

Yes, it does not matter what you believe or disbelieve, whether you accept or deny. You can either hear and take heed to or ignore His Words. You can change them to suit yourself or take them as they are written. You can eat, drink, and be merry for a while, or you can love, worship, and serve. That is your God-given choice. That is your only choice in God's only plan. Remember, it is your soul that must face its eternal place. You may wish that you were left out and had no place, but that is not in the plan. Check it out: John 3:36, 15:6; Matthew 26:41; Revelation 20:13--15, 21:8.

You know this world cannot go on forever. Look at the shape and mess we have made of it. Yes, the Lord Jesus will be coming soon. Do not be naïve; take a good look around. A blind man can see the end is coming. You have to be insane or totally misled to think that we can go on much longer.

These are trying times. These are the days of great tribulations. We cannot survive them. We draw further and further away from the mercies of God. Therefore, we are closer and draw closer daily to God's judgment. If Christ does not come soon, all will be deceived (Matthew 24:21--22). Man will utterly destroy himself, if time allows. Just look at the hate and abuse that is in our lives. Look at what we do to one another and the very world in which we live. Yet we call this progress, for the betterment of man and the coexistence of lifestyles.

Because we now say, against God's Word, "You can believe what you want, you can practice any faith you want, you can have whatever kind of god you want." We are facing more problems today than ever before, not because there are more people but because more and more people are neglecting the Word of God.

Look at America fifty years ago . . . Love, world respect, morals, and families who loved and raised their families were evident. Look at the victories we won, the battles that were fought side by side, the prayers of the nation heard and answered by God, the children and families raised in the Word of God. Where has it all gone? Who took it away? Who stole the very heart of our nation from us? Remember "In God We Trust?" In home, church, school, and government, let us trust in God was our prayer.

Now in most places, we are not allowed to pray. Now we say, "Why should we trust God? Who is He? Who said He has all power?" We say, "Who is God? Is He to be trusted?" Yet we allow this to go on and on, ignoring the fact that the more we drift away from God's Word, the closer God's Word comes to being fulfilled. We must think man can teach man to know more than God! Tell me who is kidding whom?

Let's see. Yes, there are a lot more people today than ever before. But there is also more crime per person than ever before.

There are more people in jails and prisons on Sunday mornings than in all the churches. We now think that it is okay for men to marry men, women to marry women, and then to teach our children that this is acceptable. We have taken prayer and disobedience out of our homes and schools. Now our children pack guns, gang-bang, and kill us.

Now is that progress? Where is our wisdom? In whom do we put our trust? What in the name of God the Father are we doing to ourselves? Here is an example: 1) How many shootings and stabbings do you either hear about or read about in or around your major city? Keep track for a period of a month, and write that number down. 2) Now do the same on rape and all sex crimes and crimes on men, women, and children; and write that down. 3) Do this also with robberies and break-ins. 4) Look at divorces, and write those down. Just using these numbers, add them together then multiply that number by twelve months. Then multiply that by, let's say, the major cities in the United States, maybe by three hundred? WOW!

All those crimes yearly just in America, just because we ignore the teaching of God's Word. Man, are we smart? We cannot blame this on God.

Here is another example of our wisdom. We now tell women to go have sex, and if you become pregnant, do not worry, we will "kill" it for you. We also say to the married couples, if you want someone else, that is okay too. Get a divorce and find a new spouse. All this because we think we know more than God. All these things are not of God!

How has man benefited by drifting away from the true teachings of God? How have we improved our lives? Do we think all these crimes against ourselves are an improvement? Do we think that we know more than God about raising children? We must, for we deny His teaching, and we teach all sorts of other things. We have learned how to raise our children by a man who has never had children. Smart, huh?

We, as parents, spend more money and time on sex, either reading about, watching, or practicing in the lust of the flesh, than we spend on teaching and reading the Word of God to our children. Yet our children are being molested and raped by us because of this lust. What is wrong with us?

We kill numbers of unborn infants daily; some babies are killed by those who just do not want them. Yet when a baby just dies, we blame God. When a crime is committed against someone we love, we blame God. We have made this world a Godless place. We blame God for the mess.

Look! God had no part in our Godlessness. He holds no part with sin. This is our bed. We made it, and we must lie in it or change it! We must turn it over to God. He can remake us through Christ. He can save us of our sins. But no, we refuse Him. We just keep on listening to man. We just drift further away from God and close to God's wrath. We are very smart, huh?

We would rather teach ourselves to have orgasms than to seek the salvation of our souls. We want the lust of flesh over the Son of God. We would rather do drugs and alcohol to forget the terrible mess we are in than to allow God to make a change for us.

You see, God did not teach us to kill one another. He does not teach us to be homosexuals. He does not teach us to hate, to steal, or to get high. These are the results of man's wisdom actually out the misleading and trickery of Satan. Yet we think we know best.

If it is not the use of these things of sin, which causes enough crime, we commit crime to get money to commit more crimes. We are killing ourselves more today than ever, teens and adults alike. What has our disobedience to God gotten us?

It does not stop at crime. Look at the hospitals---babies being born addicted to drugs, born with aids and other sexual-sin sicknesses, and beds full of overdoses, suicide attempts, and mental sickness. All these are the result of a sin-plan sin.

However, we still think we are capable of working it out on our terms. We have not yet, and we are not going to. Instead of ignoring or claiming the Word of God to be used as we see fit, we need to trust God and follow His teachings, by the power of the Holy Spirit through the salvation of Christ our Lord. Amen and Amen!

Yes, we need to know the wisdom of man is foolishness in God's sight. We need to let God lead us through this sin-sick world. Let Him bless us with His love, mercy, and grace. Then when this mess is over, to be led into His wondrous glory, where sin and pain, crime, sickness, and death are no more.

Admit to God, "I am wrong. Satan has tricked me. I do not want my pride to be the fuel for the fires of hell. Save me, Lord."

It is not bad enough what we are doing to our bodies and minds. No, now we are spoiling the very land and water we need to live and grow our crops. We say it is okay to poison our crops if they yield us more profit. Whose profit?

Not that is enough. I think we got the message. No! Now here we add to our problems with wars. We call it war so that it is legal to kill. We are told by man, "Peace is at hand." Look around; never is there more war between or within countries as there is today.

We even have people killing people to prove they love and serve the real God. (Now that takes the cake!) Let's see. I know more than God, so I will kill people to prove that I am right. (That is really Godly!) That is what they did to Jesus; they thought they knew His Father more than He, so they just killed Him.

Let us not be blinded. Look at our leaders, banks, industries, large companies, and government. Look how greed has taken over. Companies are moving overseas for cheap labor, y et prices are still going up. We put people into temporary jobs to lower employment and cut wages and benefits for more profit. Whose profit? Let us make healthcare so high that only the rich can use it. Profit? Whose profit?

We say that crime is rampant because of the judicial system. Who made the system? Do not blame God for this one; this is man's baby. We do not know how to do anything right, yet we ignore the teaching of One who is righteous. God tells us what to do about crime and bad people, but we know better . . . right?

God did not put loopholes into His Word. Man does this. That is why a rapist can go free just because a police officer made a mistake in gathering evidence. I could go on and on . . . but why?

I know that I have painted an ugly picture. I know it seems there is no way out. But there is. God can and will deliver. Remember, our only crime is the rejection of God's Word. We are punished because we rejected His Holy Son. Our punishment is for all eternity, and our only atonement is the blood of Christ.

Our escape is through the salvation of our Lord; our reward is in this life as well as receiving the glorious Kingdom of God.

Man does not want to believe in God's plan, but if God's plan is fulfilled, man does not deal with God being angry with him. Man does not want to pay for his crime. But he will if he does not stop his crimes and live a life without willful sin.

We serve a just God, and He pulls no punches. He does not care who or what you are. You will have no excuses. There will be our hotshot lawyers to plead your case before God. You must and will stand before God for yourself. You alone will answer and pay for your crimes against God.

I know you know this world is in a terrible mess. Satan does not want you to see the truth. That is why I brought it up. You need to see the whole truth, not just the joys of sin but also the results.

Satan would have you to be ignorant. He does not want all to be told. If all were told, Satan will say it is a lie. He would have us to believe a lie and die in our sins. He does this and then lays claim to your soul. Here is what is sad: we let him. We even help him.

I know that so far, I have painted an ugly picture. This can cause bitterness in your heart toward the world. I just want you to see the awful mess we have created. I also just want you to see what the devil does not want you to see, for if you know the end of your path, if you could see the destruction, you are headed for, then you would change. Satan could no longer keep you from seeking your soul's salvation.

I do not want you to dwell on the miseries of this life but seek you a better life, the way of truth. While you enjoy the many pleasures and joy of serving God, not only does God warn you of the troublesome times, but He also gives you an escape. These times are bad, and they are going to get worse. We all know that. This life is like the schoolyard game of follow the leader. We follow what others do. Who are you following? Where are they headed?

It is okay to put the thought of them in the back of your mind just as long as we recognize them and understand why and how they come about. It is not healthy to dwell on all the misfortunes of the world. Our way of life because of sin and the father of sin paint a horrible picture---a picture full of hate, hunger, crime, and death . . . a picture without any escape.

Do not give up! There is hope for you, and there is an escape.

While the gate of salvation is open, you must enter therein. Many people still have hope. I just hope their hope lies with the one who delivers. Do not look at all the bad. God still has people who love you, people who pray for your soul, people who will tell you about the Holy Lamb of God, the One who will save you from the destruction of sin and the mighty wrath of God the Father.

There is still good in this world. It should get better. God has not yet removed His mercy and compassion from us. You still have time to turn to God. We need to take our thoughts away from the ways of this world and the wisdom of man. We need to turn our thoughts toward the Word and teaching of our Lord, for only by His power and wisdom can this world be put back to the way God had first intended for it to be.

Look, we have trusted man and tried all sorts of ways to help ourselves. Look at where that has gotten us. We have given Satan and his lies a chance; now it is time to give God a chance. He cannot make things any worse, and He just might make a difference. Satan does not want you to believe that, but you have believed his lies long enough. Trust the Word of God and see the truth revealed.

This world could get better, but time is short, and it must pass away. It cannot be perfect because of sin. Because sin and Satan have blinded the eyes of so many. Because of sin, the hearts of many have been hardened cold. Because of sin, we have shut off our mind to the Word of God. Yes, Satan will cause many souls to follow him; he will cause them to spend all eternity in the hellfire of God's angry wrath. Yes, eternal punishment for a life of neglecting His Word and rejecting His Son is our future.

This world will not have peace because we have forgotten who the peacemaker is. However, that does not mean you cannot have peace. All you have to do is trust fully in the Word of God, be born of His spirit, and enjoy the peace within instead of ignoring the love and mercy of our Lord. Ignore the foolishness of man and his deceiving ways.

You can overcome these troublesome times just by depending on the divine wisdom of God. Then you can enjoy your life and have peace everlasting, for you are now obeying God the Father. You will dwell in the midst of God's love abundantly, there to rejoice until you inherit His glorious Kingdom.

God helps us all to be in this part of your plan, not having to face thy wrath as it is poured out over this land; helps us not to be foolish in man's wisdom; helps us not to be misled by the shortcomings of sin; and helps us get off this vicious circle. We will temporarily solve one problem as we create another. Round and around we go; where will it stop? When God says so. He holds our destiny in His hands.

Do not take me wrong. I do not want you to think that I hate life because I do not. I love living on this beautiful planet. I truly love living in America, for I know that God loves and blesses the United States. He does so because we are the land of freedom; we care about people; we hold our hands out to all those in need. We should be a Godly country, thanking God every day for His many blessings.

That is our foundation, and it is time we stand on and take to heart our motto "In God We Trust." It is time we take our America back to the basics. It is time we tell all the cults, clubs, associations, order of whatever, lawyers, doctors, and groups of whatever to BACK OFF or get out! Our forefathers knew what they were doing. They knew whom to trust. We are the ones screwing things up. We trust and listen to the foolishness of man while we ignore the wisdom and plan of God.

I know I have jumped around a lot. I have hit and missed on many subjects. I did this so you would see the whole picture. I wanted you to see the forest, not just the trees. I wanted to open your eyes to the things Satan has hidden away. You must realize what is at stake. You must take the time to see the result.

Remember, for every action, there is a reaction. What will the reaction of God be to your action?

Because God created and loves you, you ought to love Him. Because Christ died for you, you owe Him your service. If you do what God the Father asks, He will do for you. If you work for God, He has a reward for you. If you neglect or deny Him, He has His wrath for you. Remember, it is YOU who causes your soul to face the hellfire and punishment . . . not God.

I write about a lot of the bad that is in the world today. Here is why: Everyone can see and is eager to face the good things of this life. We find joy in anything we can just to ignore the mess we are in. We need to take a good hard and open-minded look at what is really going on around us. Then we need to ask ourselves this: Is this the role God intended for man to play? Is this the kind of world He intended for us to live in and endure? I think not; I know this is not what God had in mind for mankind. That is why He dealt with man as He did. That is why He gave us the Holy Prophets of old. That is why He tried to lead His people in righteousness. He promised them a land of milk and honey, yet they chose another way. That is why He gave us the law and commandments of the Old Testament. He was trying to get man to live in His plan, not in the ways of sin.

God sent His only begotten Son to save man from this world of sin. Christ lived and died so that we could get back into the plan God had and has for mankind. God gave us His Holy Spirit; the spirit of Him will lead, guide, and direct our way of life . . . if we let it. So, we can have that land of milk and honey; that is God's plan for us.

Nevertheless, because of sin, Satan has given us a misleading way. He gives man his deceiving spirit to lead us astray. He lies to man. Satan tells us we know all. Therefore, we do not need to listen to God. Isn't that the same lie he told Eve? Isn't that why we were cast out of the blissful peace of the Garden of Eden?

Isn't this world today created by all the sins of yesterday? Yes, we are in this ungodly state because we deny the true teaching of the Word of God. Can we blame God? No, because we choose to reject, alter, and ignore the Father, the Son, and the Holy Ghost. The more we deny, the more we remove ourselves from the blissful peace of God's plan. Because of our deceiving ways, we draw closer to facing the torments, pain, and death of this life that causes us to endure the endless ages of eternity in the part of God's plan where souls are punished in hellfire; because this is the role we choose to enact.

Oh, God! Save us from our ignorance. Redeem our souls through the salvation of Christ. Lead us, O Lord, according to your plan. Enable our eyes and mind to be opened to the truth. Give us your love and blessing. Grant us entrance into thy Holy Kingdom. Amen.

Please do not remove yourself from the best part of God's plan. Do not live your life as to say I do not care that Christ came and died for me. I do not want the love, mercy, and blessings of God. I do not believe in heaven and hell as it is written, but if I am wrong, then I will go to hell instead of heaven. Is this what man has come to? I do not think so. We have only allowed ourselves to be misled and deceived.

You could say someone or something has pulled the wool over my eyes. Why have I not tried to see the truth? Why have I not at least given God a chance? Because man is not as smart as he thinks he is. While we think we have all the answers, while we think we are doing what we want to do, we have actually fallen into the entrapping snares of sin. We are actually doing what Satan wants. We are walking away from the love and mercy of God. We are being led right into hell, while he uses us to mock God.

This is done before man knows the truth, before you are born again through the Holy Ghost baptism of Christ. Before you can experience the true peace and blessings of God, you are taught ungodly ways. Man, and Satan inject their deceitful ideas upon us.

Before you can find the pleasures of God, you are taught the theories of man. You are caught up in worldly pleasures; drugs, sex, lust, and self-righteous ways of life are used to entrap you.

Television, radio, and the schools we attend denounce the teaching of God. Most parents never teach or read the Word of God to their children. Therefore, you are ensnared in the short-lived joys of sin. Not knowing the condition of your soul, it is not fair to God or to you. How can you make a decision of such great value without seeing both sides of the coin? God, you win; Satan, you lose.

If that is not bad enough, man goes one step further. He makes up and teaches his own plan and expects God to honor it. What a joke! Man adds to and takes away from the Word of God that he expects to save him. This is done because Satan's lies are instilled in their hearts, not because they want you to go to hell. It is because they think they are right.

Then we have teachings of power and glory of fame and fortune; none of which is Christlike. Do you see my point? Man wants everything his way, but in the end, it will be God's way. Whose side are you on?

Look, neither this world nor mankind love or care for you. If you get in their way, if you stand up for what is Godly, they will treat you like a dog. After all, they crucified our Lord, didn't they? Because no one cares about you or your soul as much as God does. Your eyes are not open to the trouble, pain, heartache, and death brought about by sin. This will go on and on until sin is removed. This can be done.

It starts with you then through the power of the Holy Ghost. You can tell your friends and loved ones because you want them to see the danger, because you do love and care for them. You want to lead them to safety. If man could see the fiery destruction up ahead, he would try to detour you around it. Yet he does not take his own soul to safety. Taking a different route that leads to the same point is not safety. You must change directions; turn around and head for the shelter in the arms of God. It is that easy.

Once you see where you are at, once you see where it leads you, once you decide this is not a place that you want to be, then you will get off your worldly ways and stand on the Word of God. You let Him and Him alone direct your path, for He is all, and He sees all. He knows all. Let Him give you a lesson on show-and- tell. He will reveal all, for He wants to save all. Please read Psalm 119:105.

If you listen to man (meaning lies), you will not be enlightened to the end. Satan would lose the battle. If you could see the joys of this world are short term, they also fall short of the glorious blessings of God. If you could see your soul's eternal home, Satan would lose. That is why you are blinded from the truth. He wants you to go to hell. He wants you to deny and mock God.

Whether you like it or not, Satan will take advantage of you. Our ignorance is his biggest tool. Once you listen to God, Satan is defeated. Yes, once you feel just one touch of the master's hand, Satan has nothing to offer. Look at the love, mercy, blessings, promises, and rewards God grants to His people. Now look at the pain, misery, and punishment God gives to those who have not accepted Him. Do not call God a liar, for in the end, you will face the truth of His Word.

Satan is fighting a losing battle. He cannot win if you do not let him. He cannot take away from the pleasures of God, unless you put a deaf ear to the Word of God. Even though Satan and his army outnumber God, we will overcome. We will stand our ground until the end yet not alone. Christ is in us and for us. At the end, Christ will deliver us to glory, while God dismantles this world and the things of it. Then He will pour out His angry wrath upon those who took part in the thoughts, theories, ideas, and ways of man. Then He will cast them all along with Satan, into the flames of the lake of fire. Pick your place.

Everything man has come up with leads us astray. Satan knows and uses all the tricks, but it does not matter. No matter how far you drift away, no matter how bad you think you are, God still loves you. He still wants to save you. He will free you from the bonds of this world. He will give unto you sweet peace and joy for your soul. That is right . . . Joy! More joy than you have ever experienced.

Do not listen to the lies. I have heard them all. You will NOT miss out on the happiness of this world; it will be added unto you. You will not lose out on the fun. You will not miss the so-called joys of sin. You will discover what fun and joy are really like. What can sin or man offer you that is not overwhelmed by what God can offer? We already know who loves you more. Do you want the One who cares for you and your soul gives unto you more and more life abundantly than the one who could care less about you? Not the one who wants to mislead and use you; not the one who wants you to lose your very soul because his soul is lost. Think about it.

All can be saved. All should be saved. You need to cast all else aside. Just one reach of your hand toward God, just one word from your heart, brings the power and wonders of God to your rescue. Just make the first move. Christ will come from His throne; the angels in heaven will rejoice as God brings you into His family and sees to all your needs. He will be your Father, and you will be His child. He will see to your joy and safety.

Through your faith and His grace, He will put you on and guide you down the pathway of righteousness where you will live and bask in His wondrous presence. You will enjoy His many blessings as you live according to His plan. What a good life it is to be at peace with God. Though He gives us a good joyful life there in this world, this world will end to bring forth our reward of the eternal Kingdom of Heaven, a promised land in Glory, a land made just for God's people. It's all yours, just for the asking. God's people will live in heavenly bliss. Only God's people will live there; all else will spend their eternity in the pits of hell. That is their reward for neglecting and rejecting the Word of God. Hell is there. However, you do not have to go there. God does not want you to go there. I know you do not want to go there either.

So why go there?

God's Word tells us how to live in His plan and in His Word. He tells us to prepare and await the second coming of Christ. We must put our faith where it belongs, in God, the creator of man, for it is only then that we really begin to live. To live in harmony with the Word of God is life everlasting. It is the life He intended for us, and we should be ever so grateful. We should live so we can show God that we are thankful for all He has done and given to us. We should worship His love and mercy, for there is no greater love than that has God for man.

Our life should be full of love. It is a part of God's plan. We should get along with and be able to worship with our brother and sister in Christ, for we are all members of God's family. We should treat all mankind with the same love, understanding, and mercy that Christ showed us. There is no place in our life for envy, lust, hate, or the problems we face if we lived and followed God's plan. So why not put it to the test? Why not try God? You can always go back to your old ways if you choose to.

You do not have to be a bad person to need God. All have sinned (Romans 3:23). You may not lust for sex, you may not kill, and you may not steal. In fact, according to the laws of man, you may be just fine. That is good; however, man does not judge your soul. Do not be misled or tricked. In God's eye, sin is sin. Your only sin might be that you are not born again, but as I have said, sin is sin. You need to repent. Do not let the wisdom of schools are knowledge or ignorance of man or your self-righteousness bound you for hell.

You rejecting the salvation of He who died for you is the sin of sins. Everything else is just the works of that sin. Everything else is merely the tools of Satan ---tools he uses to harden the hearts of mankind, hardened to the ways, love, and knowledge of God. Is this happening to you? Are you so great that you do not need God? Do you know more truth than the father of truth does? Are you so smart you can cause God to change His plan? If you must face the wrath of God's punishment, can you save your soul from it? Do you think God will have a special plan just for you? If so, then God is a liar . . .NOT!

God hates a liar. He hates sin. Sin is an out-and-out mockery toward Him. He will do away with sin and all those who take part in it. Do not test God by getting on His bad side. You will not like the result. Death is bad enough, but the second death is far worse (Rev. 20:14). Do not put your or man's knowledge on even tilt with God. Defeat the worldly way of sin, and win for yourself a crown of glory. Inherit the Kingdom of God. Proclaim victory for your soul's sake.

Take serious note that we are in the final part of God's plan, the part where He ends this chaotic life of sin, the part where you receive you part of His plan. You cannot trade it in; you cannot refuse it. You will get the reward you chose by your lifestyle in full power.

You see, when God blows the whistle, this game is over. There will be no more death, no sin, no disbelievers, no time-outs, and no overtime. His full plan will be enacted onto every soul of every man, woman, and child. The ages of eternity began while Christ separates those who are His from those He knows not. He will direct you according to God's Word, the very same Word you rejected and/or denied. Well, at least you have now been warned. For it will be as God said it would be; there would be no excuses accepted and no exceptions. Just like when God shut the door of the ark, there will be no way in and no way out. Your destiny is sealed, and your eternity begins. Just as those of Noah's day disbelieved, they were sealed out of God's safety. Just as in the days of Sodom and Gomorrah, they were sealed in God's wrath.

There is no way into God's safe haven except through and by God's simple plan of salvation. There is no way out of the judgment and wrath except the words and teaching of Christ. Get out of the trap while there is still time. Once God seals His plan, there is no way in or out. His judgment or your death seals God's plan. Where will you place your soul?

What you must ask yourself now is "Where and how do I fit into the plan of God?" The only way to answer that is to read and understand the words of the creator. Do not expect the ways or teaching of man to tell you the truth. He cannot put away his pride, greed, or lust. He will make a way that seems right, but it is the way of sin. What can you do with your soul after death? What can man or Satan do for you after death? Nothing at all. No one can help you. Today put your soul in the hands of Him who will have the right and power to place your soul in heaven or in hell.

Use God's Word, use the guidance of the teaching of Christ, use the inspiration of the Holy Spirit, for herein lies the power over death, grave, and hell. Let HIM, whose plan it is, show you where you fit in. If you are not where you should be or, I should say, where you WANT to be, then do what Christ is begging you to do. Make things right with God. Trust in Him who sent the One who can deliver. Accept Christ. He is the Savior of your soul.

Do not listen to man, and do not put it off. Do not be misled; the stakes are too high. It is a matter far worse than life and death, for our life here will cease. Death is not the end; it is the beginning of life eternal. What is more important? Seventy or eighty or even ninety years of this life or ten million times ten billion times over and over? Being the endless ages of eternity.

You can serve God in this short life and reign with Him forever in His heavenly Kingdom, or you can reject His teaching and listen to man in this life and face the flames of hell throughout forever. Which benefits you more? Is this life or the life to come the one to prepare for? Will you face God or man after death? What will be the sentence of our judgment? Will it be the Word of God or your thoughts or theories? Face these questions now so you do not have to face the wrong answer.

People, we must all return to and learn of the Words of God. We must forget the sinful ways of this world and let Him save us from our self-destruction. Everything that is wrong in our world can be made better if we use God's plan. All we have to do is to put our trust in Him and allow room in our life for Christ. The troubles, crimes, and pains of this life will be easier if we follow the path of God's plan. His love and grace will keep us safe and free from fear. He will lead us and deliver us according to His Holy Word. If we take to His path and stay strong in His teaching, He will shelter us and bless us one day at a time. His spirit will allow us to see and avoid the deceiving ways of man and sin.

Why one day at a time? Because we have no promise of tomorrow. No one knows when he or she will face death. Death can come quickly and in so many ways. No one but God Himself knows how many days are left. Only God knows the time He will call an end to this life so that eternity can begin.

There is another day you must take into consideration. The day that God will call on you no more, the day that you are turned over to a reprobate mind, a day that God gets fed up with your rejection. One of these three days will find you unprepared. Which will come first? Which will come when? Read Prov. 1:24--31.

The knowledge of man cannot tell you. Satan, even if he could, could not tell you. God does not tell you. He tells you to get ready today for tomorrow so that you may face His judgment. However, if not tomorrow, you can rest assured it WILL be one of your tomorrows. How many tomorrows do you have left? How much longer do you expect God to put up with your rejection?

Listen, do you really want God to prove to you His Word and plan? Would you not rather prove to God that you really want to be in the better part of His plan? You know you do. You know what to do. Yet, knowing of God's plan, whether you believe it or not, you know of it. Then seeing the problem caused by man and sin, you still go on your merry way even though the competition of God's plan is at Hand you continually reject and deny the salvation of Christ.

You will not outdo God. His Word will stand the test of time. Your world and plan will cease. You will enter into the completion of God's plan. You will become a believer in His Word. I sure hope it is by choice, not fulfillment, and I pray it is in time.

So, when making plans, plan to live according to God's plan. Do not accept anything less than the true Word of the Father. Do not turn to the ways of man. Do not allow yourself to be denied the promise of God. Do not be misled into thinking that either you, man, or this world can plan out a better life for you than God. As each moment brings you closer to your day of reckoning, it is even more reason to put God into your plans. Allow His Son to give you the joys and peace of this world and your next.

Plans are being made daily, which do not include God. I cannot understand how man can say he has all this wisdom. Yet he can ignore the all-powerful wisdom of Christ. Man needs to open his eyes because he remains in the darkness of sin. He does not let the light of Christ open his eyes. Do you think if you ignore or disbelieve it will go away? You are the one who will go away. You will go away from God and His people. You will go to the place here every and all things not of God go. Are you making plans for tomorrow? If God gives you a tomorrow, are you allowing room for Him?

Man will not make plans that include God. Man does not want to change; he would rather go on his merry way, however so short, than to admit he is wrong. Man refuses to acknowledge that his church might be wrong. He does not accept that his family teachings and traditions could be keeping him from the truth about God, just like men in the day of Christ did not want to receive or believe the new covenant. They did not want to change, so they used the old traditions to deceive the people into rejecting, abusing, and even killing the Son of God, the Son who was sent to fulfill the old and bring us into the new. Christ came to bring us out of the darkness and into the light, but we must allow the switch to be turned on.

Christ has brought us into the grace of God through faith. He stands awaiting to grant unto you the inheritance of God's people: the promises, the joy, the many blessings, and the glorious Kingdom of God. He stands with outstretched arms that are full of love, mercy, and grace. As He stands, His spirit calls unto you to come unto Him. He uses His people to tell you of Him. He uses the Word of God to draw you to Him, but you and only you can let Him into your life.

That is the difference between Him and Satan. Christ stands and knocks at your heart's door; you must invite Him in. You must want Him in your life because He loves you and wants you to love Him. Satan, however, does not wait. He does not ask to come in. Satan enters your heart and mind without your invitation. He barges in and makes his abode with you. He causes you to believe any lie that leads away from the Savior. He gives you joy in sin whether or not you want it. He uses the same things on you he has always used: lust of the flesh, pride of life, and lust of the eye. I assume by now you are getting tired of using these same tools of Satan. Well, you should be tired of Satan using them on you too! See, God wants you to accept His ways. He uses the holiest of ways to call you into the fold. Satan makes you accept his ways. He uses your family, friends, trickery, and/or our knowledge against us. Remember, with God, you have a choice; with Satan, you have no choice. He makes up your mind for you.

Look, God has the power to make us all puppets. He can make us do what He wants. You cannot defy nor defeat God. He made you. But God wants you to love and serve Him because of His love, mercy, and grace, not because He is bigger, better, smarter, and more powerful. He wants to be loved because He is love.

Here is another fact: you cannot defeat Satan. He can and does control our thoughts and ways. He does not want your love; he wants to steal your soul from the eternal bliss of God. He wants to and he will use everything this world has to offer to rob you of your soul. You do not have to ask him and cannot stop him. He will beat on you and lie to you. He will offer the joys of sin, riches, and even fame just to defeat you. He will allow miracles to be performed. He will throw all kinds of false doctrines at you. He will use anyone to convince you to believe a lie. All the while, Jesus stands and awaits your call for help.

If this is not true, then why did Jesus have to come and die? Why does His spirit have to be bestowed unto us? Why do Christians enjoy the many blessings and peace while serving God? To defeat Satan, that is why. Man is sentenced to a devil's hell unless Christ pardons them, which He does to all who ask. But remember, you must ask. He will not force Himself on you. He calls, draws, pleads, and awaits your invitation.

Again, man does not like to change. The fact is Satan uses all his power to convince you not to change, even though man's life would be so much richer and fuller. There are so much peace and true joy in serving Christ. Yet man listens to the lies of Satan.

He tricks man into thinking he must have riches. He has to have more than the guy next door. He has to have enough so he can pay to enjoy himself. See, sin does have a price. Amen. While God's love, joy, and peace are free, our Lord Jesus paid for them.

Man has really put himself in a strange position. He feels he needs and deserves the best of everything. Yet he has chosen the worst lifestyle in which to live. Man has a life of pain, discomfort, crime, lust, and greed that leads him to face two deaths. First, the death of the flesh that everybody must face. The second death is for those who do not accept Christ as their Savior. That is total rejection by God from His presence, totally separated from all God and all His glories. That is the death and end of the pit of hell. That is when God casts the pit of hell and those therein into the eternal lake of fire.

Man has chosen this lifestyle over the blissful life of love, mercy, and never-ending peace, which only comes by knowing that the spirit of God dwells within you, knowing you have all the promises He bestows to His people to which He will always be with you. He will bless you and keep you safe. His joyful spirit will lead you gracefully down the road of this life. He will lead you and guide you through all that comes upon you. He will be your comfort. He will receive you into glory where He will walk you freely down the golden streets of Paradise. There you will live forever as you bask in and enjoy the marvelous glories of the heavenly homeland that He has specially prepared for you.

Even though man has chosen to reject or deny the Godly plan, who does man blame when sickness and/or death claims the life of a loved one? Why do you think you can live according to man's plan and then call upon God when trouble approaches? Why does man pray for or light candles for a departed loved one? If they died without accepting Christ as their Savior, you cannot pray them out of hell! Remember, if they chose not to serve God, they get the punishment God promised.

This is a hard fact to face. Some so-called watered down doctrine preachers console the families and friends with lies and false hope. They think it is better to lie to you than tell you the truth.

That being if anyone dies without receiving the born- again birth through Christ, their souls are in hell. There is no exception. I do not care how good you are. God does not care what wonderful things you try to do. He does not care what church you attend. Nothing matters to God except you repenting and living a holy life. Remember, His judgment is final and forever. Amen.

Why would you accept a lie and put trust in false hope? If your lost loved one could speak to you, they would beg and plead for you to listen to God and seek His way of life. "Let Christ save your soul from these flames of hell" would be their cry (Luke 16:22--28). No one in hell wants you to come there except the devil himself. There is only one thing worse than allowing yourself entrance into the pits of hell. That is not believing or knowing and waking up in eternity, engulfed by the flames of hellfire. God forbid.

I was in a hospital to see a friend in ICU. This was one day after her triple bypass surgery. My friend was now facing emergency surgery, and I went in to pray with her. I prayed, "Lord, we know you have all power. You can heal and save. I pray you touch my friend in a special way. Let her see your need for Christ. Please speak to her heart. Don't let her die lost. Heal her, O Lord. If it is in thy will. If so, Lord, show her the light. Help her, Lord, is my prayer. Please, God, be with her family. Whatever the outcome, Lord, pour out your spirit upon them. That they too will see their need to seek their soul's salvation. In Jesus's name, I pray. Amen." Now then this family all drink and get drunk. They used God's name in vain. However, they are good friends and in man's eye real good people. But they do not serve God. They do not profess to be born-again Christians. Well, while I waited for my friend to be taken into surgery, someone asked a pastor of a certain church to come to the hospital. At this time, I was not a pastor. I was only called to preach a few months before this happened. So, I understood why they called a pastor in. This pastor thanked me for praying for my friend. (What's with that?)

He then said he would pray again for both her and her family, and he prayed a beautiful prayer. He helped the family to feel a little more at ease by saying "I know this family was baptized in my church years ago. I know she is a Christian, and I know thou are with them in their time of need. I know you can bring them hope, for she is in your hands. You are the God of love and all mercy. You can touch this sister and give peace to this family. In the name of Jesus," he prayed and "Amen."

What a lie! What a deceiving way to console the loved ones of a person who may be facing death. God will not heal this woman unless she calls upon the name of the Savior. Her fate lies solely in the hands of the doctors. God will not heal a lost person just because a so-called preacher asks him to. He will not speak peace to this family if they are not a born-again member of God's family.

What should take place is the family should see their need for Christ. As death approaches their loved one, they could pray that God gives her a chance to prepare her for judgment. Then if death should take her, they all could be reunited in glory. But man thinks the truth would be too cruel. There we go, listening to man again.

Satan wants to comfort and console falsely. If the truth were preached, souls would be saved. If God's people would take off the gloves and quit pampering the whims of man, less would die lost. Everyone must die. Not all the prayers in the world will stop death. Yes, even Christians die. No prayer can stop death. Our prayer should be to the families, friends, and loved ones. Death has to come, and then judgment followed by your eternity. Pray that all prepare to face God Almighty!

Do not tell people that someone is in God's hands. Do not tell families that their loved ones, in death, went to a better place. If that person did not find Jesus as their Savior, if they did not confess to you or to someone, then they are not in good hands; they are in man's hands. They are NOT going to a better place. They died and went to hell, just as God said they would. Tell them as inspired by the Holy Spirit and give them a thread of hope that God gave them time to repent. Put it out on the table in full view. If they do not like it, let them tell God when they too die and face God.

God wants men who are men, men who will preach and teach the Holy Word of God just as it is written, men who will not sugarcoat the Word and do not try to change it to fit man, and men who do not think it will bring fame and fortune but will preach it so that souls can be saved. If you are worried about how you are received by man, you are not of God. If you worry about making a big church and being respected by all men, you are not of God. You better worry about facing God yourself. If you are of God, you will try to please and serve Him. You do not do the devil's deceiving. You preach Jesus, Jesus, Jesus!

It's Friday here in the good old' USA and for most people the end of the workweek. Like always, everyone is planning or getting ready for the weekend. Everyone is looking forward to a few days of fun and leisure. Thoughts are full of parties, camping, fishing, racing, trips, getting high, robbing, stealing, etc. Yes, the weekend brings out the whole of mankind. But man has neglected or forgotten what the weekend also brings: a day of worship.

Yes, man's plan may not include God, but one of those days off was given to us to worship the Lord. It was in God's plan for you to have a day of Sabbath, a day of rest. Yet you do not include God in yours. That is why so many people have to work on weekends today. The Sabbath was not kept holy by enough men of God, so man took it away. (That is progress!) The greed of man saw the need of sin and a way to make more money. So, the Sabbath to mankind is just another day of play.

All kinds of plans are made, but few include going to church. It is just not in their plan. Man will not even take the time to simply thank God just for allowing us to see another week passing even though God holds the power in His hand to stop all time from passing. He can call for the last and final act of His plan. The next day we see may last forever. Are you ready? Think about it.

As I was saying, the weekend was nearing, and it would soon be here. The plans of man the country over were coming together. There were dates, marriages, birthdays, and orgies of all kids to attend. Connections were being made to buy and sell drugs, some of it for kicks and some to temporarily forget the stress, pain, and problems of this world. The bars, prostitutes, drug dealers, and police were all planning for the "big haul."

There were some who just planned to stay at home, relaxing and spending time with the family. Some would watch a little television or a lot of sports. Others would see to the tasks of chores. Some would have cookouts, while others would visit friends and family. Yes, some were good, clean, and wholesome plans. However, God was not a part of these plans.

There are two other types of plans being made. One of these plans included God. Yes, God's people planned to attend church on the Sabbath. They were going to worship and praise His holy name. They would go to church to give thanks and gain strength from His Word and while at church. They would be blessed and uplifted as they sang and testified of His great love, mercy, and grace. These being the children of God, being washed in the saving blood of our Lord and Savior. These having the Holy Spirit to inspire and lead them. These relying on the Word and promises of God, which would keep them safe from being led stray while they awaited the coming of the Lord to deliver them to that which was prepared for them!

Now the other plans, which were being made, were made by a larger and more arrogant group. These are those who were also planning to go to church; however, they were going just to be seen. They use church to gain respect of man. They want people to think good of them while hoping that their attendance and membership would hide their sins (not from God. Amen!). They would give money when the plate was passed, thinking to buy God's love and mercy. (It is not for sale.)

Some of this group would attend a worldly church. What does that mean? These are the churches (and there are a lot of them) that have drifted far from the teaching of Christ. For you see, without Christ being the head, there is no church. Christ Himself set up the church, so you might as well call it what it is: an Antichrist meeting. These people still put their trust in the ways and sacraments of the Old Testament, thus denying themselves of being born again. We have passed through the law and covenant of temple worship. Christ has brought us into the later stage of God's plan. God will judge man according to whom He sent and raised from the grave (John 12:48). Who now stands as our mediator with

God? This group has also fallen in a snare. Satan has made them believe a lie.

Others of this big group will miss their entrance into heaven by going to man's church. What is that? That is meeting of people that are hoodwinked. The founder of this group is the sheep in wolves' clothing. Satan disguises himself in the form of a Godly man, a man who appears to be a great saint. Satan allows him to act out great works ---acts of healing, laying on of hands--- to which people are overcome by the Holy Ghost. Great services that include singing and beauty, great riches promised by the spirit (whose spirit?). These men perform acts of driving out spirits---acts of revelations. Some god telling them that you have

"lump" and then healing it. What a mockery to God and His Word! I have never seen so many so-called Christians having evil spirits. I have never seen so many men having powers and even more powers of the apostles. No mention at all of anyone other than the twelve and the alternate being ordained to perform such acts. Remember that which is of man is sin.

Now do not take me wrong. I do not deny the power of the gifts of the Holy Ghost. I believe in and preach in divine healing, prophesy and visions, and men being empowered through the Holy Ghost to do the will of God. But it must be done according to the teachings of Christ. Christ did not nor do His apostles get rich for doing the will of God. Golds, jewelry, diamonds, planes, limousines, stocks, and bonds, there are all of man. All are to be sold and the money used to feed and clothe the poor.

If you yourself have the power to heal, then go out into the streets; go to the people who are sick with disease and dying without being saved. Use all that God has given to you to heal and save the lost. That is what God says, and that is what Jesus did. That is what He told His apostles to do, and that is what the Word tells Christians to do. If a man claims to be empowered of God, then he will live the same as you according to God's Word (James 5:14). Now if you practice other means, then you are of other spirits. Amen. Read Acts 19:13--16, Acts 16:16--19, and Matthew 7:21--24. Be on guard of these workers of iniquity.

It is sad how man, for his own glory and fame, will cause you to turn away or to ignore God's Word. Man will believe in or put his trust in anything coming or going as long as it looks good of feels good. Remember, if you are not born again, if you go to church and feel at ease, then you are not in God's church. If you are not hearing salvation preached, you will not be saved (Galatians 1:8). Watch out for man's church. It is not of God.

So, this weekend is just like weekends of the past; there are all sorts of plans for all sorts of reasons. You can leave God out of our plans, but He will not leave you out of His plan. Man does not want to listen to God's Word, yet time has proven sin brings forth death. That is why we should turn to God, the giver of life eternal. Instead, man turns to the short-lived pleasures of sin that takes life and causes God's wrath to be upon us.

There are so much danger and death because of sin. If you really thought about it, you would be afraid to go outside your home. So, we just do not think about it, or we make excuses for it. We do not want to see what could lie ahead. That would cause us to turn to God, and Satan will not allow that to happen without a fight. So, he keeps you from the truth. He makes you think things will be all right.

Yet the facts will shock you. There will be many people killed in car wrecks just because someone is either high on drugs or drunk. Innocent people of all ages will be shot or stabbed to death because of sin. Look at how many will be raped, robbed, or beaten just because man has taken to the ways of sin. How many homes will be broken into or cars stolen? Look at the number of kids who will commit suicide. However, we ignore this part of sin. We blindly go along with life as it is.

Man will not change. In fact, he cannot change his ways until he includes God. Mankind will never change its ways. Man thinks that he is too big or too smart to serve God. But that does not stop you. You still have the right and chance to ask God to come into your life. He will make your life worth living. He will deliver you from this sinful world and give you a home in heaven.

If you escape death this weekend, you very well might see the second coming of Christ. God could change all plans. He might be fed up with our sinful ways. Yes, God can put an end to time and plans we have made for it. And there is nothing we can do about it, for God's plan will be fulfilled just as it is written. It does not matter to God what we think or what we do, either we accept or we reject, for at that day here is God's plan. Every knee will bend, every tongue shall confess, and every single person will be a believer. It will be clear to all, for at that time, all will see and acknowledge the Son of God in all His glory as they witness the enactment of the Word of God.

If man or when you turn to God, things will change for the better. Love enters the picture ---true love. Man will begin to love man as himself. Then we will show our love for our fellow man with our labor of love and kindness. Instead of hate and greed, we will look past the color of skin; we will live in peace and harmony just as in God's plan.

By becoming a child of God, you will see the terrible end that sin brings. Our whole outlook changes; we now want our fellow man to be enlightened to the many wonders and joys in serving God. We do not want anyone to die lost and perish in the pits of hell. That is the difference between God's people and the people of the world . . . sin.

People of the world want to show off what they have. If they have latched onto something that is really great, they want you to know, but they will not tell you how they got it. God's people tell you that they have found it, and they will not stop until they tell everyone how they can have it too. If worldly people help you gain something, it will cost you. If God's people do not help you to obtain God's gain, it will cost them. God's way seems to be far better.

However, man and his plans go on. They never give a thought to changing because man does not listen to God. Yet it takes God to draw man out of his sinful ways. If you do not look, you will not see the danger. If you do not change, you have no choice. You will die in your sins. That is why God is reaching out to you. That is why He uses His people to tell you and show you the means of salvation.

One such person is Reverend Evans, a man of God who was called to preach the gospel. He, along with a few Christians, was out working for the Lord this weekend. They, knowing the week-end brought the Sabbath, were out on the streets. They were out visiting people in their homes. Reverend Evans would pair them up, and they would go door to door and invite people to attend church on Sunday, telling them if they did not have a way, the church would pick them up and bring them home.

They would tell people about Jesus and about the love of God. Some of the people they visited said they would at least consider it; a few planned to attend. Yet most people told Reverend Evans their plans were already made. Some said they were simply not interested or just not ready for church, while others just said, "No way!"

Along with the visitation team was a man by the name of Brother Reynolds. He, like the other members of the team, was a man of God. Brother Reynolds has been a Christian for some time and knew about the Words and glory of God. He could not understand why people would not at least give God a chance to show and prove unto them His love and mercy, why one after another rejected their invitation just to come and visit their services.

On the way back to church, Brother Reynolds asked Reverend Evans, "I wonder if the people who do not go to church put their faith into God's Word. Would they change their plans or ways if Christ Himself would ask them?" Reverend Evans answered, "I don't think most of them would, for you see, when Christ lived among men, He taught and showed man God's ways. He also showed them the powers of God and His Words. He gave man promises made to all who love and serve God. Yet they turned Christ away. In fact, because He wanted to bring them from the law into grace, they crucified Him. They, just like people today, do not want to change.

Today man is so set in his ways for whatever reason even a direct invitation of Christ would be ignored or put off. See, the spirit of sin causes man to push away from God. Satan would have man to put off God until it would fit into his plans. Only God does not fit into the plans of man. We cannot dictate to God the terms on which we will deal with Him. God does not have to fit into man's plans, for God has a plan that we all fit in. Man must deal with God on His terms. He must get man to ignore the lies of sin and see where he stands in the truth and the throne of judgment.

I added the ways of man have turned the whole world inside out. Parents used to read and teach the Word of God to their children. Parents used to live close to Christ. We had an example to follow. We could see the power of prayer in action. This made it hard for Satan to get his claws into our young people. He would have to work hard to turn our children into a life of sin. Now it is the other way around. Not telling them where sin takes their souls, then we leave it up to God to draw them into salvation.

Today God must use His people and the Holy Spirit in order to reach and teach our children who are already entrapped by the powers (yes, I said the powers) of sin. It gets harder and harder to get man to hear the Word of God. That makes it hard for Christ to bring them into the saving power of His blood. Satan treats them like puppets. He lets them kick around in and tangle freely until they hear God's Word. Then he lures them in; he lies, deceives, and tricks them into submission.

Brother Reynolds spoke up and said, "You know, even churches today have compromised to and accepted the ways and toys of sin. They know if they preach the true Word of God, they would lose some members. Man is so impressed with numbers and money that churches have jumped on the bandwagon. They deceive the very souls and some who are searching for the truth. Satan uses many tools to keep man away from the teaching of God's Word. He will use our church unless we stand strong and ray long."

I replied, "Man has to be careful before choosing a church. Some churches have their own way to obtain membership. You may have to study their ways and doctrine. Some, you can buy your membership. Some others sprinkle you with water into the church. They use this as an act of baptism, while others ask you to sign the book of membership and do your part. However, I am glad not all churches fit into these categories. I praise God that it is only man's churches which make up their own rules, rituals, and doctrines."

The rules and doctrine of God's church are set up by Christ. He is the One who brought us out from the ways of old by His death into the grace of faith. To be a member of His family and church to inherit the new covenant, you must be born into it, not by natural birth but by a spiritual birth. Man's ways will only reward you with the things of man. God's reward is not of man. His reward is given with all power, glory, and it is eternal.

Brother Reynolds jumped in with "Why does man build his hopes and beliefs in the ways of man's knowledge when the reward for this is something of this world---man-made? For when we die, we take nothing of this world with us. Man cannot even take his false hope or doctrine. For at death, you will see the truth. You will have to face the doctrine of Christ. Why not take something into death that is not of this world? Take the Holy Ghost of God, the Words, and teachings of Christ, for these will prove just where you fit in God's plan."

But all is not lost. God does have a people He knows as His, children born unto Him through the blood of Christ, those whose plans are in alignment with His Words. There are still God's people who, after accepting Christ, preach, teach, tell, and even show others of the enjoyment and pleasures in serving the Son of God. There are still those who stand on the Words and promises of God. These are those who will inherit the glorious

Kingdom of Eternity; their place with God is in heaven. Amen. God has never been pleased nor is He pleased with man today.

Because of man's acceptance to sinful ways, God's feelings are hurt. He is angry with the ways of this world and with man. God will punish man for rejecting His beloved Son, of this you can be sure. He did not give His Son to man to die and be punished for our sins just to have us mock His salvation with false doctrines and teachings, without setting things straight and punishing those who re-punish Christ daily by their disbelief.

God loves and calls each man and woman unto repentance through the Holy Spirit. He has done this since Christ brought salvation to the souls of man. He will keep calling on man until He calls for this world to end and eternity to begin. He is obligated to do this by His Word. He calls on each of us until we are turned over to a reprobate mind. In other words, we have totally given ourselves over to Satan. Yes, this does happen. Just look around and see how Satan controls the minds of many people today. However, God has not given up on you. You still have a choice. You still have time to choose your eternal home. Why leave it to chance? You will lose.

God calls on your heart to accept Christ as your Savior. He is doing all He can to give you the promise of heaven. He wants you to be blessed in this world. He wants you to take your burdens and problems into His care. He loves you so much. He wants to give unto you all the glories of His power and mercy. He wants you to enjoy the fulfillment of His Word to His people, not the wrath of His judgment. He does not, Christ does not, and the Spirit is telling you not to wait until the fulfillment to find out you are to face God's wrath. God's people love you also; they are trying to help you to not choose the fulfillment of His punishment. You will not like that choice. You still have a chance to change. Take it.

Do not drift so far away to where you can't hear God's call or the spirit's knock. Do not let sin or the ways therein harden your heart. Do not let Satan blind your eyes to the truth. Do not turn a deaf ear to God's Words. You could slip into the flames of hell. Death can come quick and in so many ways, so could the final be coming of Christ. Sadly, death comes to all. Sin brought it, and death brings judgment. Judgment brings the final stage of God's plan. Are you innocent, or are you guilty? Will you be sentenced to a devil's hell or rewarded with the Kingdom of God. That day is coming. When? Maybe within the hour. The flames are getting higher, and souls are already burning. It is time to jump in or jump out.

As time goes on and so does the ways of this world, plans all over are being made daily, plans filled with sin and the pleasures therein, plans that do not include God. If time would allow, these plans would all come to pass. That is unless someone heard the soft sweet call of our Lord and answered it. We must take time to worship and praise God. We must thank Him for the saving power of Christ, for these are the gifts of God that enable some who had their weekends planned to change their plans, for they were smart enough and cared for their souls enough to heed the warning and to answer to the voice of our Lord.

Now they are sheltered in the arms of God and protected from the lies and tricks of man. They have received the spirit of Christ. He changes them into the newness of life. He leads them through the pitfalls of sin. He shows them the truth. They changed their plans by putting Satan behind them and the Son of God within them. This makes them children of God. Just a man who of sin was set free. Now they must rely on God's Word and promises. They must live day to day, one day at a time, always being strengthened and led by the Holy Spirit, because Satan and man are out there, waiting to drag you down.

Even though man refuses to alter his plans for God, he expects God to alter His plans for man. Does this make any sense? There are many reasons why man should allow room for God in his plans. A few of these are the following:

1. There is no better time than now to start receiving the goodness of God. You do not know nor can you imagine what not being of God is causing you to miss out on.
2. Remember, the hands of God's clock might be ticking the last tick. Time will cease to allow eternity to start.
3. All man must face death. No man knows how or when. That is also God's call.
4. Before Satan gets his claws in you, he is the monkey on your back. Do not be an addict. You could get hooked on sin.
5. Remember, God has a place and a plan for you. You get to decide which place and plan you want.

These are just five reasons for turning your life over the wondrous ways of our Lord. There are a lot more. God's Word is full of reason for serving Him. It is also full of reasons why you should STOP serving Satan, man's knowledge, worldly ways, and the things of the flesh. How important are the above reasons? That is up to you. Think about them. Read them again. Now I ask you, what reasons can you give for not serving our loving Savior? How does your reasoning stack up to God's?

With the world in the shape it is in, with so many false doctrines and false teachings, with the way sin has been so acceptable, it must really please God to see there are still some who will both here and obey His Word. Even the angels rejoice when a man or woman changes their plans and turns their love to God. God allows time to go on because there are still some who accept Christ and are thankful that He came and gave His life just so that we can be saved. Why do you try to anger or hurt God? Why are you driving the nails back into the hands of Jesus? Why is man still crucifying Him?

You know all man has to do is to stop listening to the knowledge of man. It is nothing compared to the mighty wisdom of God. We must quit following the ways of man, for we now know from where man's ways came. We must not listen to scientists or psychiatrists; they only know what was taught to them by man. They can only guess or make up excuses for the shape you or this world is in. Unless they are men of God, led by God, they cannot tell you the reason you are what you are. Stop making excuses! Do not accept excuses. Get results through God. Man calls rapists, murderers, thieves, and pedophiles a form of sickness. God calls them sin-sick. Man gives pills or tells us to cope with the stress and strain of this life. God cures stress and strain with the gospel. Man digs himself out of one pit into another. God has a permanent pit for man. He has a heavenly home for the men of God. Man is born into sin, lives in sin, and will die in sin. God hates sin. Christ will save you from sin. The Holy Ghost will lead you away from sin. The problem with man is SIN. The solution is GOD. Try to solve any problem without the right formula, and you will fail.

Man must turn a deaf ear to all ungodly teachings, preaching, and traditions. Remember, do not forget that all who preach are not of God. All churches are not built on Christ. Most traditions are of the past, and just like the law, we must leave them in the past. It is sad to say but these ungodly ways fit so easily into the ways of man. I wonder why. Here is a thought to ponder on: man does not want to change his ways to please God. Yet the fact that he knows he has to change proves his need TO change.

Man thinks if he rejects that he is wrong, does not admit that he is wrong, denies that he is wrong, believes that he is not wrong, THIS makes him right. NO! This makes him a fool. This makes him ignorant to the knowledge and wisdom of righteousness that is found in the Word of God. This also makes him lazy, for he will not take it upon himself to read the Word of or to be led of the Spirit of God. You must receive Christ today. Do not put it off any longer.

That is unless you say "I want to live my life my way." But this also makes you a fool because if you are not living for Christ, you are not doing what you want. You are doing what Satan tells you. If you do not believe that, try to stop, and sin no more. Do what no one else has ever done.

Maybe you are thinking "I will just take my chances. God will not send me to hell. He is a loving God and too kind of a God. He is full of mercy and grace." Remember, God is also truthful. He said He would punish all who reject the gospel of His Son, and so it will be done. Do you think that God lies? Do not be that big of a fool.

God does not care about your doctrine, your denomination, your tradition, or your excuses. He will do exactly what He says to the letter. Our Father has warned what He will do to you if you do not obey. What He has told you to do is what He wants. So do not blame God if you get burned. You do not have to, but if your soul does burn, it is because you chose for it to happen. I hope you do not need proof.

See, God's plan is like night and day. Man knows by man's knowledge that night will turn to day. He also knows there is nothing he can do to stop it. He can disbelieve, he can hide his face from it, and he can tell himself anything he wants. But unless God says different, this night will turn into day. We accept that as a fact.

Death is another example. Man knows that once born, you face death, sooner or later. Nothing man has or ever will have defies death. But God says man must die, and die we will. We accept that as a fact. You could say, "God will not let me die. He is too kind," or "God will not let my mom die because I asked him not to." Yet death comes. Why? Because He said it would, and God cannot lie. So do not even ask.

Why does not the same go for the rest of God's Words and plans? We cannot do anything about these two examples of His Word, so what makes us think we can do anything about the rest? Look, the Word says you will enjoy the glorious Kingdom of God, or you will face the fury of His wrath. Can anything we can do, say, or think stop, alter, or change these two parts of His Words? I think not. These two are the same as the two I gave as an example. They too are facts because God said it. Therefore, accept it. Just because we witness the two examples daily does not mean one is any less a fact than the other. It just means we do not have faith in God's Word. We just trust what we can see. Well, just guess which part of God's judgment you will see. Just think which part of God's plan you will have to accept then because you decided not to accept all parts now.

If you really want to be a somebody, be somebody who takes advantage of the time and choices you have. Do not be a pushover for Satan. If you want help, comfort, and peace in this life, if you want the treasures and wonders in the next life, then get off your high horse! Get off your deadbeat rump!

Do something about it. No one can do it for you. Stop wishing things were better, and better yourself. Let God change you and make you what you should be. Live in the blessed plan of God, and stop living a life doomed by His Word. Doggone it! Wise up! You are in a fight for your soul. Allow God to give you victory over Satan and salvation for your sins.

In a way, I hope the last part of this chapter has made you upset or even angry. Yes, angry enough to cause you to go into God's Word and prove me wrong. Yeah, that's it . . . Go into His Word, read, and look for the truth yourself. That is the way it should be. Then the power of His Word through His spirit can deal with your heart and draw your soul unto repentance.

If you do not believe in His Word, if you think the Bible is just man's writings, then do not be shy. Jump on in! Get your feet wet! There have been bigger and better people than you who thought there was no truth in the power of God's Word. Put it to the test. Better yet, go to a bible-preaching church. Get down to the very nitty-gritty, and see if you do not feel the soft, sweet touch of God's hand. I know the power therein. I know firsthand what God can do. I also know and accept His Word as fact. Do not let the memory of what I told you burn in your mind while your soul feels, tastes, and smells the burning of itself. Do not let your eyes witness the pain and torture of sin. Do not let your ears hear the horrible cries for mercy, the begging and pleading, for just one more chance to believe. No, as the saying goes, "Don't go there!"

This weekend started like most other weekends. The plans and ways of men went on as before, for life goes on. Yet because of man's worldly ways, some people's lives would not continue, while others would face the problems and stresses of this life, not accepting the fact that nothing good can come of this life or of the flesh not being of God.

But praise God for the few souls who listen to the call of our Lord and are saved! Thanks be to Jesus for those who use this life to draw closer and closer to His merciful grace, thus enabling Him to use them for His work and glory. You need to become part of this precious group, for God loves you. He also needs you. He wants you to become one of His. He wants so much to give unto you the glorious gift of life and life eternal. All you have to do is make plans to make room for God in your life. Do not push Him out. Do not evict His love and mercy from your soul. Come let Him make His abode with you.

Do not listen to Satan. You need to make peace with God the very minute Satan tells you not to and when this thought enters into your mind: "Maybe I should make this Godly thing. Maybe I am not truly a child of God. Just maybe I am mistaken." Could this reborn life be the right way? These thoughts are of God. Amen? The "I can't!" "I will not!" "I am not ready!" "I am too young!" "I do not believe!" and "I will miss out of the pleasures of sinning!" These, along with whatever else is holding you back, all are of Satan.

Why is it every time a Godly thought comes to mind, Satan replaces it with one of his?

Think about it. Why do I not search for the truth? Why will I not make up my mind to at least hear God's Word preached? If there is no truth in His Word, why is there a battle against it? If there is not a better life with God than without, then everyone who accepted it would prove it untrue. Remember, a lie will not last for two thousand and some years. A lie cannot wipe away tears or heal the sick. A lie cannot bless and protect you. A lie is a lie. It deceives you. It tricks you. It causes you to not accept the truth.

Why did you say "God, if you are the Almighty, if you are the truth of life, if you do want me to become one of your blessed, if this is truly what I need to do, if there is a better way of life for me and my family, if I will go to hell, if I do not accept Christ, hen show me the way. Help me to forget all I know and believe and give me the knowledge from your wisdom?" What are you afraid of? The truth?

Do not be afraid of God. Fear His judgment just like when you go to your daddy. "Dad, I need to know what I should do." Dad says, "I cannot make the decision for you, son. I can only tell you the benefits of your choice. If you do this, you are promised a peaceful life. You will have someone who will always go before you just to lead the way. Then when it is time, you will receive a crown of glory. If you do not do this, you must face life alone. You will face death alone, plus you will be punished if you do not obey." Dad says, "I cannot make that decision for you, for I must make the same decision for myself."

If your dad says, "Go this way, son. I will be with you," then says, "Do not go there! Oh, son, it is terrible! If you go there, I will punish you," you know your dad loves you. He wants what is best for you. Do you obey him because you are scared of him or because you are scared of his punishment? Will your dad punish you if you do not do wrong, or will he be proud? Should you fear his love or his wrath?

If a police officer is chasing you for doing wrong, do you fear him or what will happen if you are caught? When you go to court, do you fear the judge as man, or do you fear the power and authority the judge has over you? Do you fear HIM or your sentence of punishment?

Well, it is the same with God. He is proud and happy when you obey. He too will punish. He has power and authority over you. He will also sentence you. The term of your sentence is the endless ages of eternity. Your place of confinement is the eternal lake of fire. There will be no parole and no chances of an appeal, for you see, God is the supreme judge. He wrote the law. Praise God!

Do not be afraid to choose God because with God, you have choice. You can decide to listen and obey, or you can decide not to follow the inspiration of His spirit or His Word. You can decide to walk a path that leads toward heaven or a path that leads to wrath. God does not make you do right. He wants you to love Him because He is God. God does not lie, trick, or deceive you. He does not manipulate you. He just tells you like it is. Please do not make Him prove His judgment to you. Come to God now. Do not expect favoritism from the throne of judgment. He will not know you.

With God, there is a choice. With Satan, you have no choice, no chance. The ways of sin are doomed from the start. If you live out of God's plan, Satan rules. He also has powers over you; however, his powers are subject to God. Satan misuses and abuses. He makes you do what he wants. He knows how far he can push before you seek the light. He can push some a lot further than others, while some he does not push at all. He just gives them a false security. All he has to do to them is cause them to believe a lie. He paints a pretty picture over the bottomless pit just for you. Do not get sucked in by its beauty.

And next weekend will be just like this one if time allows. It will bring Sunday services, and preachers called of God will bring the gospel of Christ. I am glad to have known a few of these. Reverend Evans, as I have said before, is one such man. Reverend Evans, after accepting Christ as his Savior, was called to preach and pastor a church, a church that stands on and holds up the entire Word of God, a church that does all it can to teach about Jesus, a church that I know God is pleased with. Now do not get me wrong. It is not my purpose to lead you to this one church. Nor do I want you to think that this is God's only church. God has a lot of true believing churches and many members in the church family. This just happens to be one I personally know of, one that still does the work of our Lord. We need all the ones we have plus some. God needs all of us to help in the battle against the ways of man and sin. The more who teach, preach, and obey God's Word, the more souls can hear the truth, the more that man can be spared of the trouble, stress, and pain of this world.

We desperately need man to turn his ways to the way of the cross. We need the love and guidance of Jesus in our plans. The more man does for God, the more God can do for man. The more man listens to man, the less he hears from God. The further we get from God, the more pain, trouble, and death we cause for man. We cannot and we will not make things better until we reach for the giver of knowledge. No one can help us out of this rut unless we reach up to the one above.

Last weekend found Reverend Evans greeting those coming to the church where he was the pastor. He and the deacons loved greeting God's people and the visitors who came. They wanted all to feel the love of God's people. They wanted you to feel welcomed and at home in God's house. The church should also extend friendship to all who come so you too can feel welcome in the house of worship.

As Reverend Evans started the service, he noticed a very large man had come in. This man looked angry or displeased as he took a seat toward the back pew. As the services began, you could feel the presence of the Holy Ghost. The service obeyed the spirit as it led. God was worshipped in spirit and in truth. The songs and testimonies of praise were in accordance with the Word. The spirit was blessing. Some cried, some shouted, and some stood with their arms reaching toward heaven! Now came the time for the Word.

Now I did not mention the format nor did I mention the steps of the service, for it does not matter in what order you do worship. It only matters that you worship in order. I know what you must be thinking; "This must be a Holy Roller church." That is a man-made phrase to describe the praising of God, for you ee, man does not want you to see someone being touched by the Holy Spirit. Man, or you know who, does not want you to see tears of pure joy and delight for the wonders of God toward His people. Satan would have you believe this lie. The power of the Holy Spirit cannot make a child of God so happy. He has to tell someone, or he has to stand and shout, praising unto the Savior and keeper of his soul.

Satan wants you to think this is an act. He tells you God cannot make a man jump with joy. He cannot overwhelm you with His love. That is because he has never felt the power of the Holy Ghost. Have you? Then do not try to tell me of things you know nothing about. Yes, even man tells us to sit and be quiet. Do not show any emotion. Just sit there and ignore the spirit. It will go away. Some churches feel that way.

In part, they are right. If you ignore the Holy Spirit, it will go away from you. It will pour out its blessing on one who will accept it. Again, I tell you, God does not force His will or blessings on anyone. Sadly, man and some churches miss the mark. The Holy Spirit has gone away. It went out to God's people who would hear and obey.

Man, and even some churches have put the Holy Spirit out of their service. They either limit the power thereof and/or deny the power. Here is another lie that Satan would have you to believe: man can only act out his joy over man-made things or the things of this life. He is telling you that man or worldly things can give you more reason to rejoice, cry, shout, or jump with joy than what God Almighty can. What a joke! Worldly churches believe this same lie. They too want you to believe there is no emotion or big deal in worshipping God. They think it is just sacraments, rituals, or lip service, and yet they claim to believe in God's Word.

First, look at those types of churches. The Old Testament is full of Godly men showing emotion. Prophets fell on their faces and Ried to God. David leaped for joy. Psalm tells us to make a joyful noise unto our Lord. David tells us to sing songs, play music, and bang the cymbal. Prophets shouted over the victories God gave them. Abraham was stopped in the act of killing his firstborn just to show God his faith. Yet today's churches say no . . . NO.

In the New Testament, Jesus says give thanks in all things. He did not say "in silence." He also tells us that we must confess of our salvation unto man. He tells us that even the angels in heaven rejoice over souls being born again. Paul tells us the Holy Ghost will give you gifts: gifts to prophesy, testify, and rejoice. He also tells us how to keep it in order in the church, and he tells us that it is okay to greet the brother in Christ with a holy kiss. What church or man can tell God? "We do not want the spirit to lead us to do this or that? We do not like it? We do not act that way? That is not how we do it?" A church not of God, that is who. Now let us look at man. The devil has really got him screwed up. It is okay to jump, shout, boo, and even get angry over a ball game. Man pays cheerleaders to root for their teams. Man jumps with joy over the birth of a child knowing that he is bringing this child into a terrible mess. Today we laugh and cry, and some have orgasms over movies. And all this is okay. Just do not show motion toward God. "It just isn't right!"

Today man pays to get excited. He will pay for things to make him happy. Man will go and do anything to find peace and joy, which only lasts for a while. Then man tells God's people how they should behave when God gives them all the things man is searching for. But God gives it freely and more abundantly. God's pleasures, joys, and excitements go all the way to man's soul. Yet we are supposed to walk around all stiff-necked and upright, keep it all inside. Why?

Why? I will tell you why. Man, or Satan do not want the world to see the sheer joys and excitement in serving God. They want you to think there is nothing to it. Just go to church and try to be good. Help others when it does not interfere with your life, and you will be okay. Liars!

The fact is it is a sin to ignore or stop the spirit. But why should they care? They live in sin. They know not God. They have not received the power or gifts of the Holy Ghost, yet they tell us what it is all about. Do not listen to these lies. Do not be misled. Do not have your mind made up on how to worship or praise God. Wait until you receive the spirit of Christ, and then do whatever you are led to do.

Without the spirit, you cannot please God. If in fact He does not know you, He only knows that you are lost. Remember, all things done in the spirit are in order. These are done to glorify and edify our God. He knows what He likes. God does not need man to tell Him or us anything about His spirit. Man needs to realize just what is what. Man is man. He is here, he lives, and he will die all because of God. God is God. There is no other. He is all power and wisdom. He can and He will do unto us as He and only He sees fit. So wise up or shut up . . . God has the last word.

Wow! I need to get back to my train of thought, but I had to bring this up. We need to know and tell the truth. God warned us this would come to pass. In His Word, God said this would happen. It has happened, yet we do not trust His Word. The prophets said that Jesus would come and call unto God, a holy nation. He has come. He has called man, and yet we disbelieve. Jesus said He would come for His church. He also said those not of His church will go to hell. You had better believe it!

As the Sunday service went on, it came time for the preacher. Reverend Evans began to preach on the man who had two sons. He gave both sons a good life, much like the one God gives to His children. Well, one son got worldly ideas and listened to his self-will. He decided to take what was his and leave. The son then took all his possessions and left the safety and the presence of his father. In addition, he took to the world.

This son felt he could make it on his own. He did not think about or expect the dangers and problems he might encounter. "Now is not this just like some Christians today? Is not this like man?" asked the preacher. He too thinks he can make it on his own. Reverend Evans then added that man and some Christians have this same idea. They do not think they need the wisdom or the power of God's spirit to help or to guide them. "Amen!" some-one shouted.

Reverend Evans went on to say they forget Satan is out there, just waiting. He will trick, and he will deceive. He will cause you problems to no end. Then the son journeyed into sin. Farther and farther, he went away from his father's teachings. The son ran out of friends. His buddies left him when his money ran out. No one cared if he ate or slept. Are we not like that today? Man will use and abuse then cast it away. Now the son knows about bad times.

Yes, the world gave him more problems than he could handle. Man, and the ways of sin were teaching him a lesson. Reverend Evans continued. The world was destroying his morals as well as his life. The son now was hungry, broke, and confused. But unlike some of us today, he did not give up. He did not continue on this beaten path. He did not make excuses for the ways of man. He saw the problem and knew the solution. The lost son also knew where he could get help. Unlike man, he planned to do something.

Reverend Evans added that this boy, like mankind, could have just given up, but he had his mind made up. He sent word to his father that he wanted to come home. He did this without knowing whether his father would take him back. But Christians know our heavenly Father welcomes us back if we get off on the wrong path. "Believe a lie," Satan tells them. "Do not go back. He does not want you." Therefore, they listen to him who took them astray. Reverend Evans said, "I praise God that his son did not listen to any more of Satan's deceiving ways. I am glad he made plans to return to the shelter and grace of his father's home."

The reverend went on with his message, although he noticed the man near the back pew. He was being a bit restless. The mes-sage then told how the son planned to see if the father would take him back. "The son sent word to the father," the preacher said. "He told him, 'If I can come home, hang a white rag.'" "Dad," the boy said, "hang the white rag in the big tree, the one out front where I used to play." This was done so he would know before he entered the gates if he was welcome back at home. See, the boy wanted to go home. He needed to go home. He was hoping he could go home.

The son was ashamed. He was burdened with his wrongdoings and for leaving the ways of his father. Christians too can find themselves in the same position when they drift away out of the grace and safety of God the Father. The preacher drew a verbal picture as he continued. He said the son had traveled for days. He was almost at life's end. "It is sad," said Reverend Evans, "that sometimes we must get or be at our lowest point before we will look up and ask the Father to pick us up."

The lost son was full of pain and hurt and weakened from the absence of food and rest. Yet he drudged on ever so slowly, one foot in front of the other. Each step brought him closer to his home. Step after step he knew would get him there. Reverend Evans said, "I wonder many times did he ask himself 'Will I be welcome there? Will my father forgive me? Will he take me in?'" That thought had to be burning in his heart and mind as he approached the homeland he missed and needed so bad. With his worn and torn clothing, with his heart in his hand, as tears of both hope and joy ran down his dirty and beaten face, the son was nearing the point where the big tree could be seen. Soon, he would know. Soon, he hoped he would be home. Oh, how he earned to be home.

The preacher told us he finally crawled to the top of the last hill. This would give him a full view of his home, his father, and the true way of life. "O God!" he cried. What a glorious sight he saw. He saw bedsheets hanging all over that big ol' tree! "Praise God!" somebody shouted. "Amen!" The whole church was in tears. The son was welcome! The preacher then said, "It's the same with God. He, being our heavenly Father, He too wants all who are lost to come home. And it just gets better. Whether you are lost or wondering about trying to find your way home, God does not just hang out a white sheet, but He also sent his Holy Son to bring you back! He is asking you to "Please, please, please come home!"

Upon seeing his lost son afar off, the father could not wait. He ran to meet and greet the son who had come home. Reverend Evans said, "God does more than that. All you have to do is to make the first step. He will send the spirit to bring you on in." Oh, the joy of it all! They embraced as the tears of love and peace ran down their cheeks. Both of their hearts were overwhelmed with compassion. Do you know that Christ will also greet you and embrace you with all the love and mercy of God? It does not matter if you are a lost child or one who has just left His grace. He loves you, and He died to make a way to bring you into the Father's embrace.

The message then told what the father said to his other son. He said, "Kill the fattest calf, and go prepare a feast. Go get the family ring for this son." His other son asked, "Why? Why do you do this for him, Father? I have been here and worked all along. This one left. He went astray. He ignored the goodness and peace of this life." The father replied, "Yes, you have been faithful. You have stayed by being here. You have enjoyed the riches and blessings herein. You have not done without. You are a good son. I love you, and I am proud of you. You knew what was right."

"However, my faithful son," the father went on to say, "we must feast in praise and thanksgiving, for there is no greater joy in heaven than this. For one that which is lost has come home. Why, even the saints and angels of heaven stand and rejoice at such a sight. Is not that a blessing?" Reverend Evans asked, "Isn't He a wondrous God? NO matter where you go or what you do, as soon as your heart is sorrowful for your ways, God the Father, through the salvation of Jesus, welcomes your home."

Reverend Evans then preached a heartwarming message. I am sure everyone was able to see the full picture, for God truly blessed his sermon. It lasted about forty-five minutes, at which time, the preacher asked, "I wonder if there is anyone who is lost or just away from the teachings of the heavenly Father. Is there any like prodigal son who wishes to come home? You know you do not have to wait to see if you are welcome. Christ is standing with open arms, pleading, 'My child, come on home. I will bless and keep you safe. I am here. Do not wait for a sign. I am calling you now. I cannot help you if you do not take that first step. Then I will walk with you all the way, even through the ages of eternity.'" Reverend Evans asked, "Will you come?"

God was well pleased, and the church was full of joy and gladness when four souls came forth and made peace with God. Yes, they took the step to meet and receive Christ as their Savior. One of those four born-again children of God was the man from the back of the church. After being born again, he confessed Christ as His Lord and Savior and then testified, "This was not the reason I came today, but praise God! I am so glad I came. I never knew what it was like to be touched by God. I am not the same man I was when I came in. I will never be the same. I have been reborn. I know and feel the power of the Holy Spirit. I will tell you why I came to church today. I was very angry at this preacher. I wanted to know who he thought he was! I really came here to hit him in the mouth and to tell him to stay out of my marriage." He said, "My wife has been coming here for a while. My wife told me she heard and felt the power of God's Word. Then she said she gave her life to God and accepted Jesus Christ. I said, 'So what? It isn't got nothing to do with me. But it did. I did not like the new her. She started reading the Bible, she stopped cursing, she prays. She changed. I saw her living for God. I had to list to 'church' stuff. She would not stop! She would not do the things I liked to do. I was fine just the way I was. She changed, and I did not like it. My marriage was being destroyed because of what this preacher told her. I know other women who go to church. They do not act like her, so I came to set this man straight. But God set me straight."

"Praise the Lord!" Brother Reynolds yelled. The church then listened to the other three who had received the gift of God--- life. They too told how they just happened to come to this service. They had not planned to do anything. They were invited and came to see how the services went. But you see, God spoke to them throughout the preaching of His anointed Word. The big man had a plan; however, because of God, his plans were changed. God was not going to allow this man to disrupt His worship or allow His anointed man to be harmed while preaching God's Word. Nothing will stop the Word of God!

Man has tried to stop or alter the preaching of His Word since the days of Christ. Man killed Christ, but Christ finished what He came to do and teach before He ALLOWED man to kill Him. The key word here is ALLOWED.

Jesus arose just like the prophets said He would.

Man, stoned Stephen to death but only after Stephen preached Jesus to them.

Man chased Peter and took off his head but not until Peter had preached and taught the power of Christ and the Holy Ghost.

Man chased Paul because of his preaching and teaching but not until he had finished what Christ told him to do.

There are so many others, but God's Word is still preached in every nation today, just as He said it would be.

I wonder how does God get men to do His work. How are they willing to leave friends, family, and jobs just because the Spirit asks them to? Why would man give his life up just to preach God's Word? If there is no truth, there is no power. If there is no heaven to gain, if God cannot give you more than man or the Word, how can He just speak and men follow? If God's Word is not what He said it is, why does man try to stop the teaching of God's Word? Why are you afraid to hear God's Word?

Look, there have been great armies, kings after kings, nations, and even the devil himself who have tried to shut up the Word. And yet it is still here. It still has power, and it still saves. Look into the history books. This fine country is here because man wanted to serve and worship God. Look at our national motto, "In God We Trust." Why are you here if not because of God? And do you know what? If you are not here tomorrow, it is because God says so. That is why I mention throughout this book that you need to make your peace with God, for I do not know and you do not know if God will allow you to live to finish this book. Think about it!

Well, again, another week was passing, and as before, another weekend was approaching. Plans, like always, were being made. One such plan was being made by David. He had the weekend all planned out for his family; they were just going to have some fun, relax, and then rest. This was a normal American family--- David, his wife, and two sons. This was a good moral family just trying to make it, a family who loved one another and cared for their fellow man. However, their plans like so many others did not include going to church. They had not even thought about it, so it was not in the plan.

After work on Friday, Dave and his wife planned to take their children to the sitters, and then they were going out for a little while. They would go to their favorite lounge and meet up with some friends and listen to the band, whom Dave knew, and they would dance to the music. Dave and his wife enjoyed music, dancing, and having a fun time with friends. They would have a few drinks then pick up the kids and go home.

Saturday after breakfast, they planned to visit some other friends at an afternoon pool party. There they would have sandwiches and beer, and the kids would have some sodas, and from there, they would leave and go to his parents' house for dinner and a game or two of cards. They planned to go bowling around 9:00 p.m. after leaving his parents. It would be late when they got home that night, so they had planned to sleep in on Sunday morning. After getting up, there were no plans except that Dave wanted to watch a ball game on television, so they just planned to sit around with their boys and relax.

Now you could not call this a fun-filled weekend, and man would not call this a sin-filled weekend either. However, there was no room for or mention of God. Dave and his wife taught their kids to mind and to respect their elders; they had taught them to have manners, but they did not teach their boys that they should love and serve God. Dave and his wife did not think they need the ways or teachings of God in their way of life. Why is this so acceptable in today's life? This family, like so many others, did not even know the need of salvation and the guidance of the Holy Spirit.

Dave and his family did not hate God or Christians. They just did the best they could. They did not hurt anyone; they did not break any laws (except for speeding . . . and driving after drinking, maybe lying on their taxes a little). All in all, they were good people. If you need help, they would be there. They took good care of their boys. They felt the boys were in good enough shape without attending church, and when the boys felt ready (maybe when they were a little older), then they would go to church. Right now, Dave and his wife were pretty satisfied with their plans for the future. Little did they know that their plans were about to be altered.

Dave did not know about God's plan, nor did he know he was going to be touched by the mighty hand of God. It was Friday, and the workweek was over. After taking the boys to the babysitter, Dave and his wife went about carrying out their plans. They went out to meet their friends at the bar, had a couple of drinks, and danced a few times. Mostly, they just sat with their friends and talked. It was starting to get late, and Dave asked his wife if she was ready to leave. They said their good-byes and headed home. After picking up the boys, going home, they got them ready for bed. Both Dave and his wife were tired, so they decided to retire for a night of rest. After a sweet kiss, they embraced as always and drifted off to sleep. Dave was looking forward to a good night's sleep. What he did not know that tonight, God the Father would pay him a visit. The Holy Spirit would knock at the innermost parts of his heart. Yes, this night, Dave would feel God's touch and hear his call.

After being asleep for a while, Dave suddenly woke up trembling. He was scared to no end and managed to look at the clock. It was 3:00 a.m. Dave realized that he had just had a terrible dream, not just a dream but also one that he would never forget. It was not just the dream that bothered him, it was the actuality of it . . . the details of the dream. Plus, the fact that he remembered to whole ordeal. He had never been awakened by a dream before. He knew this was more than just a dream. Let us look at Dave's dream.

Dave dreamed he was dying. He could see himself lying in bed as he was drawing his last breath. He watched as he saw himself grab and fight to hold onto anything he could find. He heard himself cry out in pain! The expression on his face was of fear and agony. He saw his body being engulfed with the flames of hell, and the pain was so unbearable and would not stop. He could even smell the burning of his own body's flesh. That is when he woke up.

Dave could not understand the realness of his dream. He felt his head; it was hot and sweaty. His eyes were wet from his tears. He now was feeling both scared and guilty, but why? He could not understand why he would have such a dream. Needless to say, Dave did not get a good night's sleep. He kept thinking about his dream. He knew he was a good dad and a good husband to his wife. He worked hard and had a lot of friends. He tried to treat people right. Why this dream? And why did he feel so guilty? These questions kept running through his mind. Over and over, he wondered why did he dream of his death and body burning.

About nine o'clock Saturday morning, Dave and his wife got up. Dave did not say anything about his dream, yet it was still in his mind. He did ask his wife if she ever thought about dying. "What brought this on?" she asked. Dave just smiled and asked, "What do you think happens when someone dies?" His wife replied, "Will you please change the subject! Who in his right mind wants to talk or even think about dying?" Little did she know that Dave was thinking about it. He also wondered why he was now afraid of dying. He was so concerned that he thought about taking his family to church on Sunday.

However, just like the rest of mankind that God speaks to, as time, so did the thoughts. Now I know you do not have to say it; "God has never done something like that to me." Well, He does not have to. God touches and calls each of us on the level we need. We are all different. God knows how to speak to us so that each of us hear. Some He reaches out to by just a soft tug at the heart. Others it takes being down and out, while some it takes a slap to the head. What will it take for you? Maybe God has already tried tugging at your heart. What will it take? Maybe you felt the tug and just ignored it. Do you think He will call on you gain? I pray He will. Does He have to call again? Or did you miss your last chance? Listen, He might be calling you right now.

As Saturday went on, things were going back to normal. Dave and his wife were busy doing all the things they had planned. Dave was not blocking that nightmare out of his thoughts. They were having fun with their friends. Oh yeah, the thought about going to church . . . well, that was put on the back burner. Dave felt he maybe should go to church, but he felt there would be plenty of time for that later. So, they headed to dinner with his parents, and after dinner, bowling, then home to bed. Dave was a little more tired than his wife, so he fell asleep before she could ask him, "Want to watch a movie?" She kissed him, pushed his legs over, and made him give up some of the covers; then she too fell asleep.

It was Sunday morning about five o'clock when Dave awoke suddenly . . . again. He had just had another dream! Only this one was different. He was not scared, only confused and feeling guilty . . . again. He had tears on his cheeks . . . again. Dave dreamed of a story he had heard in church when he was just a boy; only now, Dave was in the story. "Now how could something from so long ago come to me now so fresh?" he asked himself. He had only gone to church to see this girl and to meet her. He really did not pay much attention to what was being said. So, he thought!

See, God uses all sorts of things to bring you to the point where you can be called. He could use something a Christian said to you, maybe a statement you read. He could use a gospel song or the birth of a child or even the angel of death. These are the times when people realize that a higher power does exist. But no matter, there is the truth and the thought I pray you will never forget. I truly ask God to implant this into you hear and your mind.

If you really look, you can see sweet Jesus standing on the clouds of glory. He is reaching His arms out for you. Why, you can even see the holes where they drove the nails into His hands. Listen as He speaks. If you try, you can hear Him saying "My dear child, I gave my life for you just so that through you, you could gain peace with God and inherit His eternal Kingdom." Look, there are two tears in his eyes as He says, "Please, come unto me. Do not make my death be in vain. I love you. I want you to take part in my salvation. I gladly died for you. Please, call upon my name. I will come and make my abode with you. God the Father is waiting. He sent me in spirit to beg you. Let me be your Savior." Now you have heard the gospel. You know the truth lies in it. You have been told throughout the anointing of these words, and God has spoken to you. Nothing or no one can erase this thought from your mind. Now your heart must deal with it. What are you going to do about this call of God? If you reject this call, you better hope and beg that you get another call. Ask yourself this: "How many times will God allow you to push

Christ away before He goes away to stay?"

Now back to David on that Sunday morning. Not only was the thought of the dream still on his mind, but he also thought about the time when he was a child riding in the back of his dad's car. It was late, and the moon was full. Dave looked at the clouds in the sky and thought he saw two hands reaching down through the clouds; then they were gone. *Why did this come to his mind?* he wondered. Then he thought of Reverend Cobb, the man who married Dave and his wife. He remembers the reverend saying "If you want this love to last, then God must be in it." The preacher said, "God is love, and He will make a house a home."

The first dream . . . the second dream . . . and now all these thoughts ---the fear of dying, the guilty thoughts. Dave was confused, but he knew he had to do something; he just did not know what. But he did decide that he would go to a church. Why? He did not know why, just that it was a good idea. He could just go and listen. "What could it hurt? My kids need to go to church every once in a while, anyway. I guess we all should go at least to show God thanks, even if it is just for our home and good health." In fact, Dave had asked God to help his wife during labor, which she had trouble with. He thought, *I guess God has been good to us.*

While Dave was getting dressed to go to church, his wife awoke and raised in the bed. Dave had tried to get dressed for church before he woke the family up. His wife could not imagine what Dave was doing. He looked at her and smiled then asked, "Why don't you get up and get dressed? Let's take the boys to church." Now that really blew her mind. She, being still sleepy, said, "Honey, we will go some other time. Okay? Now get back in bed before you wake the kids up." Dave replied, "No, I think we should go today." His wife asked, "Why does it have to be today? I thought we would sleep in and just relax today. Look, Dave," she said, "we have got plenty of time for that later. Let us enjoy our life a little. There are a lot of things we still want to do. Going to church is for older folks. It's for people who feel guilty. What have we got or done to be guilty? Dave, there is nothing wrong with going to church, but look at the boys. We like to go away on the weekends. They enjoy camping. It is not fair to make them miss out on what they like. How about sports? We run all week to this practice or to this game. We need one day just to do nothing. Okay? Besides," she went on, "I am not ready. I do not want to be like some people. I do not want to go out on Fridays or Saturdays and then go to church on Sunday. I like to drink a little and gamble. I like to have fun. I do not want to give up what I like. Honey," she said, "look how kids treat kids who go to church all the time. We are not ready for all that."

She added, "We are just as good if not better than half the people in church. We even act better than some of the pastors. I am not lying to myself or to God like those people do. Besides, that church would we go to? There are so many different kinds. Who is right? I think we can have church at home. Why should we listen to a man who is wrong? Churches think they are right, and the other churches are wrong. Churches cannot get along with each other, and the members cannot get along with each other. They are talking about what the other one did or worse. Most of it is just for show anyway. Dave, when we are sure about it, we will go. Right now, can we please go back to sleep? But before you get back in bed, put on the coffee."

Boy, did that woman cover all the bases. She pulled out every excuse I think there is. The sad part is half of them are true. That is because there are so many false doctrines and false teachings. Look, it is easy. If churches cannot get along, in fact, if they are not in one accord, then they are not of God. If members cannot get along, then they are not of God. If you do not put away your old ways and walk in the newness of Christ, then you are not of God.

If you rely on water baptism, lighting candles, giving money, saying Hail Mary's, doing penance, taking communion, being on the church books, not eating unclean meats, speaking in tongues, having someone pray for you, kneeling before a statue, wearing a cross or rosary, trying to live a good life, living out of the Old Testament, making up your own Bible, discrediting the Holy Bible, being a Jew by birth or traditions, having birthrights, and paying alms to any man like a pope, bishop, pastor . . . Helloooo! You are not of God, for God says that you must be born again. You must accept Christ as your Savior, and you must accept the Holy Spirit into your soul. Then you must let it and God's Word lead you. That is God's Word. That is the truth. Anything else is an out-and-out lie.

Yes, the ways of man are full of excuses. Where do these excuses come from? By man. If man would not listen to Satan and himself, if churches would not listen to false doctrines, if they would worship in Spirit, if everyone would put Christ as their head, then there would be no excuses. Satan tells you of all the church's ways that are pretending to be right. But when it comes to a true church or a true man of God, we make fun of their ways. Why? So, he can keep you right where you are, in sin. Why will not man see what is going on? Because he does not want to.

But David was not listening to her excuses. He said, "Honey, I'm mixed up and confused. I worried about two dreams I had, one on Friday night and one on Saturday night." Dave went on to tell her about the two dreams. He gave her full details. He then told her, "Please get dressed, and let's go to church today. I don't know what it all means. All I know is that I do not like the feelings I have."

She answered, "This is silly. Don't let two dreams get you so riled up. They're just dreams. Chances are they don't mean anything." She then turned over and said, "Let's go back to sleep and discuss it later." She could not understand what the dreams had to do with going to church. "If you feel bad," she said, "we'll try to be better people. You know, God is love. He likes people who do good. Besides, there are a lot of people who need church more than us. Maybe your dream is telling you that. We don't have to change our lives because you have a dream. We live by what we know, not by what we dream. If God wants us to do something, He can tell both of us. Now let's talk later. Okay?"

For some reason, Dave did not want to accept that. He said, "I'll go by myself if you won't go. As silly as you may think it sounds, I think I want to go to church today. You don't know what I feel. I think that if I die, I will go to hell. How, what, when, or where, I don't know. I just know I need to do this." He added, "I don't even know where I should go. Maybe I'll go somewhere each week until I find a church that I like. Then you and the boys can start going with me."

Little did Dave know what was going on. God was getting ready to speak to Dave's soul. You see, God was tugging at Dave's heart, just like He does at yours. When you have that thought of "maybe I should go" or "maybe there is something to this being born again," maybe you are afraid of death and the next life, maybe you see the destruction of this life. These thoughts are from God. He is trying to open your heart, eyes, and mind to His goodness and mercy. Take a moment and listen . . . Is He tugging at your heart right now?

Dave got ready for church. Little did he know this would be the "D-Day," the day that God would touch his soul and call unto him through the Holy Spirit, the day he would be faced with the decision. He would have to answer the call of the Lord or reject and deny His soul of the sweet peace of knowing God as His heavenly Father. See, when you deny God's call, you not only reject what He wants, but you also deny yourself all the gifts of life, love, mercy, and powers of God. You not only cheat God, but you also cheat yourself. But Dave would not sell himself short. His D-Day would send him home a changed man. He would come home as a child of God. He would now walk in the guidance and inspiration of Christ; he would be blessed of the Holy Spirit.

Upon entering the church where Reverend Evans was the pastor, Dave was greeted by some of the deacons and members who shook his hand and made him feel very welcome. The service started soon after he was seated, and Dave was a little edgy. He did not know what to expect. The service started with choir singing "I'd Rather Be an Old-Time Christian." Then they sang "Love Lifted Me." Reverend Evans took prayer requests, and someone led out in prayer. Some people prayed to themselves, while others joined in and prayed aloud. Dave just closed his eyes.

He could hear the pureness and pleas of those praying aloud.

People were praying for those who were sick, in trouble, lost, or just not close to God. They were praying for their family, friends, and even neighbors. Some prayed for the service, that God would use it for His glory, that the Spirit would take charge, and that souls would find Christ. Now this was different for Dave. He did not know what to think . . . so he did not. He just listened. He heard an elderly woman say, "God, give me the wisdom of thy Word. Help me to grow strong and close to you through your grace, O Lord. Use me, O Lord, in the way you see fit, and if there be one here who don't know you, God, touch them is a way that their soul may be saved. Have your way, Lord. In the name of Jesus, I pray, Amen."

That sound stood out. Dave later learned the woman's name was Ma Clay, a sweet, dear, and Godly lady who later had a special place in Dave's heart. The service then went on with testimonies and songs of praise. One lady, known as Sister Dessie, got up and sang. *Boy*, thought Dave, *she has a beautiful voice.* The song was called "Thank You Lord for Your Blessings on Me." This song touched Dave. He felt something that he could not describe, but he felt it.

As the service went on, people were crying. Some were shouting praises unto God, singing, and others were shaking hands and hugging. Something was going on. Dave did not know what to think. He had never seen people this happy or excited in church before. Now do not get the wrong idea. Everything was done in order and in the Spirit. Dave was witnessing the pouring out of the Holy Ghost. People were praising God, glorifying Christ and His salvation.

Now do not think that every church service has to be a barn burner. All services do not have to follow these steps. People do not have to have what churches call family prayer. Services must, however, go in the order of God's direction. People must worship in spirit and in truth. Move as the spirit moves you.

That is the order of service; the steps of the service are not what matters just as long as there is time for praying, praising, and preaching. Then give God time to do HIS business. He wants people to come unto Him by repenting, accepting, and confessing, or He will take His business elsewhere, which He has done in so many cases.

Dave is a lot like you and others. He saw people get excited with Johnny Bench hit a home run to win the game. He has sent the reaction of fans when their team wins the "big one." Dave will never forget the reaction of thousands when Elvis took the stage. But he had never witnessed the reaction of people being blessed of God. He had never seen people get excited over something he could not see. That is when he knew it had to come from within or by some means other than what was visible. That is when he felt a cold chill run through like he had never felt before.

The devil started talking to Dave. How? By the thoughts he was putting into Dave's mind, the same thoughts he is telling you. "People don't act like that in church. These people are silly. They are Holy Rollers. They are fanatics." Satan wants to deceive you with the emotion and pleasure of sin, but he does not want you to see or experience the overwhelming joy and excitement of God's blessings. He wants you to go to a church that limits or denies the power or joy of the Holy Spirit. "Have joy in the world, not in church," he says. The kind of church Satan wants you go to is one where you sit; do not read your Bible; go through steps 1, 2, and 3; and then leave. Satan will deceive you by letting you to think you are doing right, but he will keep you from the true power of God's Word and Spirit. It is simple: Satan and man want you to celebrate in the things of the world, not to rejoice in the things of God. Do not get sucked in! Experience what God has for you.

All people are different. People react to their own taste, and that is okay. God loves us all. All must be born again. All must be led by God's spirit. All must worship and praise God the Father. You do not have to do it just like the other guy. Find God. Then find a church of God that best suits your spiritual emotion, one that fits your spiritual needs. Just do not limit God's needs. If He wants some people to shout out, sing, cry, or pray aloud, rejoice for them in your own way. Mind the spirit; do not quench it! Rejoice your way. React in your own way. Praise God because others have that same freedom. In other words, do not listen to Satan, and do not listen to man. Do not listen to a church that does not listen to God. Once you have the spirit of God in you, listen and obey.

Dave could feel the love and warmth within these people, and he knew it had to be of God. Man could not conjure up peace and love on this level. It was hard to describe, but it was like you could almost see the spirit. Dave felt something else also. He could not quite put his finger on it, but he was glad he had come. He was also glad he had come to THIS church. This just happened to be the church where Reverend Evans was the pastor. I should say that Dave was glad he had come to the Lord's house . . . the Lord's church, a place where the Lord's people rejoiced and praised God.

Dave had witnessed the family of God being led of God. He heard of the power and wisdom of God through the songs and testimonies of Christians. But he felt kind of left out. That is okay too, for you see, man cannot ask or get anything from God except through His faith in God. Then he can claim all the goodness and mercies of His Kingdom. God has a plan for His people. He also has a plan for those who reject the salvation of Christ. And God has a plan to bring you into repentance also. Dave was fitting in that part of God's plan. For the first time, he thought he was missing something in his life. He was about to find out just what.

When it came time for God's Word, the pastor started by asking the church, "Please turn to John 3:16, and read with me. Then pray God will use me and anoint His Word that we may learn of it." Reverend Evans then read, "For God so loved the world, that he gave his only begotten Son, that whosoever believeth in him should not perish, but have everlasting life." He went on reading and stopped at the verse that says, "He who believeth not is condemned already." Reverend Evans then began to bring the message from the guidance of the Holy Spirit. As he preached, Dave noticed a change in his voice. It was like he was being led to speak.

Reverend Evans began to get really excited. He started walking around. He was almost crying. Dave could not imagine a grown man crying and acting like that in front of so many people.

His sermon was now hitting on the main course of the gospel. He was preaching on the love and salvation of Christ, and how these were man's gift though the grace of God. The preacher went on by saying that God saw the condition that the world and man were in. Because of sin and worldly knowledge, man was doomed to death and destruction. Satan had full reign. He had deceived all, and this displeased God. Because of God's love for man, He sent a Savior; unlike the prophets and kings of old, God sent a perfect man. This time God sent His only begotten Son to the aid of man.

He allowed Jesus to come with power and from glory to die. This was man's only hope, for Jesus, being perfect and being of God and not conceived of man, was sent from His home in glory to shed His blood for the sins of man. Jesus was the supreme sacrifice. HE is the salvation of man. And yet man still goes on in his sinful ways even though

Christ paid our debt with His death;

Arose from the grave to give us eternal life; Sends the Holy Ghost to comfort and to lead;

Man, still listens to and believes a lie. Man refuses to accept

Christ as the true Son of the Almighty God. Amen.

Blood had always been the only remission of sin, but because man had drifted so far away from the teachings of God, because all mankind was lost, it took holy blood for the remission of man's sin. God wants to save man. He wants you to be in His family. He wants you to enjoy and inherit all His blessings and wonders. That is why God sent unto us a means of redemption, a way to become a holy nation, a way to be a child of God from the inside out. You must be born again. You must allow Christ to dwell within.

Man has tried to please God in many ways but to no avail. Man is not born of God. This body is born of sin. The preacher went on to say that our soul is dead until it is born of God. Our eyes are blinded to God's ways until He gives us sight. We cannot understand God's plan until we belong to God. We do not know or understand the wisdom of God until He gives us the knowledge. We cannot receive our heavenly home until we know Jesus. The only thing we can do without God is to go to hell. That is the eternal place for sin because God hates sin. Therefore, the wrath of God befalls on all those who live within the ways of sin.

Reverend Evans stated, "The ways of man is sin. The wisdom of man is sin. The ruin of man is sin. They cause man to reject and deny the love, mercy, and Word of God. Because you reject the Savior's call, God will reject you. Do not think you are something special to God! His Word puts you in your place. His judgment by His Word will put your soul into its place. You do not want your soul to fall into the hands of the living God without being introduced. You must be prepared to meet thy God. You do not want to go into His judgment without being one of His."

These words were ringing in Dave's ear, and he was having a lot of thoughts. Dave was actually hearing the Holy Words of God for the first time. He also wanted the sermon to end.

Something was telling him that he had heard enough. "You better leave if you want to eat and get ready to enjoy the ball game." Dave thought about his wife. She would want to talk now. He even thought about having a few beers with his meal. Then he remembered his friends. They had made plans to play poker after the game. Dave looked around to see if anybody knew him. He sure did not want people asking him "Why did you go to church?" He said to himself, "I'll try and do better. I don't need to be here. As soon as this is over, I will just tell Kathy, 'Let's be better people,' and later on, we'll start going to a church. Not all the time, just once in a while. After all, I've got a life of my own. I got things I still want to do." *Boy! I'm getting hungry*, he thought. The sermon lasted about forty-five minutes. All through the message, Dave felt that the preacher was looking right at him. Dave thought, *this man doesn't know me. Why is he staring at me?* Dave's thoughts were going back and forth. He would think about the things he enjoyed and wanted. Then he would think about what was being said. He could not ignore the preaching. The sermon was answering all his wonderings and thoughts. At times Dave would begin to feel guilty and even ashamed that he did not know Jesus in the way this man was preaching. Dave thought, *if this salvation thing is what God wants man to do, it doesn't seem right to ignore all that Christ has done. Did He die for me?* He asked himself, "Does God want me to be saved?" Then his thoughts jumped elsewhere.

What really hit Dave hard was the last few minutes of the sermon. Reverend Evans preached that it did not matter what and how much good or bad you do in this life. For not being a child of God, you only have to answer to yourself and to man. What really matters is there will come a time when you must answer to God. You can do as much as you want. You can believe what you want, but when you face God, if you reject His Son or His Words and His calling, God will reject you. You can listen to receiving thoughts. You can choose to leave here today rejecting God's call.

God gives you that choice. The preacher then hit home when he said, "You can choose to reject His love, His Words, and even His salvation. But this fact you can take to the grave: You will be proof, for not you or anyone else can reject the wrath of God's judgment. Do not make God prove to you that His Word is truth and justice for all. The truth is by not accepting His Word now, you are already doomed, and you do not even know it. Satan will tell you anything to get you to reject God. By doing nothing, God has promised that you will face an everlasting fire-burning hell. Take Him at His Word! Fear His wrath. Love His Son." Now that got Dave's attention. As the sermon went on, Dave knew this was the reason he had that first dream. A thought came to him to leave. *Your wife told you this was SILLY. You will not be able to do the things you like to do.* Dave ignored those thoughts. HE kept coming back to the other thoughts. As the preacher was finishing, everything was being put into place.

At this point, his sermon came together, and it all made sense. Everything that was being said hit home to Dave. Dave felt a tear in his eye and quickly wiped it away. He did not want anyone to see it. Too late, for God saw it. God's spirit was hard at work. Dave kept telling himself, "I'm glad I came. But I only came to listen and learn." God had other plans. Dave was hearing and about to obey.

That is how God works. If you listen, He will let you hear the truth. If you allow time for His teaching, He will bring you to His throne of grace. Satan knows he is on losing ground. He cannot stand up to the anointed Word of God. Both he and your old way of life are trying to trick you. But if you will listen, then you will hear. If you hear God's Word, there will be no doubt. You will know it through its power. All you have to do is to give God a chance. He will send His spirit to the rescue, and that is what was going on with Dave. God was sending the spirit a calling, the same He did for you. Just like He is doing now. Listen . . . can't you hear Him?

After the sermon, Reverend Evans gave the altar call, an invitation for those who need to come and pray. He asked if anyone wanted to come and ask Jesus to come into their life. The church sang an invitational song, and the members prayed for the Holy Spirit to have its way. The pastor said, "We will wait another few minutes. I feel God is dealing with someone." He said, "God is knocking at a heart's door. He is asking a special soul to come and receive their salvation." Preacher Evans asked the church to sing "Oh Why Not Tonight." He asked everyone to listen to the spirit as it deals and beckons for you to come.

Dave knew something was happening. His heart had a yearning. There was a tug at his heart. He did not know it, but God was calling out to Dave's soul. His heart wanted him to move, but his feet just would not move. Dave was being pulled in two different directions. He now understood the two spirits of this world. While his heart and soul were longing to answer the call of God, his brain was thinking about his friends, fun, how would he act, and what kind of life would he have. He started to think of all the excuses his wife had mentioned. He did not listen to her. He went to church anyway. Now he was using the same excuses.

See, you must understand the power and plan of Satan. The reason we doubt and deny the Words of our Savior is because he wants to keep us from answering the call of God. Satan is bound to the devil's hell, and he thrives on taking us with him. He wants man to tramp on the blood of Jesus under our feet.

Why is it when you seek or listen for God's call, all the excuses in the world will pop up? If there was nothing to it, why are there so many powers trying to prevent you from hearing God's Word? Remember this, all excuses used are of this world, yet the purpose of God's plan is for your soul in the next world. Think about it. Satan does not tell you what he offers in the life hereafter. He just uses lies to make you think there is no life or punishment in the hereafter. What you must be willing to accept is if God's Word is true. "I will go to hell, and my soul will forever burn." You had better make a change while you have the chance. You are playing for keeps.

Dave was at the crossroads of his life. He needed to accept what he knew his soul wanted and needed, or he would listen to the voice and excuses of Satan and ignore the sweet call of God. Dave grabbed the back of the pew where he was standing. He began to shake inside. He felt a tear trickle down his check, and his heart yearned for peace. His soul wanted Jesus. Dave wanted to get out of there. He thought about leaving, but he could not. He wanted to go and pray, but he did not. He wanted to do what was right, yet he did nothing.

God was using the Holy Spirit to speak to Dave's heart and soul. It was a soft, sweet feeling. God was gently calling Dave in the family of God. Dave was like the lost son, and God was trying to welcome him home. On the other hand, Satan was hard at work using thoughts of "This is silly. You are not like these people. Get out of here!"

Why will Satan or man never say, "Go ahead. Go up there and ask God to save you. Then you will see that this is a joke"? Why? Because even Satan knows the power of God's Son. He knows that Jesus will come into your life and reveal the blessings and glory of God. You do not have to believe me. Seek God and listen to the excuses that pop up. Then ask God and watch as He delivers just as He said He would.

Dave was in turmoil. He wanted to receive the love, peace, and grace of God, but Satan would not let up. He told Dave's mind to "Go home. You should not have come here. You should have listened to your wife." A voice was telling Dave to ignore what he felt in his heart, but it was not working. Satan was losing this battle.

Satan had a final plan. He put a party into Dave's memory. Dave thought of the party that he and his wife planned to attend next Friday. They had been looking forward to it. There would be lots of food, cool beers, and drinks and a great band with lots of dancing and a wild time. That caused Dave to take notice. He ignored his heart and was ready to leave. In fact, Dave had let go of the pew and turned toward the aisle. But the war inside Dave was not over.

At that point, Dave looked up. He did not see anything or anyone except the preacher. Reverend Evans had tears in his eyes and a plea in his voice as he spoke. His words burned like a hot iron. He said, "Church, pray. My heart is mourning. Christ is calling out to a lost soul." Dave knew it was him . . . The preaching was talking about him. Reverend Evans said, "Soul, Jesus is waiting with open arms. His nail-scarred hands are reaching out for you. The bloodstains that He shed as He gave His life for your soul's sake are still there. Christ is begging, 'Come unto me.' He is pleading for the salvation of your soul. Please come and receive the peace and love of God. He is asking you 'Why? Why do you forsake me? I am the truth. I am the light. I did so you might live. Harden not your heart.' As Christ stands and waits, please turn to Him, not away."

Dave knew this was the answer to his dreams. He knew God was pleading, and Jesus was waiting. He could not just stand there. He also knew he was not going to leave. The war was over, and Satan was defeated. As soon as Dave made the decision to listen to God, Satan fled. Dave only remembers taking that first step. The next thing he knew, he was kneeling at the altar, pouring his heart out to God. Dave cried and prayed, "Oh, dear Lord, save me. I don't know what to do or what I expect. I just want to be saved. I want to be a child of God."

He prayed, "Take me, God, and make out of me what you want me to be." He begged, "Please, I need your help. I don't understand. I just know I want Jesus in my life. I know He loves me and died for me. I want to receive the Kingdom of God. I will trust your Word and grace to lead me. O God, forgive me! I accept Jesus as my Savior. God, help me." That was Dave's prayer. Oh, what a prayer it was. Oh, how the angels in heaven rejoiced.

Dave prayed very hard for a while; however, nothing happened. He did not know what was supposed to happen or what he should feel, but he was sure something had to happen. Dave stopped praying. He had no more tears. He felt empty. He no longer had the yearning to pray. "Was this it?" he asked himself. "Did I do it wrong?" Dave was confused and disappointed. "What is wrong?" Had he done what he was supposed to do? Dave then heard a soft voice. The voice was coming from Brother Paul, a man of God.

Brother Paul told Dave, "God hears your prayer. He loves you, son. The salvation you seek is a gift of God. It's been bought and paid for by the Son of God through His love, mercy, and grace. There are no works or deeds that can earn it. You don't have to beg and plead for it. All you have to do is ask and then accept it. It's yours. However, you must accept it by faith. You did what God asks all of mankind to do. Now you must believe He did what He said He would.

"Just confer your acceptance of Christ on His Word, for it is written with the heart man believeth, but with the mouth, confession is made unto salvation (Romans 10:10). The Bible tells us that he who believes shall be saved. Not MIGHT BE but SHALL BE. A deaf ear to the cry of a lost soul. Remember, son, it's by grace through faith that you are saved, not of works, lest any many should boast. It's a gift of God (Ephesians 2:8--9)."

Brother Paul then hugged Dave, and they both stood. The preacher asked Dave, "Do you feel better? Are things right between you and God?" Dave remembered what Paul had revealed to him and answered, "I confess the salvation of my soul through the Lord Jesus Christ." At that point, there was no doubt.

Dave felt a warm feeling pass through him. He then felt the Holy Spirit in the deepest parts of his heart and soul. A glorious feeling like no other! It just swept over him. Praise God! He began to cry and shout praises unto God. The joy was overwhelming! He had never experienced such a feeling. He could feel Jesus inside him. Dave knew now he was just where he should be. He was now a child of God being blessed by the Father.

Listen, that is a feeling man cannot achieve by any other means. Nothing can compare to the feeling when you accept and know Jesus has received you as a child of God the Father. Nothing known of man, nothing Satan can conjure up, and nothing of this world can measure up to just one touch from the throne of God. This is what Satan is depriving you of and replaces with things of this world. When God destroys this world (and He will), what does that leave you with? What? God's judgment and His wrath! Is that what you really want? Are you going to be denied?

You too can have the blessings and rewards of God. Just as Dave did, you can have the feeling of sweet peace in your soul. You can know without any doubt that you are a child of God and entitled to a home in glory. What a grand and glorious feeling it is to know "I will not have to face the angry wrath of God Almighty."

What a joy and peace Dave felt. At the same time, Dave now knew God is the truth. He wanted to shout praises unto God. He wanted to enjoy and share the peace he had within. He wanted to cry. He did not know what to do. He just basked in the glory of God, knowing he had the Savior living within his heart ---a Savior that would bless, keep, and lead him to his home in the Kingdom of God; One that will never leave or forsake him; a true

Savior; One who has the power to deliver his soul from the wrath of sin. All his cares and troubles were now in the hands of the caretaker. All his sins were under the blood.

You too can have the same fulfillment for your soul. God makes the same promise to you. You can have Jesus. Jesus loves you. Jesus came and died for you. Jesus will be your closest friend. Jesus will go all the way with you, even to the end. Jesus will see you through the darkest times and deliver you in the bright city of God, whose portals and streets are made of pure God. You too can have the Words and teachings of the Father through the Son. Yes, you can also have and enjoy the many wonders of an Almighty God.

Please, let God love and inspire you in the ways not known by man. God holds all wisdom and power.

Let God unleash His glory unto you. Just make room in your plans for the father. Just ignore the ways and teachings of man. Listen and hear the voice of God. All you have to do is put your faith in His Holy Word; accept the death, burial, and resurrection of His Son; and be united with the Father as a child of God. It is all there, just for the asking. Remember, you must ask God. Satan does not give you a choice.

So do not be denied. Do not be led astray. Do not let the ways of sin cause you to face the wrath of God. Your rejection of His Word does not change the Word. Do not let the foolish knowledge of man deceive you or allow Satan to trick you. You deserve better. You deserve the best there is. You are special to God. Christ died to give you a glorious eternity. Do you want what is yours? Then do not let Satan rob you of your inheritance. Remember, if nothing else, if you do not ask for the best, you will be left with the worst.

Dave is now called Brother Dave because he has begun a new life. He is a child of God living in the teachings of Christ. He thanks God daily for the peace, joy, and salvation in his soul.

He was far happier now than he has ever been. Dave now knew and understood what life was all about. It did not take long for Dave to feel the importance of serving the Lord. The urgency of winning his family and friends set in at once. He wanted everyone to know the glorious way of life that Christ leads you through.

That is the way the love of God is. Once you get it, you want everyone to have it! You do not want to keep it to yourself. You want to tell everybody about the deceiving ways and lies of man. You have such a love in your heart you want to share it with everyone.

Dave wanted to learn and know all he could about the ways of Christ. He wanted all the blessings God had to offer. He wanted to work for the Lord, so he began to read and study the Word of God. He did not want to miss out on anything. Dave had such a zeal to learn. He gave his heart and soul to Christ and now wanted to give his brain to God. He wanted God's wisdom, not men. He knew he must learn all he could. This would help him when witnessing to others.

Dave wanted man to see Christ in his life, so he must grow in the Word. He must know how to tell people about the love of Jesus. He had to know what to say and how to say it. Dave taught his family and lived by it. If something is worth doing, then do it the best you can do it.

Dave lived and learned the ways of man. He got all he could from his life without Christ. Dave also found out the more you try to do for Christ, the more He does for you. The joy, the peace, the blessings, and the love of God are overwhelming and never ending.

Dave was growing closer and closer to God. He now saw why it is more important and rewarding to work just as hard to receive the many riches and joys of God as it is to gain the life and riches of this world. Dave was learning to put all his faith and trust in

God's Word. He was growing in grace and strengthened by the promises of God.

Now Dave was not anyone special; this is how God's people live. The love, peace, wisdom, and promises are given to all who believe. It is all found in the New Testament (which is the new and better covenant). So that is where Dave began his study. He learned so much about the love, life, mercy, power, and salvation of Christ. His heart was so overjoyed! He was willing to do whatever God wanted him to do.

Dave began to go to church as much as he could. The thoughts of his life had changed. He now enjoyed the ways and plans of God. He detested his former way of sin. He no longer enjoyed the things he used to. Now he enjoyed the things he thought he would detest. He had a new love in his heart, a high step in his walk, and a spiritual talk. He truly was a new man. For man to say there is nothing to this being born again, to them there is not. But to those who have been, there is nothing like it. Amen.

Because of Dave's study prayer, praise, and worship and his growing in God's grace, the Lord's blessings on his life were abundant. As Dave read and studied the Bible, he underlined all the scriptures he thought would help him witness to others and improve his life with Christ. Dave just wanted to please God. He had to learn from God's wisdom that there is so much power and knowledge in the scriptures. So many "how-tos" and "do not dos!" But there is the "why tos" and the "why not tos" also. Then there is the "what happens if you do not" and the "if your dues." Dave was in a new world . . . right here! He could not get enough. But you know what? God just kept growing and giving.

This could be you. You could put your name where Dave's name is. You could be the one coming out of the darkness of this life. It could be you receiving the pouring out of God's spirit. Do not forget Christ died for you also. He came and died for all who will believe. It does not take a lot of work or giving. It is yours, just for he asking, for you see, God gives you just what you accept. He is there for you, but you must come to Him on His terms.

Remember, once you accept His Word and Son, you will never be the same. If you are, you have met an imposter. If you do not receive the fulfillment of the promises of the Holy Ghost, you have accepted a deceiving spirit, a wolf in sheep's clothing. You have met up with Satan; he just changed appearance. You must be careful, for all who call themselves a church are not of God. There is nothing in a name. God looks upon the heart; He looks for the blood. Avoid the ways and teachings of man. Do not be bound by sin; it will take you further away than you want to go, and it will keep you longer that you want to stay. Believe me, it will cost you more than you ever want to pay!

After being a Christian for a while, Dave began hearing a lot of different doctrines. He had met and talked with a lot of people from all sorts of denominations. People began tell him all kinds of things he was supposed to do. People said he had to prove with signs that he had received the Holy Ghost. He was told being saved was not enough. He had to go back to God and ask for more. He was also told that the church he was attending was not following the full Word of God.

Some asked, "Do you have powers to do this or that?" Some even said, "If you do not worship the way we do, you will not please God. Our church is the only church. We do not recognize any other denomination." One woman even told Dave that God had called her to pastor a church. Now all this was blowing Dave's mind. Some of it was funny. Some of it was just plain stupid. Dave had to say something.

So, when people brought this stuff to him, he very nicely replied, "Look, I love God and want to please Him, not you or your church. If there is something I need to do or be, bring it to me with God's Word backing it up. Do not tell me 'We believe' or 'we think' or 'my pastor believes or teaches it this way.' Bring me the Bible, chapter, and verse. I believe in God's Word, every word. I live by the New Testament teachings of Christ, for it was He who saved me. If God's Word says so, that makes it so." He also told them, "Look, I am in this for my soul. This is the most important thing in my or anyone's life, so I will search the scriptures. I will pour out God's Word in my heart. I will not sin against Him."

A few never came back. Some came back with a verse, but they had to tell Dave what it meant. These were the ones he wrote down and went into God's Word to find. Hardly any of these things were found to be the way they were told to him. A lot of things pertained to the old covenant and to the laws and orders of the Old Testament. Some of the beliefs were in direct conflict with the Words of Christ. Dave found what he needed to know. He found the one person who could teach and lead him; he found Jesus Christ, the author of the book.

Dave knew he was a child of God. He also knew the Holy Spirit lived within him. He could feel the presence of the Lord. There was no doubt; however, he did not know how people could say he did not have what it took. He asked God to forgive him and save him . . . God did. He accepted it by faith, and God says that makes it so. He also knew the only way Jesus could get into his soul was through the Holy Ghost. He knew this had taken place because he was changed. He loved the Lord and all mankind. He looked at life with a new sight. How can anyone tell you something that conflicts with what God says, then try to use His Word to back it up? What is wrong with these people?

I will tell you what is wrong. They are listening to man. They are being deceived. God's Word does not contradict itself. Man without God's spirit just misinterprets it. They think they know more about the plan of salvation than Christ does. They must think Jesus left something out so they could put in what they want.

Jesus did not need man to bring us salvation. God said it was Jesus who paid for the sin of man. Jesus did not need man to build the church on. God said, "Upon this rock, Jesus, I will build my church." God did not ask man how to instruct His people. He moved holy men to write what He wanted. Why do people think God needs man to add or take away from His ways now? The answer to that is . . . He does not!

People need to quit building themselves up. Jesus was a servant. Jesus and the apostles all served man and God. Jesus never said, "Look at me. I am big." He said, "Look at me and see the Father and His glory." So, do you think man should say "I am this" or "I am that"? No! Man needs to lose his pride and humble himself before God. God knows all and allows us to know what we need to know when we need it. Then we need to use if for His glory, not ours.

After salvation, what did Christ give unto His people? The Holy Ghost. After the Comforter, what was given? The church. No name, just the church. How can you be a member to the church? Through salvation. What and who is Christ coming to receive? The church. Who is the church built upon? Jesus Christ, the Son of God. Now leave it alone. God knows best.

Just one more short paragraph on the matter. Jesus never said you must speak in tongues or that you must have this gift or that. He never died so water baptism could wash away sin. The Bible only mentions the twelve apostles with one replacement, which was dealt with God and the eleven. No others were replaced, so why do some think they are now apostles? Jesus never asked the priest to pray for your sins; He never said to say "Hail Mary's" or penance. So, get real; read God's Word and accept it.

Dave not only heard all these different directions of thought, but he also even witnessed people of God argue about God's Word (which is stupid to do). God's Word says what it means, and God means what He says. There is no "in some case" or "it might mean" or "I think God really meant to say or is saying!" It is God's Word. You must listen to Him. What you think, what you want, what you believe do not matter. Accept nothing but the Word, for the truth is therein.

If you do not accept it, then leave it alone. God has something else for you that you will accept. With it, you have no choice. With God, you do not have to come this way, but that means that you will go the other way ---hell. That was what the letters were written to the early churches. Read them. The letters were full of warnings to those who were being led astray.

They got power-hungry, gift happy, and prideful, relying upon the traditions of the old law and covenant. Paul's letters put them back on track. Paul even told the early church, "After we are gone, there will arise within you false doctrines. There will be false preachers." All you have to do is to read it. Start with Romans, and go to Revelation. Let God show you what is what. Remember, it was the so-called religious leaders who wanted Christ crucified. They did not want to accept the new covenant either. Did they change it? No! Will you? NO! Will Satan? No!

If you ask me, God needs to write a few hundred letters to the so-called churches of today. I wonder if they would accept them. Would they think the letter was for someone else? Would they change them to fit their ways? I guess that is why He does not write them a letter. After all, that is what they have done to the letters already recorded in His Word. If they do not accept the already written Word of God as it is written, then why write more?

Dave could not believe that all these different ways and doctrines could come from the same Word of God. He could not understand, but he knew the reason. Men with carnal minds or deceiving spirits (or both) were trying to master the spiritual realms of God. God wrote His Word for two reasons: to show that you must be born again and then to lead and instruct His people. If you are not a child of God through the salvation of Christ, you cannot understand His teachings. If you do not have the Holy Spirit giving you the true understanding and knowledge of what God's Word means, why do you (or man) try to tell someone else what God's Word means?

Man, being the proud, boastful, never wrong "idiot" that he is, will not rely on the spirit. He wants to figure it out for himself, but he cannot. He cannot get saved by himself. He cannot please God by himself. He cannot make it to heaven by himself. Man is nothing to God until he becomes of God. That is why He gave us His Son, His spirit, and His Word---His Son to save, His Word to instruct, and His spirit to lead, inspire, and give us the true understanding of His Word. Without the three, you are lost. You are lost to His blessings, His grace, and the ability to rightly divide His Word. So why does man try to teach or tell someone about something he cannot understand?

Dave did not want any false doctrine being put into his head. Dave wanted to find out why the world and churches were in this awful shape, so he went into God's Word. Dave also asked God for holy wisdom and knowledge to understand and discern the Words and teachings of God, not so he could be better than anyone else, not for worldly gain or power, but for glorifying the Father, to make himself a better witness and a better Christian. It would enable him to serve His Lord to the best of his ability.

The Word is easy to understand if you get your knowledge from God. He teaches you by four basic means. By reading the Bible, you understand the words you read. Spiritually, you understand according to what you can digest. God uses fellowship with other Christians through their prayers, testimonies, and experiences. And then God uses preachers. In His Word, you will find "How can you believe if not heard? How can you hear if not preached?" Even then, you only grasp what

He knows you are going to take to heart.

You see, God knows best. You advance in understanding when you grow in your Christian life; that is why we call the Bible the living word. The more you study, the more you learn. None of us knows it all. God gives you what you need to understand when you need it. That is where man gets into trouble.

Man does not want to ask God or wait on Him. He wants what he wants . . . NOW. So, he uses man's knowledge to try and figure out the meaning of God's Word. Who are they? I will tell you. They are men getting rich because you put your money and faith in them instead of in God. If God does not give you the teaching you think you must have, then why do you think man can?

Dave was being led by the spirit. He was studying and praying daily. He was growing in his Christian life just like a baby grows into adulthood. And just like you cannot teach a baby everything they will ever need to know in a year (or twenty), you must learn daily of the Words and ways of the heavenly Father. This is what Dave was doing, learning and growing daily in the way of God, not the doctrine of man or Satan or of a church. He read, he studied, he prayed, and he waited on the spirit for understanding. Christians do this.

Dave discovered the Bible is written in six parts. Well, that is not "official," but the Bible can be broken down into many parts and subparts and so on and so on. Dave used the basic six parts. He called the first one creation and the priesthood. The second is the mosaic law and orders. The third part is the teaching and salvation of Christ. The fourth is the setup of the spirit and the church. The fifth is the letters to the church, and the sixth and final is the revelation (visionary summary) of the past, present, and future. This is the breakdown that Dave used. It is not God's way, and it does not have to be your way. It just worked for Dave, but just like Dave, you must know the time frames of the Bible.

When Dave reads the Bible, he asks himself, "In what time frame am I reading? What people are being read about?" By doing this, Dave found out everything leads or points to the promise of salvation. First, through the law and now through the Son of God. Why, even the youngest Christians know Christ fulfilled the old and brought us into the new. Dave knew he was among God's people. The Bible taught him he was one of many within the holy nation. You must know this also. The Bible teaches us Christ came to call all mankind unto repentance. "For all have sinned and fall short" (Romans 3:23). Please be one of the whosoever's; do not be one of the whatever's.

Things were going good for Dave. His learning and prayer were paying off. He was experiencing a time he did not understand. Dave loved serving God. It was his life. He loved going to church, to worship and praise the Lord and Savior. He enjoyed the fellowship with God's people. He loved the singing and spiritual uplifting of the anointed preaching. He was leading a good Christian life, yet he had a feeling of emptiness or envy or something.

Dave did not know what was wrong. He just felt different. He always wanted to do more, but something was not right. Dave helped with the Sunday school, and he gave some of the most heartwarming testimonies. People would get blessed hearing him tell of his love for God and the many wonders of serving Christ. People would even listen to Dave pray. They later told him it did them good to hear him pouring his heart out to God. Yet he felt something was not right, but what? He did not know. He knew he was doing the best he could, but that sweet inner pace that he received and felt was sort of not there.

He did not question that he was a child of God. He did not have any question about his salvation. He did not fear the eternal life to come. But why did the altar calls bother him? Why was that inner peace still there, but something was different? Dave was troubled; he read, prayed, worshipped, witnessed, and talked to theirs, but he could not seem to find the answers.

At one service, Dave was really bothered by the sermon. But why? The topic was to not limit the power of God by disobeying the spirit. Dave could not understand why the sermon touched him is such a way. When the Reverend Evans gave the altar call, Dave felt he wanted to go and pray, but pray for what? He thought, *I serve and I love God. I know I am in His grace. He blesses me and answers my prayers. I know that He is the power and strength of my soul.*

Dave went on soul-searching. "I know God is using me, for I feel the Holy Spirit leading, inspiring, and empowering my life and witnessing. God has worked in my life at home and on the job. He has moved in my family. He has saved both my mother and father and my two brothers. Things could not be better." But something kept drawing him to the altar. He wrestled with it for a bit, but he knew enough to listen to God. Dave did not know what the problem was, but he knew where he could find the solution. He obeyed the spirit and moved to the altar, kneeling before God the Father and seeking help.

Dave began agonizing with God, and while he was praying, a word kept coming to him, a word he knew but could not conceive. God's people joined around Dave to pray for him. He felt the warmth of their love and the spirit of their prayers. You could feel the power as their prayers reached the throne of God.

Then Reverend Evans knelt beside Dave. He said, "Dave, if there is something between you and God, you must remove it. You must lay your life in God's hands. If there is something God wants from you, you must obey. If it is something He wants you to do, you must let Him have His way with you, or you will not be happy. I know what He has in store, and so do you. You cannot limit the power of God. You cannot tell God what you will or will not do. Dave, it is not enough to just love God. You must be willing to obey His spirit. He will not ask of you something you have to do alone. He is with you, and He will go with you. You must go where He sends you. Remember, Dave, if you quench the spirit, you hinder your service. You limit what God can do for you and with you. God will not make you do anything, but He will sure make you wish you had."

With that said, the power of God swept over Dave, and the solution was revealed. Dave began to cry and shout praises unto God. He knew and accepted what God was wanting of Him. God was calling Dave to preach His Holy Word. "YES, LORD! Oh yes!" cried Dave. "I will do what you ask. I am not worthy nor do I think I can, but I am yours, Lord. Take me and make out of me what you will. Use me, O Lord, for your glory! Praise your holy name!"

After the service, Dave told Reverend Evans what God expected of him. Dave announced that God had called him to preach

His Word, and he had accepted His calling. Dave told his pastor that he was unsure of himself and plenty scared but that he also knew this was not something he wanted and that he was not worthy. "Pastor, God knows I have not had much schooling. I am not very smart. God knows I am afraid, and I have so much to learn. Yet He called me to preach. How? Why?"

The pastor replied, "Dave, God does not care about those kinds of things. He is only concerned about your love for Him and your total giving of yourself to Him. He only cares that you are willing to be led by and obey the Holy Spirit. God has called you, and you have answered. Do not forget that because He will be with you and guide you. Dave, God has asked you to do a holy thing. Hold it in the highest regard and close to your heart.

"Dave . . . son, you know what you are capable of doing according to man's knowledge. But you do not know what God is capable of doing with you according to His power and wisdom. God will give you and show you what you need. He will not call you and leave you empty-handed. He will teach you what to do and how to do it. God has and will always bless and inspire man for the task He has asked of him."

Dave could feel a warm glow in his heart as he spoke. He said, "I love the Lord with all that is within me. If He can use me as a preacher of His Word to lead and win souls, then I say, 'Here I am. O Lord, use me for the upbuilding of thy Kingdom. I submit all to you and praise your holy name, for I know thou art God."

After a few services at Dave's church, the pastor made announcement. He said, "Someone will be helping to bring today's sermon. A new preacher will deliver an opening sermon before I preach. Be much in prayer for his sermon to be anointed by the power of the spirit." Everyone, including Dave, looked around. They wanted to see who the visiting preacher was. This was nothing new. Other preachers would drip in from time to time. The pastor would recognize them and open the pulpit to these men called of God.

The service started as usual. There were prayers, praises, and songs. But when it came time for the bringing of God's Word,

Reverend Evans took the pulpit and said, "Now be much in prayer for Brother Dave Stevens as he comes to bring tonight's sermon." Well, what a shock! You could have knocked Dave over with a breath. Dave was melting in his seat. He could not budge. He was scared and shaking. He thought, *Oh no! Not tonight. Not now. I am not ready!*

Satan was telling Dave to run. "Do not get up there. You will make a fool of yourself. You made a big mistake."

Dave thought, *God did not call me to preach. I cannot preach. It is all in my head.* The thoughts continued. *I do not want to preach. I cannot preach. Who will listen? What will I say? O Lord, what am I going to do?* Then the spirit spoke to Dave's heart. "I am with you." It then reminded Dave what he had promised God. This all took place in just a few seconds, and yet it felt like an hour. Dave remembered how God had dealt with him and called him. He also knew he had accepted his calling. He now knew he had to answer by obeying.

Dave stood. But he did not stand alone. Just as God was with him when he took his first step toward salvation, God stood with him. Dave knew in his heart and by the Word of God that he could trust and depend upon the Holy Spirit to guide and inspire. As Dave neared the pulpit, he felt weak. He was so afraid, and as he hung his head, tears rolled down his cheek. He did not know what to say or do. He only knew he had to stand as a man called of God. Upon reaching the pulpit, he felt so alone, so humble, and so afraid of this task. He was scared to stand before the church, scared to stand before his fellow Christians as a man called of God to the honor and responsibility of delivering God's Word. But most of all, Dave was scared to stand before God knowing he would be held accountable for what he said. Worried that he would misquote or mislead, he thought to himself, *O God, I need you now.*

When Dave took note of reality, he was standing at the pulpit. His eyes were closed, and he began to lead the church in prayer. You know what Dave prayed for? Help! After the prayer, Dave was still waiting for the Holy Ghost to save him. He opened the Bible and began to read. He really did not know what else to do. Somehow Dave read the scriptures pertaining to the second coming of Christ and the need to be prepared. Upon reading the Words of God, God came to his aid in the form of overflowing warmth. Dave knew he had been delivered. Praise God. He could not hold the feeling.

The warmth and blessing sent him into a testimonial praise unto God. Dave praised the Lord for the love of Christ and for his love for Christ. He was a man anointed! He preached on the end of time either by death or Christ's second coming. He preached on the need to prepare yourself for the just judgment of God. The church could feel the power of spirit as it spoke through the new preacher.

Dave's message only lasted about fifteen minutes, but he had said what God knew needed to be heard. When Dave had finished, he did not get another word out. A woman came to the altar and knelt to pray. She came to give her life to God. You could feel the power of God in the service. The spirit was touching and blessing souls. Dave was overwhelmed at the pouring out of the Holy Spirit. His heart was in his throat, and he knew he was where God wanted him. Amen.

Now do not get all bent out of shape. This does not happen every time a man answers his call to preach. This event does not mean Dave is any better than any other preacher. It simply means God placed a woman in that service who needed to hear that she needed to be saved. It did not matter who told it; she just needed to hear it. It did not matter that this was Dave's church, for you see, only God calls, and only God has the power to save. Praise His name!

The woman could have been saved with the preaching. God could have called her with a song or a testimony. The only thing that mattered was that she was among God's people who obeyed the spirit. Brother Dave might preach and did preach a lot of sermons, some much longer and some harder, where no one was saved. That does not matter either.

YOU do not save people. YOU do not bless them. YOU do not build yourself up by how many souls come to Christ when you preach, sing, testify, or witness. That is God's business. He will take care of that. You just do what He lays upon your heart to do. Your reward is not with man; it is with God. Remember, God's work will get done with or without you. God needs and wants you to be included, yet you will not prevent it. If you do not do what God is asking of you, He will ask someone else who will.

Do not let someone else get the wonders God had in store for you. Do not deprive yourself of one touch from the portals of heaven. Listen to God. Obey the spirit. Give God a chance. He will make a change in you. Choose now to serve the Son of God while you still have a choice because at judgment, you give God no choice.

Dave continued to grow in grace and in the knowledge of the Lord. He was becoming a good preacher. He would preach at his home as well as others whom he visited. He would go and preach or witness at every chance. He was really enjoying working and preaching for the Lord, and the Lord continued to lead and bless Dave's efforts, not because it was Dave or because of his church, not to build him up in the eyes of man, but because it was done to glorify and edify God the Father, Jesus Christ the Son, and the Holy Spirit.

The church that Dave attended was growing. It had about 250 members, all of whom proclaimed to be born-again children of God. But something was not going too well. The more inspired the pastor preached the Words of God, the more displeased the members became and started missing services. He was called to please God, but seeing the members dropping out troubled his soul.

A few of them started attending other churches, while others stopped going to church altogether. See, it happens in church as well as in the world. People do not like to be told what they should do, even God's people. They rebel when they listen to Satan.

The true preaching of the Word puts you in your place. Some do not like that. They want to feel at ease. They want to be told they are good enough. Man is the same all over, but there is power in God's Word. It cuts to the heart. Instead of listening and obeying, man does not accept it that way and runs. Are you a runner?

Will you listen and learn? Will you obey or deny? Will God accept you or reject you? It is in your hands. There is power in the Word and spirit of God, but you hold the controls. God does not overpower; He empowers.

What was going on troubled Dave also. He could not understand why anyone would stop going to church after they had experienced a relationship with God the Father. How could anyone give up the wonders of serving God? How could they turn away from the hope and promises given to God's people? How could they go back to a life and world of the pain and crimes of sin? How could they live with themselves knowing they now faced the mighty wrath of God?

The pastor and Dave discussed the problem in great detail. Then they went into the Word of God and searched the scriptures for advice. They did not try to figure it out on their own, nor would they ignore the spirit and try to preach to the likings of man. That is what so many so-called churches have done today. That is why these churches have a lot of people in their services. They cater to the whims of man instead of pleasing God.

So, man preachers today are taught by schools not to hurt anybody or group of people's feelings. Do not step on toes and tone it down. You will lose people. They do not want to hear "repent or die" and face the fiery pit of hell. Many churches have even taken that out of their man-made doctrine. Listen and read it for yourself. The fact is (and I do mean fact!) Christ came and died so none of us would have to go to hell. If you do not believe that, you have chosen a reserved seat in hell.

I am not the judge nor do I control the judgment. I cannot accept a false doctrine, nor will I stand back without calling an Antichrist doctrine just what it is. Any man-church or doctrine that does not teach, preach, and allow the born-again experience through the acceptance of Christ by the baptism of the Holy Spirit is not of God. That is plain and simple, so be careful. If you allow yourself to be deceived into believing a lie, you are lost forever.

God accepts no excuses, and remember that neither ignorance nor "oops" is an excuse. God has no respect of persons. He does not care who or what you think you are. He does not care how much good you try to do or by what name you call yourself. It is His Word and His way; there is no middle ground. Either you accept His Son or you are bound for hell. Would not you rather go UP than DOWN?

As the pastor and Dave looked into the Word, they found the answer to the problem. God's Word says before the end of time, in the last days, there would be a falling away of those who followed Christ. It says the love of many will wax cold (1 Thessalonians 2:3). God took time to warn us of this, so as you see this taking place, you know that we are IN the last days. You had better take note: the more the people of God fall away, the nearer we are to the coming of our Lord.

Just look around. How many preachers and churches have fallen into being man-made doctrines? How many of God's people do you hear about falling away from the gospel to whatever? How many people do you know of who just play church? Now I ask you, how near are we to the end?

But do you notice? Does mankind? The longer time goes on, the less man feels he needs God. This is so lame! The truth is the longer time goes on, the more we fall away to the deceiving and misleading ways of man and sin. The more this takes place, the nearer to the end we come.

The closer that day approaches, the more we need to depend upon God. But do we? Do you? Let me say this: Christ is coming for His church. You had better make sure you are a member to THAT church, the one that is built on Him, by Him, and for Him. Amen.

There will be a great awakening on that day. Christ is not coming to call the Catholic, Apostolic, Methodist, Baptist, or those of the Jewish faith, etc.; He is coming for the born-again

Christians. But you do not have to take my word for it. Read God's Word or ask God to show you the truth. Do not get so wrapped up in the doctrine of man or tradition that you are blinded or deceived to the teaching of Christ.

God's Word warned Reverend Evans and Brother Dave to the deceiving spirit of the latter days. Instead of compromising to the ways of the worldly acceptance of sinful lust, this put a spark in their preaching. They both preached hard on the gospel of Christ, but they were not the only ones who saw and took heed to the warning. There was still a lot of old-time, Bible-pounding preachers serving their members the meat of the Word. God made sure of that.

No matter what you or I or man believes, God will always have someone who will preach the Word His way. He will get the job done with or without you or me. Nothing will stop his plan. No one will stop the spreading of the gospel. They have tried it since the first sermon Christ preached, and they are still trying today. That alone should tell you something.

Reverend Evans preached under the power of God. His sermons would raise the hair on your back. Because of his willingness to be led by the spirit, his preaching would put the fear of God in the hearts of anyone who heard them. Or it made them see what they were, and they ran. But instead of toning his sermons down, the spirit would fire them up, for the need of God in our ways and plans grows stronger every day. We need to prepare for the day of our Lord, which by our every deed of disobedience brings closer and closer the last tick of God's clock. Christ could come before you finish this book. How do you stand?

As I said, this was not happening at Dave's church alone; it is going on all over the world. A lot of churches in the family of God were having problems. Members were leaving, some were getting upset with the preaching and with one another. The churches were finding it hard to keep the ways of man and sin out of their services and the spirit and teachings of God in them. Satan was launching his final attack on God's people, for he knew also there was not much time left.

However, as time passed, the men called of God stood up to the task. They armed themselves with the Word and power of God. They were in a battle, and they fought to win it. They knew how to win: preach the Word, teach the Word, accept nothing short of the Word, and live the Word. Then let God take care of the war. God would draw in those who believed and run out those of disbelief. He was making ready for the great Day of Judgment.

Therefore, the sermons of the gospel of Christ, the preaching of His salvation, and the second coming were ringing out all over the world. They were telling people of all so-called faith and those who had no faith to take heed to the warning to listen to the call of God. Prepare to face the judgment of and in His Word. Christ is readying to come and claim those who are His. He is just waiting for God to become so displeased and hurt to the point of "I have had enough!"

"Go . . . Redeem my people! Leave the rest to my wrath. I will take revenge upon the disbelievers. They will know that I am God. They will fall and cry out to your sweet name. They will know that thou art my son. They will see and endure the truth of my Word. They have ignored al the warnings. They have chosen to give me no choice. They will have hell to pay."

This day is swiftly approaching, and this day will come. Do you dare to tempt God with your disbelief? Are you going to make God prove to you His Word and judgment are at hand? His Word says that those not under the bloodshed salvation of His Son will perish and be punished forever in torment and hellfire. Will you cause Him to let you go to hell? His Word is true. God cannot lie. If you do not choose His glory, you give Him no choice. You have chosen to take your chances with those left behind. Remember, in God's plan, all have a place.

A few heard the Word and believed. They made their peace with God. But so many others ran from the truth, while others turned a deaf ear to His Word. The ones who ran ran to all sorts of deceiving doctrines. They found false hope in the teachings and traditions of self-made churches. They allowed themselves to be misled by the thoughts and theories Satan has instilled in the minds of those who he has brainwashed with power, fame, and ignorance.

Can you imagine the hurt and anger this mockery causes God? Just think of the pain this must cause Him: to see the blood of His beloved Son trampled under the feet of men as they reject and deny

His redemption. They might as well be driving the nails back into His hands as they crucify Him daily. You can know this: God will get even. These acts will not go unpunished. Please do not be the one holding the hammer.

Those who hold the hammer, those who crucify Christ daily, these are those who do not accept His bloodshed salvation. Either they deafen their ears to His Words or they patronize themselves with the false teachings of man. They accept ways of churches set up and built by man, man used by Satan to mislead. Man-made religion accepts whatever pleases man, not God. Man has made churches to fit whatever you want or believe. Some use some form of God's Word, while others use nothing from His Word, but they are all of man who teach anything but the whole Word of God. Do not be misled by this deception. Do not rely on the ways of man. Look at the mess that man has gotten us into.

Do not think that because man has been put into a high so-called religious office that he is of God. Do not think that because a so-called church of a so-called denomination has big beautiful buildings that it is of God. Do not think that degrees given by schools make a man called of God. Do not think that

man having many followers, fine robes or jewelry, jet planes, or TV programs is of God. Remember, Jesus lived a life of doing without. He was not dressed in fine linen. He did not travel first class. God only saw to His needs.

To be of God is to be Christlike, not full of riches and price. Remember whom Christ used to preach His Word: men who felt unworthy of so great an honor. Did He use high-ranking religious leaders? No, He used the common person, men who would trust completely the Words of His teaching. Did Christ say to build churches full of gold, brass, and silver? No. Did He tell His apostles to get rich or churches to buy businesses or a lot of property? No.

Man has done all this. Man has set himself up a devilish scheme, a scheme to gain from those who seek spiritual guidance. Greed is not of God. Riches are not of God. Charging people for prayer is not of God. Getting rich on the hopes and faith of people is not of God. If you want to be like Christ, preach and teach God's Word just for the love of God. Do it because you love and want to help mankind. God knows and will see to your needs. You do not have to beg His people for your desires. Amen. God does not call men to act like this. He does not have churches that are interested in worldly possessions. What does God want with what man has? God's only interest lies in your soul. He does not love what you have or what you are. He gave His only begotten Son because He loves you. He also gives eternal life through His Son. If anyone says that you can gain the glory of God except by faith, then he is a liar. If any church accepts you as a member except through the Holy Ghost experience of being born again, leave it quickly! That church is on their way to the fiery pits of hell, along with all other false doctrines.

God calls men who will preach the Word with the power of the Spirit. His churches teach love, mercy, and grace. You are born into this membership when you accept Christ Jesus. God does not need men with worldly power or knowledge, for He holds all power in heaven and on this earth. He is the maker of wisdom; He holds all knowledge. God only uses those who rely on Him, who obey Him, who glorify Him, who humble themselves to Him. Let me say this: money is not the answer to man's problems . . . God is.

God's Word is truth. His plan will be carried out to the smallest detail. God is not the author of confusion; man is. Man, always wants things his way. Man needs to forget what the idiots have to say and trust in the wisdom of God. But will they? No, they allow more room for the ways of Satan in their life than the ways of God.

That is why Reverend Evans and all the churches and preachers in God's family were facing a falling away of their people, not because God does not love or save anymore but because man has chosen the worldly approach. But even with this falling away, God's people who stayed true were being blessed with the fullest of the Holy Spirit. Souls were being saved, and the worshipping of our Lord was in high gear. God's people knew as the end was nearing, so did their promise of His glorious eternity. They knew that on the day of our Lord, they would spend their forever in the presence of an Almighty God.

All this to offer the peace and joy of this life and eternity in the Kingdom of God. And yet man turns away. Oh, how Christ must hurt. The sorrow must be great in His heart just to see man denying His love and gifts only to accept the temptation of worldly sin. But worse than that, accepting some man-made doctrine instead of His teaching.

No one else, no group of people, no so-called church has done for man what Jesus did. Jesus bore our pain. He bore our sin. He suffered in the hands of those He came to save. He gave His life just so you could be accepted into the family of God. Jesus is the only way to heaven. God gave Him the power over all. Jesus gave

Himself and left us His teaching and used His apostles to help set up His church, a place to learn of worship and serve God the Father. He sent us His Holy Spirit, and the spirit keeps and guides us and is the only means by which we have fellowship with heaven.

God does not hear or answer our prayers except that we be born of Jesus. We cannot be inspired, blessed, or feel the joy and peace that God want to rain upon us except we be of Jesus. Jesus knows the Words and plan of the Father. He knows it all will come to pass. He knows that without Him, all will perish and face the punishment for denying, mocking, and turning away from the Word and power of God. He got up from the grave that we may have victory over death and hell.

He did all this just because He loved us. He wanted to give us a means to receive God's heavenly Kingdom instead of the angry wrath of God's judgment. Yet as He reaches for us, calls unto us, has men of God warn us, we push Him away. Instead of asking for the greatest gift to be had both in heaven and on earth, we accept the filth of this world. Do you really know the pain you are causing Jesus? Do you really know the pain you are causing yourself? If you are not feeling the pain of being unsaved, believe this . . . you will.

Man was set up in the blissful Garden of Eden. He had no sin. God had placed him there to live forever, but because man allowed sin to enter in, this was taken away. Now Jesus has gone to prepare another place for us. This time, when man is placed there, no sin will enter in.

In the garden, man could not resist the temptation of sin. He turned from God. In the days and life of Noah, man turned away. In the days of Abraham, Moses, Jacob, and even King David, man turned away. But this time man turns away from the Son of God who died for us to give us the power to resist and overcome the temptation of sin. How it must cut deep into his heart as He catches man resists the power to overcome by choosing to be misled. By choice, we add to and take away from the Words and teaching of our Savior. So many have chosen to ignore all God's Word, but Jesus does not give up on us. He still calls and waits for you to say yes. Yes, Lord, I do need and want to be saved.

Because Jesus truly loves us, He beckons and calls until God says, "Call your people home. I am putting an end to man's mockery. I am not going to allow man to defraud the authority of heaven any longer. You went to give salvation. Our Spirit gave them power and hope. It is time to take my children out of the midst of this sinful place. Man has had enough time to make up their mind. As I promised, bring my children to safety and unleash my wrath."

How long before this takes place? No one knows exactly, but the signs are sure right. How much longer do you think God should stand back and let man do whatever he thinks is right? How much longer should He put up with man blaspheming His beloved Son? How much more will He allow His children to face the sin, pain, sickness, and death of this unbelieving and anything-goes world? Is He fed up? Only God knows.

One thing is for sure; this world and its so-called religion is in complete confusion. There are more troubles and crimes that we can handle. Never in history were there so many false doctrines and false gods. The name of, the number of, and the status of the church appear more important than salvation. Pastors and preachers all know that something has to happen soon. If not, the power that this world and man have given to Satan will prevail. All will be misled, brainwashed, and deceived. God will not let this happen to His people.

He will deliver them to His glorious Kingdom. He will put an end in all disbelief. Man will no longer want things his way. All rejection of His Son will stop. All denial of His Word will stop. All will cry out to the Almighty God. Their cries however will not top. They will ring out for death and mercy forever. There will be no escaping, for the awful wrath of God will be here. Our days will have run out, and eternity will begin.

As that day approaches, here we are. God loved us and saw that we were lost. He gave us salvation. He told us what we should do. He told us what to look out for. He told us how we can overcome. He told us of the end. He gave us signs of His coming. He told us of the place our soul will inherit after judgment, be it good or bad. Yet we seek not His Words and instead find favor in lust, greed, and sin. It is sad, but we accept the words of everybody else and deny the Words of God, which will destroy everything else.

The terrible truth is that man has decided to follow the ways of man instead of listening to the ways of God. This is done to hide oneself from the truth. Man accepts the false hope of man-made religion, or he allows Satan to blind him to and bound him from all forms of religion. All this is done to deny God. Who tells man to go to this church and give your money? Try to be good; do not hurt or rob anyone. You will be rewarded for your effort. It is not God. God says to repent or be damned.

You must accept Christ to be of God. You have to forget family or church tradition. You have to ignore our ungodly leaders who because of their sinful ways pass bills and make laws defying the teachings of God's Word. You must be of God to please God. You cannot pick and choose how much you will believe. There is no middle ground. God will not and cannot have mercy upon your soul if you reject and deny His Son. Why should He?

How can He? God is not a liar. Remember that. His Word says you will spend eternity either in heaven or in hell. His Word also says you have until your life ends or this world ends or until you harden your heart to the point of no return to accept His salvation.

His Word then says that those who have asked and accepted are His, while those who do not are not His people.

If you are not of God, then whose are you? If you choose not His ways, then who are you following? His Word declares that "I have a place for my children. I also have a place for everyone else."

You still have a choice, but if you do not make room in your plans for you, then you give Him no choice. It is not God but you who has picked your place. You do not have a choice being in God's plan. Every man, woman, and child fit into the whole plan of God. You have no choice in facing death. You will die. Then you will have no choice but to face the white throne of judgment. You have been given one choice, not three wishes. There are no

I want to, I meant to, or now I will. It is either "Yea, I want to serve God through Christ our Lord. I want to receive the promise to His people" or "Nay, I do not accept His ways or Words as they are written. I WILL TAKE MY CHANCES IN WHAT I THINK OR WHAT I WANT TO BELIEVE." It is your choice, and it is you who will have to pay because the Word of God says so. Christ will have His day, and God will have His way. Amen.

Do not choose to be one of the whatsoever who accepted anything except the doctrine of the gospel. Nothing, no man, no man-made way, no church, no laws, and no other anything you call it can save you.

If man could save man, if the laws and traditions of the Old Testament could save man, then why didn't it? God destroyed this life with the great flood. Why? Because man would not listen. He allowed His people to die in the wilderness without receiving the promised land. Why? Man did not want and could not listen. God destroyed cities, armies, and kingdoms. Why? Ungodliness. Why do you think you and your so-called ways make you any better than them?

If God could not protect His Word from the evil hands and minds of man, if He was going to use a man of today to show us a better or new way of salvation, if one or any of these thoughts of and could save us, then why did they not work before after man saw the mercy and powers of God through Christ? After they saw Jesus raise the dead and heal the sick and dumb, after they heard with their own ears the Words of Christ, why did He have to die? Why? Because man is born of sin until he is reborn of God. Christ had to come, suffer, die, and come out of the grave to give us the power of His spirit. To resist and overcome the temptation that overrules man's world, Christ died to save our souls. Satan exists to rob us of our soul.

If there was any other way, then why did Christ give His life? Christ gave us the power and gift of salvation. Man did not kill Jesus. Jesus willingly gave of Himself on that wooden cross. He did not have to, if He did not love us so and if He did not want to save us. He allowed man to drive the nails into His hands and feet. He came knowing He would bare our sins and shed His blood so we could have peace with God. There was and is no other way. Then why do we reject such a gift? Why do we turn away what He died for? Why does man pour salt into the wounds He suffered for us? Why does man always hurt the One who loves him most?

Because of the way this world was going, because of man's denial of God's teaching, God was using His born-again, called- of-Him preachers. He had them preach in the power of the spirit so as to warn man of the great day of His wrath. He was using His Word through His people to draw the last ones in, for His day is at hand. He was also having His called-again people to wake up the church and those who professed to follow Christ. There was and is a lot to get done. It is not God's will for any to perish.

Reverend Evans and Brother Dave were preaching on living our lives as a testimony of God's love, mercy, and grace. They preached on the final days and the great Day of Judgment. Now not only them, but also this type of preaching was going out all around the world. It was being preached and taught in all he churches of God's family. God, through the Holy Spirit, was telling all who would listen about the gospel of salvation. He was bringing souls out of darkness. His spirit was telling all mankind whomsoever calls on the name of Christ before time is no longer shall be saved.

Eyes were being opened. The truth was being revealed regardless of thought, theory, or belief. If you want to take part in the rapture of the church, you must partake in the salvation of Christ. His holy blood must be applied to your heart. You must ask Him to come into your life and obey His teaching. This is your only means of membership. If you do not choose to take part in the rapture of His church, you cannot and will not enter into God's glorious Kingdom. You must and you will take part in the awful wrath of God.

You will be cast by your choices into the eternal lake of fire. There you will burn forever. Your soul will never have peace or rest. The pain, agony, and torment will never stop. Your suffering will have no ending, and there will be no doubt; you will know that you should have made Christ your Savior while you could have. Do not miss out the wondrous grace of God. Do not let this burn in your memory: "I wish I would have throughout endless ages."

Brother Dave had a friend who also preached. He did not attend the same church Dave did, but that did not matter. They often worshipped together. That is how God works. You do not have to go to the same church; you just have to have the same builder---Christ. It is easy to understand. God wants all His members to love one another. His members must be able to worship and serve God in unity because they are of the same spirit. No one church is better than another as long as they preach, teach, and live by the Words of Christ. No one way of worshipping or order of worship is better than another is just as long as we all worship in and through the same spirit. Remember, God does not have different strokes for different folks. We must all belong to the same body, and Christ Jesus is at the head.

Dave's friend was a good Christian. He attended the church where Brother OJ was the pastor. Dave's friend, whose name is Oscar, invited Dave to attend their revival where a Reverend Newman would be preaching. Brother Dave and Pastor Evans decided they would go to some of the services. In the first service they attended, the special singers were led by Brother Willard.

Dave knew this group, for they had been going from church to church, singing praises unto God for quite some time. God had used them to bless many of His people, for you see, it does not matter what the name of the church is or who the pastor is. It does not matter how many people attend. The only thing that matters is that the people are in one accord. You have the same spirit living within and that spirit being the Holy Spirit of God through Christ his Son.

The service went a little different from Dave's services, but it was all done in order and according to the teachings of Christ. The visiting preacher was anointed by God's spirit and delivered a good sermon. He was preaching on the turmoil and confusion in and between the churches of today.

He showed how the churches in the New Testament went astray soon after Christ went away. As soon as the apostles went on their way, the churches went on their own way. In other words, every time man does not look to Jesus, who does man look to? It does not matter; when you do not look to Christ, you will pull away from the ways of God. Why? Because Satan is there, waiting for the chance to trick, deceive, and mislead. Christ, through the Holy Spirit, is the only way to stay tuned to God. You cannot waiver in thought, deed, or faith.

He told the church to take time and read the books of Romans, Corinthians, and Hebrews, how these letters need to be applied to the churches even so much more today because the so-called churches of today are so far on track. They cannot see the train is coming. They will not be onboard when the train of salvation pulls out for the hills of glory. They have been sidetracked by their own choosing.

They are headed for a head-on collision with the wrath of God. “Churches today,” he said, “cannot even hear the warning. Why? I will tell you. They have followed the wrong goals instead of striving to serve and please God. They are striving to be holier than each other. They want to make themselves better than someone else. God calls this pride when people are striving for their own glory.

"Yet God tells all and whomsoever how to be what He wants them to be. He tells us how to pray and how to worship. He then tells us how to live in the ways of Him according to His plan. But now, as then, it did not take long before man got his eyes on Christ and added his own ways to it, which cannot please God. It is not just what man has added, but it is also what man has taken out that puts him off track. You cannot take out the power of the spirit. It enables man to be born again. You cannot take out the gift of salvation and still be of God, so why does man try?"

I know this will not sit well. I know these words cut deep, but God's Word is like a two-edged sword. It cuts out the root: lust of the flesh, lust of the eyes, and pride of life, of the bad. At the same time, it cuts and instills into the heart the love of God. The fact is if you are not born of God through the spirit, you can do nothing to please God. In turn, if you are not reborn into His family, He will not hear and answer your prayers (John 9:31). He will do nothing for you because you do nothing for Him. You and the ways of sin are on your own. I do not care what you say or what you were told. If something good came to you, if you are not a born-again Christian, then it did not come from God.

Satan will do whatever he can to make you be a whatsoever you call yourself. God only does what He did for me. No one is different or special. With God, there is no respect of person. He will do for you and for me the same as He did and does for all mankind. He sent Jesus to save us. God sends His spirit to draw and call us unto repentance, and then He calls us unto judgment and then puts us in our place. Now know this: God's Word is truth; all else is a lie. If you can find anything in His Word to show you get special attention, you better get of your high horse and read it again!

Churches today are a lot worse off. Today they ignore the early letters. Man has so injected his thoughts and theories that the church has split into so many directions they have to write their own false doctrine. God instructed His church to be of one accord. In His letters, He told the church to get back to the basics. Teach, preach, and live the gospel of Christ, for therein is your salvation. Amen.

Do not take my word for it. The preacher said, "Read it!" The early church started what we have mastered, the denial and rejection for everything Christ died for. Do you think this is something to be proud of? "I hope not," he replied. The early church did not get as far off track as we have. If they did, they got right back on track. They listened to the Words of God. They straightened up. Why don't we? We can read the same messages preached by the same spirit.

Now I am not judging you; the Word of God is. I make mistakes just like you. The reverend went on to say, "I've had people, some of which were loved ones, tell me all sorts of things pertaining to the Word, wills, and ways of God. Some I accepted as the truth. That is until through His Word and spirit I was showed differently. Then I listened to God just as the early church did and just as you must do."

Do not think because you do not see things they saw someone thinks you should that you are wrong. Remember that God warns us of false teaching and doctrine. He tells us of spirits put there that are not of Him. They will entice and lure you into deception. Do not fall into their trap. Trust God. Depend upon His spirit for guidance. How can I do this you ask? The preacher answered, "Don't look to man. Look to Jesus. If He is with you, then you will not be led astray. Do just like the early church of Christians. Hear the Word of God and then obey."

Remember Christ had many followers, but out of the thousands, only twelve were chosen to be apostles. Only twelve were commissioned of God to carry out His work with full power. They were commissioned to carry out the deliverance of the Holy Ghost. They were to establish and protect the teaching of Christ in the early church. They had special powers and gifts, but they used them for God's glory. None of them maintained worldly possessions, and they all died broke.

God said there was no man greater than John the Baptist was, and yet when he died, no one was put in his place. When we read of the death of the apostles, they were not replaced. When Christ died, no one took His place. These people were here for a reason and a purpose. They finished what needed to be done. They fulfilled the task at hand. What they did no one else can do. Why? Because nothing has changed. What they completed still holds true. Everything is done. It is ready. Judgment is at hand.

Today churches hold men up to be something special. Look, if you are doing what God asks of you, then you are special. No man is better than you are. You are to bow to no man or figure of man or woman. God does not need nor does He commission apostles today. He just wants people who will accept what Jesus taught the apostles to teach.

Some churches say that you do not get the Holy Ghost upon salvation. But Christ said, "Greater is He that lives in you than he that is in the world." How can Christ live in you except through the Holy Ghost? Everyone is not powered with the same gift of the spirit. Everyone does not get all the gifts. God uses His gifts or His purpose. He uses them only when He sees fit, not when man wants.

When Paul set up the offices of the church, he did not set in them healers or speakers of some unknown tongue. He did not set up some man who you kiss his ring or some woman to pray to. The church was instructed to preach the blood of Jesus, to be born again, to live and teach according to His Word, not to rewrite it.

Both man and man-made churches had better get on their high horse and quit power-hunting. They need to get their nose in the book of knowledge---God's Word. They better get back to doing what Christ died and gave His spirit for them to do. That is to preach and teach His gospel.

Remember, if you come to God, it is through being born of the spirit. If you serve God, it is through His spirit. If you worship God, it must be through His spirit. If you pray, it must be done through His Son. If you want anything of God, it must be through Christ Jesus. Anything else will lead you through the gates of hell.

When Paul wrote the first letter to the church at Corinth, the church was in an uproar of chaos. The early Christians had been misled. Some wanted powers to do this and power to do that.

Others wanted to know and have the best power. Now read the second letter, and you will see all this power play stopped. God's Word, through the teaching of Christ, put them back into shape. Look at Romans 16:17--18. In so many words, he who causes division in the doctrine of Christ feeds his own belly and serves not the Lord Jesus Christ. When God says he, man, mankind, and whomsoever, it means you, anybody, and any group and everybody. You can put your name or your church's name; you can put the pope, bishop, pastor, father, dad, mother, aunt, uncle, grandma, or grandpa; it does not matter, for God's Word applies to all.

Man cannot undo, redo, or change what God says. The preacher was really anointed. He was touching a lot of people. Brother Dave and Reverend Evans were being inspired. Their questions were being answered through the power of the spirit. The preacher went on to say that God said man will work for his support and he has to. He said woman would suffer in childbearing, so she does. God said that man must die, and we do. God said He has a place for those who, or for whatsoever reason, reject His Son's teaching will go. So, you will find out that if you made your bed, you will lie in it.

The preacher said there is only one Christ, and He has only one spirit. He promised that spirit to whomsoever believes and asks of Him and accepts His salvation by faith. If you, for whatsoever reason then, are not of God, then you are not a Christian. You are not serving Christ. You are not a member of the church, and you are not going to heaven.

Now I know this is plain, and I cannot do anything about that, for this is God's Word. It is not me saying it, but it is God revealing it through me to you. You can take it or leave it. It is your soul. It is your choice. Get mad and be hurt, or get saved and be glad. But first, read His Word.

All the answers are found in his Word as well as the dos and the do nots. God's Word does not need man's help. You cannot do anything for it except accept it and teach it. God does not accept man's doctrine. Why should He? Who are we? We were made of

God for His glory. We are to serve and worship Him. We must please Him to inherit His Kingdom. If not, then you will get exactly what we asked for. If you do not ask to be born again, then you are asking God to prove to you what He said is true. I just do not believe it. You had better think long and hard before pushing that button.

Reverend Evans and Brother Dave enjoyed the sermon very much, even though some of it him hit them. But thanks be to

God that is how you grow. You hear the Word or read the Word and then obey according to the guidance of the Holy Spirit. The church that held the revival seemed to grow stronger from it. There were people saved and some who rededicated their life to God. One thing is for sure; God was using this preacher to give sermons to strengthen and guide His people.

Reverend Evans talked to Brother Dave about a Saturday night service at their church. The pastor said that they could invite some singers and a visiting preacher. "We could have a big worship and praise service!" Dave answered, "I wonder if our members would come out and support it. Would they ask and invite others to come with them?" "Well," said the preacher, "we will soon find out."

At Wednesday night service, Brother Dave's sermon was that to fear God is the beginning of wisdom. To ignore Him or be afraid is the act of foolishness. He preached that man is to fear the power and authority of God, not the fear of getting to know Him. He showed man should not fear one who can just take his life but to fear the One who after He takes your life away has the power to cast your soul into hell.

Do not be afraid to come unto God, for God is love and full of mercy and grace. He says to lay your burdens on Him, and He will give you rest. He will watch over and protect you. He has made a promise to you. If you make peace with Him, He will make a home in glory for you.

What you must fear is the truth and power of His Word. He promises a heaven for those who accept His son as their Savior, but He also promises a hell of fire for those who reject or ignore

His Son's teaching. God keeps His Word because God cannot lie. You had better have fear of His power over death, hell, grave, and your soul, but again, I say do not be afraid to meet Him.

Look at it this way. When you are in trouble, the police can help. You are not afraid to call them when your life or home is in anger. You only fear them when you are breaking the law. It is not them as a person you fear. It is the power and authority they represent because you do not agree with the law. Does that mean you can break it?

Now you can get away with it until you are caught and face the judge. Then you are punished whether you want his judgment, whether He really wants to punish. You give him no choice. You face your sentence no matter what you think or say, no matter who stands up for your defense. If you are found guilty, then you face the sentence; the judge does not care if you did not understand or know . . . Too bad. Ignorance is no excuse. If you did wrong and are caught, you have to pay the consequence.

Now if this is true in the laws of man, how much truer is it in the law of God? The only differences between the two are these:

1. In God's law, everyone is treated the same. It does not matter how rich or poor or what color you are. It does not matter what you call yourself. The punishment is hell, and the sentence is for eternity.

2. In God's law, no one escapes the long arm of His law. There are no loopholes. God sees and knows all. You are caught as soon as you decide to do wrong.

3. With God, all will face the same judge and the same judgment. All will receive the same sentence because all have broken the same law, the failure to call upon the name of the Lord Jesus for remission of sin. Guilty because we did not obey the very words of His law.

Why is it we can accept the law and punishment of man, but we cannot accept God's law? Man uses lies and trickery in our courtrooms. Do you think this will work when you stand before the white throne of God's judgment? You had better think again.

Brother Dave brought his sermon to a close and gave an altar call. Three souls came forward to pray. It was a good service and very enlightening message. Before ending the service, Dave called the pastor to the pulpit. Reverend Evans thanked Brother Dave and God for the message.

He then made some announcements, one of which was "Two weeks from this Saturday, we are going to have a Saturday night service. I urge you all to pray for this service. Invite everyone you know and those you do not know to attend this service. Bring your family, friends, and foes. If no one will come along, then come alone. Let us all plan to come and worship His holy name both in spirit and in truth." Then the pastor closed the service with a prayer.

It was not long before word got around, and some people were upset. That meant there would be church on a Saturday night, Sunday morning, Sunday evening, and Wednesday evening, for you see, even God's people slip back into the ways of man and want things their way. It seems that everybody drifts into a rut or gets lazy in their service when they exclude God's plan from theirs.

The pastor did not do this on his own. It was what God had laid it upon his heart, so he knew that God had His reasons. It was not for him to question God but his duty to obey God. It is your duty too. Amen. However, people forget their duty sometimes. We all need to be reminded. It is not enough just to be saved. Being saved is not for God; it is for our soul.

After salvation, it is our duty to serve His Word and His son. We show our faith and fruit by our service. One such service to God is preaching, telling the wonderful news that Jesus came and died to save our souls, reminding the church to be on their toes. The devil is waiting on the sideline. He wants to switch you on track, teaching and telling the children of God to dedicate your life to Him. Allow Him to enrich and bless your soul. All this is done for one purpose: so, we can hear, believe, grow, and obey. God does take care of those who are His. Praise His holy name!

Reverend Evans was hoping for a big turnout for the Saturday night service, which was just a week away. The word about the service was being talked about all over the area. However, as before, men could change his mind and make other plans. It seems you can have all the good intentions, but somehow something always comes up. I wonder why. Has this ever happened to you?

Have you ever thought about going to church or maybe to a different kind of church and then something comes up, or for some reason, it just slips your mind? I wonder why. Have you ever told God, "If you help me, I will do right?" But then you did not. Why? Have you ever been in church and thought you should go to the altar but did not? Do you go to a church that just talks about living for God instead of preaching and teaching the spiritual act of being born again? Why? You know why.

Satan is using what he knows works for you. He wants you to think you are living right to keep you living wrong. He put thoughts in your mind that are not of God or God's ways just to rob your soul of its heavenly inheritance. He makes things come up just to keep you down where he is. He does not want you to read God's Word. He knows the power therein. He wants you to go somewhere to be misled with false hope. If you do not think this is true, make up your mind just as Dave did. Make the decision to go to a true Bible-preaching church, and then watch what comes up.

If you are truly sincere, you will have to tell yourself over and over "I am going." If not, something will come up, or you will change your mind. If you go to a nonspiritual-filled church, watch what your friends will say when they hear that you are going to that kind of church. Ask your pastor about you attending a born-again Christian church, one that allows the Holy Spirit free to touch, bless, and save anyone hearing and obeying the call.

You might be surprised. A lot of people will tell you that you do not need to attend a church that acts like that. You do not need to hear hellfire and heaven taught that way. You do not have to receive the Holy Ghost. You might hear that you do not have to believe in being born again of the spirit. We teach it this way. We believe it this way. Look, there is only one way, and God says it is through the salvation of Christ and the acceptance of His Holy Spirit in your soul.

Do you not owe it to yourself to be sure you are serving God according to the teachings of Christ and not just wasting your time playing religion? I do not mean to go from a nonspiritual church to a drummed-up, spirit-filled church. I mean a church that preaches the whole Word of God as it is written for the glory, praise, and honor of God Almighty. That is done for the salvation of lost souls through the blood of Christ Jesus our Lord. What would it hurt? What is there to be afraid of? The truth? No one there will make you do anything that you do not want to do just the same as no one not having the spirit can tell you what it is to be touched of God. Better yet, take a moment now and bow before God in prayer. Ask Him to make things right between you; tell Him you want to be filled with the Holy Spirit. YOU accept His Word and the salvation of your soul through faith. YOU want to serve Him. YOU want to walk with Christ and reign with Him forever and then confess that "I have been born again! I am a child of God." Then read His Word and obey the spirit.

Do not take any chances. Trust in the Word of God, not in doctrines, pamphlets, traditions, or experiences of a man-made doctrine. Trust in Him who died for you. He will not allow you to be misled. He will keep you safely wrapped in His arms. He will fill your heart and soul with His spirit. He will always be there with you. Then one day soon, He will come for you because your sins are covered by His blood. He will lead you through those pearly gates, down those streets of gold, alongside of the walls of asper as you enter into the glorious Kingdom of God, which was prepared by Him for you. Praise His holy name, for He is the Son of God!

The sad thing is that some will never change. They will go on being misled and deceived. I hope and pray you are not one of the whatsoever. For whatsoever reason, I hope you are one the many whosoever's, those who have called upon the name of Jesus for redemption. For you to die lost and face God not being born again would be tragic. I have such a burden for the souls who are not of God. I want to bring the gospel of Christ to them all, not my ideas, not my church, not my doctrine . . . just Jesus.

Do not get angry. Let His Word bring you into repentance. You might not like the way I made a point or the way I said it, and for that, I am sorry. But blame me for the way I brought it across. However, I am not sorry for the message, for it is of God. Man needs to know the truth. You may never get to tell me "I hated your book," or "I really liked it." We may never meet again in this world, but praise God! I hope to meet you in glory. Amen.

Here is another sad thing: we want God to be at our beckoned call. Yet we ignore His plea and call. It is like we want all that man and sin has to offer, but when we need more than this world can give, we call on God. You cannot have it both ways. You cannot tell God "Don't call me. I'll call you!" for God will not be a part of your plan. You must accept and be a part of His plan. His plan is that there is a place for those who do and a place for those who do not. You can choose not to make a place for God in your plans, but because He gave us His Word, He does not have that choice, for everyone has a place in His plans. Where do you fit in?

Now at Reverend Evans's church, the Saturday night service was at hand. It is now the Wednesday before. The pastor knew some of the members would not want to give up their Saturday night for church. Some had other plans. Be he trusted God. He knew there were those who would be there. God still has people who will give of their time and effort just to serve Him. There are still those who want and are striving to make heaven their home.

Yes, there are still Christians who will give all they have to serve Christ. After all, He gave up His home in glory to come and suffer for us. He was mocked, spat upon, beaten, and even crucified just to bring us a means of salvation. But He did not stop there. He came out of the grave for us then went back to the Father and sent us His spirit, which calls us and keeps us out of sin's ways.

I know you really want to go to heaven too. I know you might think that you are doing what is right. I also know you do not think you have to do this or that. You do not want to give up this or that. What you do not know is GOD. If you are a child of God, through the redeeming power and blood of Christ, do not look at it as a chore. Don't think of it as an "I have to." It is an "I want to." I count it as an honor to serve the risen Savior. It is a loving desire filled with blessings and rewards to do all I can for the precious Son of God.

Here is something else I know: it is not enough to just want to go to heaven, even if you do not accept the plan of God, which includes you in heaven or hell. When you face hell, you will want heaven. But it is too late and not enough. When Noah was making the ark, nobody wanted in. When Noah built the ark, God chose who went in, and then God sealed the door. But when the wrath of the flood came, everyone wanted in. No one wanted to die in the flood as the raging waters climbed. So did the desire of those who faced God's wrath. But it was too late and not enough. You better get in and out of the rain. You cannot walk on water.

Finally, Saturday night came. When Brother Dave drove into the parking lot, he was a little disappointed. There did not look to be many people, but he was not about to let that damper his spirits. He came to worship and to have a good time in His Lord. The service started with a bang. The singers were filled with the Holy Spirit from the start. People began to clap, cry, and shout. One fellow just had to get up and walk; he could not sit still. All was done in order, and God received all the praise. I could go on and on. The service was really blessed. But we need to get down to the brass tacks. It came time for the preaching, time for God to send a message to the hearts of His people and to the souls of the lost.

The visiting preacher took the pulpit very slowly. You could barely hear him. He led out in a prayer, asking for the anointed Word, and began to speak clearly. He did not open his Bible, just began to deliver his message. You see, it does not matter how you go about bringing the message; it just matters that you let God lead you.

He began to preach on the gospels of the Bible: Matthew, Mark, Luke, and John. The preacher said these books teach the life and ways of Christ. He brings man into grace, for the law could not deliver man from sin. Christ left nothing unturned. He taught in depth what sin is, who has sinned, and the way to overcome sin. Christ brought us salvation and the new covenant.

These books show man how to praise, worship, and live in accordance with God. Jesus goes on to tell man of his just reward and the just punishment for all those who rejected or denied any part of the new covenant, for the new order included all, not just for the Jews, Greeks, or Romans and not just for the religious leaders or the rich or the poor. Now it was for everyone. Now it was for all mankind to do what God expects or face the results of their rejections. It cost Christ his life, but He laid it all out for us. The preacher went into detail on the points of the gospel: what Christ said about each lifestyle, the believers, and the nonbelievers. Christ made sure that no one would be left out, for that way, you will have no excuse. He preached that Christ aid, "I am the truth and the light. If you live without me, you live in darkness. You cannot see the way of God. I am the door. If any man, woman, or child comes to the Father, He must come through me. There is no other way."

Christ promised, "I will go and prepare a place for you. I will come again and receive you." This is Jesus's way of telling you that "If you do not accept what I came and died to give unto you, you will not enter into My heaven. It was not made for you." Now He also tells us that you do not have to do anything to go to hell. It is what you do not do. "By not accepting My salvation, you are already condemned, and you will face the full wrath of God" (John 3:18 and 36).

The reverend then went on to say that if you do not want to accept the true teaching of the gospel, then do not try and change it or use it to make you into something you are not. Leave it alone. Do not take out of it what you want. Do not be guilty of misleading others. Stop trying to tell me what God expects out of me. Do not tell me you love God and deny His teaching. Do not tell the Christians how to worship or how to serve God when you do not even know the Father because you cannot accept the Words and teachings of His Son.

Now I have only highlighted the main points. The sermon covered a lot. The man of God gave all he had to the deliverance of this message. All in all, it was a very moving sermon. It lasted about an hour. I guess God had a lot to get across. It was a very awakening message. You might say it was a verbal letter to this church, saying, "Do not get on a high horse. Remember who died for you. Remember what I taught you. Do not be led by society or man or tradition. Let me live in you as you can live in peace with God."

Man must accept the preaching of God's anointed Word. This is His way of putting you on the right track. He does not use or need more letters to get His church back on track. Man does not accept the ones He has already written. He needs His Word preached in the power of the Holy Spirit. He needs churches to read the letter He had written to the early churches and obey them.

It would take too many letters today. There are too many places called CHURCH. There is too much confusion, too many false doctrines, too many men not called to preach that are deceiving and misleading. Yet if man would read God's Word, we would see that God warned us of this. He told us what to do. You know if Christ would come here now, there would be a lot of churches He could not preach or teach in. Would He be welcome at yours? Are you sure? Is His salvation welcome now? Is His spirit at liberty in your church? Does your church teach or mock His teachings?

If Christ wrote a letter to your church, would they accept it? If He wrote a letter to you, would you read it? Would you accept it? Would you obey it? Then mark out the name in its place because it was written for you and me. God is not going to redo what He has done because He does not have to. It was done right the first time, so take it or leave it. Leave with the Christians, or take what is coming after the church has been delivered to God's throne.

Man had better see the errors of His ways; if not, his rude awakening will see when Christ comes. He will see Jesus in all His glory. He will see the church members, the ones born into the holy congregation being called up and taken up to forever be with the Lord, for in that day, the disbelievers, deceivers, sinners, and "whatsoever" will watch as God calls His children home. Every one of them will be crying out for mercy just as all those who died in the great flood but to no avail.

Think of this: this is the only event concerning the history of man that is already recorded and is yet to come, that cannot be altered or stopped. Oh, praise God! What an event that will be, the day my Lord splits the eastern sky and calls the righteous souls to come home, calls them from the graves and the four corners of the world. Come home, my children, and receive the wonders and glory of God. "Oh, what a glorious day that will be when my Jesus I shall see."

Just to hear Him say, "Welcome home, my good and faithful servant." Because you allowed me to come into your life, God the Father allows you to inherit what was promised. Oh, how I want to see and be with the One who died for me. Just to be in His presence is more than mind or man can imagine. Do not forget you can be there too.

This is the last promise made to man. There is no need for more letters. The sign of the times is at hand. The warning is recorded. It is being preached worldwide. You must prepare to meet thy God, so read His Word, for the Word of God judges all mankind. Take heed to it. Do not be left behind as God proves Himself and His Word. Do not let His wrath be unleashed upon your lost soul. Be safe and get saved! Do not take a chance; you might be wrong. Get saved. Serve God. Worship Him. Allow Jesus to come into your heart and soul. Then see if you do not receive the promises made to God's people. If there is nothing to it, like man says, then go back to the way you were. Prove to yourself who is a liar: man, or God. Remember, it does not cost you anything. What have you to lose? Hell?

That was a good service and a good sermon. You did not want to miss anything. If it did not make you want to go and pray, it caused you to take a good look at yourself. He then went to God in prayer, for he knew the Word and the power of the Holy Spirit were the means of being free of the sins of man and the ways to draw closer to God.

You know, we all should go to the book of how to do it yourself. I do not mean the ones you see on TV or from the *Readers Digest.* I do not mean the how-to books written by Reverend this or Reverend that or by Dr. of this or Dr. of that. I mean the original and the best do-it-yourself home guide ever written. I am talking about the book that holds all the how-tos, what tos, who should, where to, and when to, the book written by all the power and authority of God. I am talking about the Bible: the Word of God, the book of truth. I am talking about the answer to all man's problems.

You really should check it out. Read it for yourself. Open your heart and mind to the wisdom and ways of God. He will open your eyes to His wondrous glory and saving grace. Then He will open the pearly gates as Christ leads you into eternal bliss. He promises you will not be sorry. But He also promises that if you do not, you will be sorry. You will be sorry for all eternity. You see, God does not mess around. He plays for keeps. He will keep His people in His holy presence forever as promised. As promised, His lake of fire will keep those not born of God's spirit in torment forever. Amen.

They knew the most important work for them to do as Christians was to win souls. They also knew this would not be easy. Sin had a strong hold on man. For whatever reason, man had decided to go his own way. It would be hard to get people into church. There is so much Antichrist doctrine that man does not know which way to turn.

Yet the answer is clear. Turn to God. Do not listen to schools, government, or man's churches. Do not look for any place for salvation but the cross. Not the cross that shows Jesus still on it; I mean the cross that He carried, the cross that He gave His life on that we might be saved, the cross that after He gave His life for us, He was taken off that cross.

Yes, the cross is empty. The supreme sacrifice has been paid. He was put into a borrowed tomb, but the tomb was also empty. Christ arose from the dead that we might live through Him. Look to the EMPTY cross! It reminds us of the price Jesus paid. Look to Him who died and arose that we might be saved. Seek the Words and wisdom of God. Do not settle for anything else. Do not be deceived or misled. Do not be deprived of your salvation. Turn to God through the inspiration and guidance of the Holy Spirit, and His truth will set you free forever. Amen.

As they talked on how to reach man, as they discussed ways to get man into a Bible-preaching church, Brother Dave came up with an idea. Reverend Evans liked the idea, and so they began to pray and ask for God's help. They knew if their idea was going to profit anything, it would have to be inspired and anointed by the Holy Spirit. They had come up with a plan, but they did not leave God out of their plan. With their idea and God's grace, they hoped to reach a lot of their friends and acquaintances.

They wanted to reach people they knew who were unsaved, the ones who did not go to church. They wanted to use their homes to witness of the never-ending joys and promises of God. They would do this by inviting their friends over for an evening of discussion and debate. No preaching, just talking and getting input from both sides. They told their friends they wanted their input about going to church and serving or not serving God. Their main idea was to use this plan to let their friends prove to themselves their need of salvation and living for God.

In fact, Reverend Evans and Brother Dave put out a challenge to their friends. At first, Brother Dave thought they were going way out on a limb, but the challenge was given. They told their friends if they could show there was more to gain, more enjoyment, better in not being a Christian or not having to go to church every week, Reverend Evans and Brother Dave would stop nagging them about going to church. "But if we can get you to see there is a need, and it is far better to follow the teaching of Christ, then you must agree to go to church for two Sundays."

"Here is the deal: if you prove us wrong, you do not have to worry about us coming to see you. We will not keep asking you to go to church with us. We will still love and pray for you. But you will not have to listen to us beg you to get into church. Now if we get you to agree on that it is better to be saved than not, then you must agree to attend one of our churches two straight Sundays. In fact," Brother Dave said, "if we do not win, if it is a total stalemate, we will do your yard work for two weeks." Now Brother Dave thought that was going out on a limb, but it was too late to back out, so the challenge was set with one understanding: this would not end up in an argument, nor would it cause bad feelings between friends.

The first meeting was set, and Reverend Evans and Brother Dave prayed all week. They now knew they were not out on a limb with their friends, for now, their friends would see the many joys and blessings in serving God. They would hear of the promises God has for His people. They would now see the wonders they have been missing out.

At the first meeting, not much was discussed. They just talked and got to know each other and their friends. Their friends were surprised the "brothers" did not bring up the Word of God. They did not preach to them, nor did they try to get them to go to church. It was just a friendly visit. In fact, it was the friends who finally opened the door for Reverend Evans and Brother Dave to mention their faith.

They wondered and asked how the two of them had so much in common. Reverend Evans was fifty years old, and his friends were between forty-five and sixty-five. Brother Dave was about thirty-two years old, and his friends ranged from twenty to forty years old. They liked different things, their personalities were different, and they went to different churches. It was discussed for a while, and then Dave answered, "I will tell you how and why we have so many differences and yet so much in common. We are of the same family.

"We both have been born again. We both love and serve the same God. Through the same spirit, we are just trying to please God. We want to inherit His Holy Kingdom, and therefore, we must love one another regardless of our differences. We share the same love for God's Word and for the souls of man. We are brothers in Christ Jesus. That is why we ignore our differences and thrive on our common ground. We want to lead all our family and friends to salvation."

Brother Dave added, "We learn from each other. We love the fellowship we have through Christ. We help each other through prayer and discussing God's Word because we know what God stands for, and we know what Christ died for. We have the same goals, so we work together. We do not think that one is better than the other. We let our spirits bear witness of each other. We ask

God to help us live and worship in one accord because we both want the same things. We want to win souls. We want to show man the love of God that is in us. We want to show how great and glorious it is to serve a most loving and merciful God." Other than that, there were questions and answers. The only other question asked was by one of Brother Dave's friends who asked, "Why do some people act so silly in church?" He added, "I went to a church and saw people who shouted and cried. I saw them going up and hugging everybody. What is up with that?"

Reverend Evans jumped right in with his reply. "By not being born of the Holy Spirit, by not knowing the sweet goodness and blessing that came from God's throne, you cannot understand the reaction one might have when touched by the mighty hand of God." The brother added, "I know what you mean. I too scorned at the action of some Christians, but bless God and thanks be to His name, I met the maker of joy. I found Jesus.

"I asked the sweet Savior to come into my life, to give me true peace and happiness. I found something in Him that could put a shout of joy in a drunkard, who could put peace in the heart of a drug addict. I found someone who could bring the biggest and proudest man to His knees in tears. Yes, I came in contact with the Holy Ghost of God, the same spirit that can move mountains and part the waters of the sea, that can heal the sick and cause the blind to see. The same power that raised Christ from the dead now lives in me. I met the son of God, the Savior of man. He raised me up to the newness of life I was reborn of---a great mighty spirit."

Brother Dave said, "Amen to that, brother! What a great testimony to the power of God and salvation. Now let me add something in different terms."

"Why do people react to music the way they do? Some will jump around and throw their partner over their heads. Others will act as if they are having a fit or tantrum. Some jerk and twitch like they are going into convulsions. Some spin on their heads, while others act like they are having sex. Still, others will get into big lines and kick and stomp all in time. Let me ask you this: why is it okay to react to this type of music but not okay for Christians to react to songs and gospel music?"

Have you seen the way people act when they just see a rock star or movie star? Why, they jump and cry and scream as if they were dying. Some people even pass out from just the sight of a superstar. Yet Christians are criticized for their reaction of meeting the Son of God, not just seeing Him but having a personal relationship with Him. Having Christ's spirit come into your souls is far greater than seeing Michael Jackson, Garth Brooks, or even Elvis Presley. Yet we are supposed to suppress our overwhelming joy to suit you. Is this fair?

Look how people react to their favorite boxers, racehorse, or sports team when they do something good or start to win. They jump up and cheer; they clap their hands and stomp their feet. Some yell at the top of their lungs, and some bounce up and down in their seats. They do this in public. They do this on TV. They even have to pay in order to act this way. All this over a game. This game of life is forever. Why, even the angels in heaven rejoice when a soul is won. God Himself rejoices when a lost soul wins the battle over Satan. Then you tell a Christian that he or she cannot express or rejoice when a friend or loved one wins out over death and hell-fire? Why don't we have the same freedom of expression as everyone else?

Let me ask you this. Why do you think that worldly pleasures can excite, motivate, or stir the heart and spirits of man more than the power of Him who created man? Why can you not acknowledge the fact that just a touch from the almighty hand of God, by the power of the Holy Ghost through Jesus Christ our Lord and Savior, can and does overwhelm the spirit and soul of man to his uttermost fulfillment?

There is no comparison to the joy of living for and serving our risen Savior. There is no greater reward, no championship, and no greater thrill than to inherit the Kingdom of God. Just the mere thought of being at peace with God, just the knowledge of knowing that you have escaped the awful wrath of God, is enough to put a shout in your heart.

There were about twenty people at the first meeting besides Brother Dave and Reverend Evans. The others left the meeting, feeling a little uneasy. It did not go the way they had expected it too either. They thought they would hear the same old "come on" by the two Christians, but it was small talk until the door was opened for them to witness about Christ by asking two questions. Now it was different. It was not going to be a hard sale discussion; it was going to be friends talking to one another, asking and answering questions. *This would be nice*, the friends thought. But it left them wondering.

The friends were ready for the "you better do this and you better do that" routine. They were expecting the end is near. You have to go to church. But now they did not know what to expect. It made them uneasy, but they really liked the brothers, and they did respect them. At least they stood up for what they believed. They did not change from day to day. However, the friends knew that church was not for them, so when it got down to the real issue, they would be ready. They were not going to have to give up the fun that this life had to offer. They were not ready to be tied down to going to church all the time.

Now after this meeting, Brother Dave and Brother Evans went to visit Reverend James and Reverend Don. Reverend James was the pastor at the church he attended. They told the two preachers of their idea and the first meeting. They also confessed, "We are a little afraid we took on more than we can handle." Both the preachers urged them to continue the meetings. Reverend Evans replied, "It is too late to back out. With God's help, you can do this." Reverend James told them, "Make sure to let God lead you, for this might be the only time your friends and loved ones will sit down and take a good look at their lives. This might be the only time they will really look at what a blessed life it is to serve God."

There Their preachers told them, "Take your time with them. Listen to what they think and feel. This will help them to be more open-minded to what you have to say." Reverend Don added, "They may ask a lot of questions. Just take a moment to ask God to guide your answers." Reverend James told them, "Do not be ashamed or too proud to say, 'I don't know.' Do not think that you must be able to answer all their questions. Just be what you are: two Christians among people whom you care about and want to lead them to Christ. Be led of His spirit. Witness and tell them of the glory, power, and love of God."

Now it was time for the next meeting. Both brothers kneeled and asked God for His support and inspiration. They knew they needed God's help; religion is a touchy subject. Some people cannot talk about it without arguing. The brothers did not want anyone getting upset, for this would spoil the whole thing. They wanted the meeting to run in accordance with the love and grace of God.

The brothers compiled a list. They listed all the good reasons for living for and serving Christ. Then they had a list of the bad reasons for being a Christian. Only that list was a blank. The friends began arriving, and it was time to start the meeting. It started with idle chitchat. Then the list was spotted lying on the table. It was spotted by Terri, one of Dave's friends. The rest of Dave's friends and family were Larry, Mary, Bill, Paul, Doug, Jim, Bob, Sally, and Frank. Now Brother Evans's friends and family included Joe, Dick, Ted, Tom, Sue, Sid, Millie, John, Peter, and his wife, Kathy.

After Terri spotted the list, she did not mention it. She just asked Dave to get everyone something to drink before they got into a deep discussion, so the brothers went into the kitchen for the refreshments. Terri then picked the list and showed it to the others. She said, "While they are in there, this will give us enough time to make of list of good and bad of our own. We will be ready for them." They quietly laughed and then got busy.

While they were in the kitchen, Brother Evans's wife came in to help them with the cofee and soda. She asked Brother Dave and her husband, "Do you two know what you are doing? You could be asking for trouble." She reminded them how touchy some people are. "Do not step on their toes. Do not belittle them if you want them to see your point. You must listen to theirs." She said, "Brother Dave, please do not start preaching to them. It will make them put up their guard. You guys said it would be a talk session, so keep it that way." Brother Evans told his wife, "Thanks for the input." She said, "I know how you two can be when you get started. Just remember to have a conversation. Both parties involved must talk and listen. Okay?"

Brother Dave said, "You are right. This is a good chance we have. We do not want to blow it." Brother Evans said, "What we do or say will be in the spirit of God. We will not attempt anything on our own because we know that is when we will get into trouble." His wife laughed and said, "Amen. Let the Lord lead, and you will be well." Then they heard the group laughing and yelling for drinks, so they returned to the living room with the refreshments.

Upon sitting, Frank said, "We have some questions we would like answered. We also have some subjects to discuss, as I am sure the two of you do also." Frank went on, "So we will take turns and not talk all at once so there will be some kind of order." Brother Dave then said, "I think we all should ask, answer, listen, and discuss things with the best intentions, respecting one another. We must not get angry at each other, and we must not launch an out-and-out attack on someone. Okay?" Because they had respect for one another, and they really liked one another, they all agreed.

Sue jumped right in and asked the first question. "Why shouldn't I wait until I am as old as you to turn into a Christian? After all, I am young. I have still got a lot of living to do. Why should I give up all the fun I am having now when I can wait until I am older?"

Brother Dave answered, "Sue, the sooner you find Christ, the sooner you can really be to live. Plus, it gives you more time to be used and blessed of God. He can use you to win souls that maybe no one else can reach, not to mention the sooner you can begin to witness and teach your family the true Word and ways of God. You might just win them to the Lord before Satan puts his hooks into them. There are many other reasons, but the most important is 'who can assure you that you will live one more day'? Death has no age limit, but our time is limited. The second coming of Christ could come with the next tick of God's clock. Listen, you only have one promise after birth, and that promise is death and then the judgment of God."

Brother Evans added, "You have no other promise. Christ promises to save your soul from the wrath of God if you ask Him to. Then the second part of your question will answer itself. Now I am not going to preach a sermon on the joys and blessings of knowing God. I will just say this: you have no idea what you are missing. If you do one thing, and it is fun, and then find a new thing that is the most fun you have ever had, which would you prefer to do? If given the choice, that is what it is like to be born again. The old stuff just isn't fun no more, not compared to the new joys. Listen, you did not know the pleasures of man until you tried them. The same applies to the pleasures and joys of God. You should let God introduce you to His world of pleasures, and then you will learn firsthand that you will not have to ask or guess."

Well, the questions kept coming from their friends. I will not detail the answers to the rest of them, for they have already been covered in previous chapters. I will say God gave Brother Evans and Brother Dave great answers in good details without preaching. The answers were full of God's grace yet with logic and in terms everyone could understand. I will just list the other questions from their friends. Frank asked, "I do not feel I do anything bad enough to go to hell for. Why do I have to ask forgiveness?" This question required a long and lengthy answer. Some were getting bored, so they did the best they could to answer. After this, there was a discussion on the answers, and then the meeting was called to a close.

It went very well. Everyone was putting in his or her points. Everyone really showed an interest to both the questions and the answers. The brothers in Christ were looking forward to the next meeting. Now I am just covering the main points and topics, not all the chitchat and joking and silly things that came up, because I too want to keep you interested.

At the next meeting, Joe started with "How do you know there is a God? How do you know everyone will be judged by His Word?" Wow! What a question. This gave Brother Dave and Brother Evans a real chance to relate to their friends about their personal relationship with God. It also allowed them to get into God's Word to answer the second part.

Millie asked, "If God loves man, why will He put man in hell?" This answer showed them how God gives man a choice. It also showed that God is a just God, and everyone faces the same judgment with the same results.

John asked, "How do you expect me to believe that the Bible is the true Word of God? Plus, if it is, why are there so many ways to believe it?" Now the questions were getting to demand a lot of thought and a lot more of God's Word plus a lot more of God's grace to answer. They had to be careful not to mention names of churches or people. Some of their friends had family in some of the churches, and the brothers had to show that not everyone follows the teaching of Christ, and some people go their own way. But God led them to answer in a way not to insult any of their friends and to still get their point across.

Next Brother David asked a question, "If what I believe is wrong, I still win because I have lived a more rewarding and blessed life than not knowing Christ. I will go wherever you go or come back as something else or whatever. But if I am right and you are wrong, then you lose. Your soul is lost, and you will spend eternity in the fiery pits of hell. Is this a chance you are willing to take?" Well, the group hee-hawed around this one. No one really came up with an out-and-out answer, but it did get them thinking.

Brother Evans asked, "If everybody went to church, if everybody tried to live by the Ten Commandments, would we be better on as a nation and a family?" The answer to that one came before anyone could think. Someone just said sure, and then everyone agreed. Then he added, "Why don't you as a group start the trend?" Now the answer was slow coming, and the answers were the same old ones . . . "I am not ready."

Next Brother Dave pulled out the list (he told the group that he and Brother Evans had compiled a list). They listed the pros and cons of living a Christian life. Terri spoke up. "We are ahead of you. We saw your list lying on the table, so we made a list of our own, didn't we?" Everyone replied, "Yes." Dave then added, "Let us read our lists and then discuss the pros and cons, but our list of cons is blank, for there is no bad point in loving and serving the risen Savior." This was done for a reason.

Brothers Dave and Evans had decided they wanted to go first. They would read their list of good points very slowly. They would draw out the good points so they could soak in really good. Dave began to read from their list of the pros. "Good points on being a born-again child of God. We start off with number 1: you are released from the bondage of sin that the devil has you in. God forgives you. He saves you through the blood of Jesus who died for you. He gives you a new life, and you are born again, this time into the holy family of God. His spirit is in you."

They took turns reading their lists. Each was listed in great care and detail. "Number 2: God through His sweet spirit and love gives peace and rest to the weary soul. He gives you inner peace that lasts forever. He ends your searching for pure peace and happiness. You no longer need to hunt or seek among what this world has to offer to fill the emptiness in your soul. God gives it to you from His throne of grace."

Number 3 read, "He sees to your every need, no matter how large or small. You can never use up His store of giving. He knows your wants and needs before you ask, and He fulfills them. Anything you ask for to enable you to be stronger and wiser, or to serve Him better, provide for your family, or to help some, just call on God. He is there for you."

Brother Dave could see the things of God were beginning to stir up the group's thoughts. You could see it on their faces. Next Brother Evans read number 4. "Christ is not only your Savior. He is your best friend. He will always be by your side. He loves you more than your own mother or a father. He will always pick you up when you are down. He will keep your feet on solid ground. No matter what comes your way, Christ will see you through. You are forever sheltered in His loving arms."

Brother Dave read number 5, "He will let nothing come upon you or happen to you that you are not able to bear, and He will always provide you a way out. You will have angels watching over you. He will lead you down the righteous path of life. He will make sure if you stumble, you will not fall. He will not forsake you in times of trouble, pain, or death. He is at your beckoned call."

Number 6 read, "The Holy Spirit is sent with the anointed power to dwell in you, to lead, guide, and direct your every thought or deed. It also empowers you to defeat Satan. It is the direct link to God the Father through Christ His Son. It is given to you for a comfort. It is also the means by which God speaks to your soul. It keeps you in tune with the power and authority from on high. Upon receiving it, you become a part of God."

At this time some remarks were made. Some sounded good, and others were made in a joking matter. Brother Dave asked the group to please "let them finish the list, and then we will hear yours." Jim said, "Your list sounds good, but it is all stuff we have heard before." Brother Dave said, "You might have heard them before but not in the form of comparing the good and bad of the two lifestyles." Doug said, "This is true, but I do not think I believe what you are saying. Just because you put it in a list does not make it so."

Dave added, "I cannot make you believe anything and neither will God. That is why we are here. We are here to ask questions and to get answers, to discuss our ways of life, and to see each other's viewpoints. I am not trying to make anyone believe the way I or Brother Evans believe. But this you can believe: I am asking you to believe something. Either I or Brother Evans have experienced firsthand everything on our lists except number 10. Trust me because that is a fact.

"Everything we have said is from the heart. All we ask and what we all agreed upon was to be truthful and to listen with an open mind to both sides."

Kathy jumped in. "I think they need to finish their list. I also think if this is bothering you that much, maybe they have already won you over." Doug just said, "Right." Then he chuckled and said, "Let's hear the rest of it."

"Okay. Number 7 is we are serving a Savior who can heal you of sickness. He can take your pain upon Himself. He will carry your burdens and lighten your load. He will bear your sorrow, taste your tears, and sweeten your tomorrow.

Number 8: you will live a most blessed and enriched life. You will not only not have to worry or have to be sad, you will be showered with joy and happiness, the likes of which is not known or even imagined by man. The joy and goodness of God is unspeakable and full of glory. It will overflow your heart and soul. There is nothing known of man or of this life that and compare to the uttermost thrill or pure joy of having the presence and power of God touch you."

Brother Evans said, "I will take number 9. I will leave number 10 to Brother Dave. I know he wants to get the last word in." He then read the next one on their list. "You will be filled with love. I mean you will feel such a love for people of all colors. You will want to tell them of all the grace and goodness of serving God, just like we are doing. You will want to teach and tell your children and family, your friends and neighbors, just what you have received. You will warn them of the judgment of God. You will be able to lead them with your life to the ways of God. No more hate in you, no more greed or envy, just pure sweet love, the same love which caused Christ to die so we could have life and have it more abundantly."

Brother Dave stated, "This is the final good point on our list. Like I said, our bad list is blank. We saved this one until last because it is the one we have not yet experienced. However, it is the most important one of all. Plus, it is a two-part point. Number 10 is that your soul will not have to burn in hell. You will not have to face the pain, the agony, or the many punishments of God's eternal wrath. That is the whole purpose of God's plan. He sent Jesus to die for our sin. He calls you to repent. He sends you the Holy Spirit to keep you and give you the victory over death and hell, but the promises do not stop there. If you accept the bloodshed salvation of Christ, if you live and worship by His Word, Christ will come and take your soul to live forever in the glorious Kingdom of God where there will be no sin, no pain, no sorrow, no tears, no sickness, and no death."

Brother Dave started going on about a place where the streets are paved with gold. I heard a few laughs, and then someone said, "Okay, preacher, cut it off. We got the point. No need to start preaching now. You have been doing really good!" Dave just laughed and said, "Okay. We are ready to hear the pros and cons on your list."

For a moment, no one said anything. Everyone just kind of sat there. Dave spoke up. "Let's hear your good and bad points on living a life without Christ, without the love and grace of God." He did this for two reasons. One was to get them talking before they lost interest and the second being he knew the good points on his and Brother Evans's list were far better than anything they could come up with. He also knew their bad points would outweigh their good points by far. This would be the icing on the cake.

Mary spoke up and said, "We are going to read the cons. The bad points first." Bill read the first one. "All the killings and murders. The next one and another one is the physical and sexual abuse on women and children. Another is the open acceptance of sex and nudity like homosexuality, wife swapping, strip clubs." "Now wait a minute," Jack said. "Don't go there!" Brother Dave threw in. "Neither should you!" That got a few laughs! Next was the worse one, the addiction of drugs and booze. Mary said, "I think that about covers the bad points." Everyone started laughing.

Brother Evans said, "Let's get on to your good points." Dave added, "Don't forget going to hell. Put that on your list of cons because whether you believe it or not, it will become a reality." They said they would add that, just for Dave's sake. "Now may we go on? Thank you so much." Terri was not about to give us a chance to speak up again.

We all know the bad points. They are on the news every day, but we have a lot a good point, and we do have a good life. Brother Dave jumped in before the good points were read. "Now remember, you have five black marks against you. One of which is facing God's wrath. Now do your good points mean so much to you that you are willing to accept all your bad points for them?" Peter spoke up then and said, "Let's do the good points. Then we can take a good look at the overall picture." Mary replied, "Let's start with me. We can go to all kinds of parties and have fun. We do not have to worry about what someone thinks." Larry read, "We can go to clubs. We can drink, dance, or just sit around with friends." "If a fight does not break out," someone added. "We also have good friends. They too would help us. We do not have to live a strict life. We can do pretty much what we want." Tom read, "We can gamble on cards or horses. I have won good money on betting. Plus, it is fun. We can enjoy the freedom of sex if we want. And we do not have to watch what we say." Terri added, "We do not have to give our money away. We can buy what we want and go where we want."

Sid spoke up. "I think enough has been said. We know what Dave and Fred were trying to do. We know what we were trying to do. But with the questions and answers, with the warm discussion, and now with these lists. Well, our list in total cannot compete with their list if only one of their points is true. We thought we could win. We thought we had a lot going for us, but folks call it like it is. I feel the agony of defeat."

Dick said, "Even with their list, our lists do not look that appealing. I for one do not think if God sent Jesus to die for us that we should be saying we do not care. I think we should give up and take some time to think about what has taken place here." Bonnie said, "I am not ready to be a Christian. But I have to admit if everything is true, then they have a better life than I do.

It is not for me, but their good points are better than ours."

Frank stood and said, "I do not want to, but I will hold up my end of the deal. How about the rest of you?" A few said, "No way! We have not lost yet. I do not see things differently." Then Terri said, "It is over. What time is church?"

The meeting ended with handshakes and some "I'll see you in church." When everyone else was gone, Brothers Dave and Fred prayed. They thanked God for His spirit and help. They prayed or their friends and family. They also thanked God for having this chance to speak free from their hearts about the joy and love of God.

Most of their friends kept their end of the deal. Four of them accepted Christ as their Savior. As for the others, most of them at least heard the Word of God preached with the anointed power of His spirit. However, they went right along with their way of life. They acted as if nothing happened. They were like so many others the world over. To them, the denial and rejection of Christ was easier and their lifestyle better than to humble themselves and ask Christ for the salvation of their souls.

That is like driving the nails into the hands of Christ all over again. Just how much more punishment and mockery shall we cause the Son of God to endure? How much longer will God allow us to curse the crucifixion of His Son? How long is it until He has had enough?

Life was going along the same as always. Now those living without God in their life were falling deeper and deeper into sin. Satan was really happy. He was robbing people of their soul left and right. He was using every trick he had, and only those strong in God's Word could withstand the lures and snares of his trap.

But all was not bad. Things in the Christian world were going strong. There were soul-winning meetings going on daily. Some of the best sermons ever were being preached. God was pouring out His spirit and the church . . . HIS church was being blessed for their effort and for their faith.

But as the Bible warns, there were those who were turning their backs on the very One who had saved them. These being those who were weak in their faith, prayer, and service, Christians who had let things of man and of this world filter into their life. See, if you get saved and do not grow in your spiritual life, if you are not studied in God's Word, Satan will cause you to believe a lie; he will rob you of your soul.

This is so sad, and yet it happens. Can you imagine the hurt, pain, and sorrow this must cause Jesus? This is worse than the spear they stuck in His side, for this reopens the wound and cuts into Him ever so deeper. This cut goes to His very soul and is felt by the Father, and it causes His spirit great pain to be returned . . . unwanted.

It is like a slap in His face. How can anyone stand before the Savior and say, "I do not want the joys and grace of God. I do not want your spirit to guide and bless me. I turn my back to your salvation. I want to be sinful. I will take God's wrath over His Kingdom."

This is not a decision that is made; however, it is the result. You do make a decision to be saved, but the choice to turn your back on God is made for you. This can only happen a little at a time. Satan waits for his chance, then little by little, he causes you to lose a blessing; and then he causes you not to listen to the spirit, then to quit doing something for God, and then convinces you to slow down. You do not have to be so gung ho. In fact, Satan knows you have given him your soul before you do. Why, some people follow the ways and teachings of man and do not even believe they are lost.

How sad. How terribly sad it would be not to listen to or hear the Word or spirit of God, to be tricked and deceived into thinking you were one of God's people; to have your mind clouded and your heart hardened to the voice and call of God. How awful it will be to face the judgment unprepared, to meet thy God unprepared or unaware. You will hear Him say, "Depart" (Matthew 7:23).

Man needs to learn that he is not his own keeper. He does not have to choose to follow Satan. He may not decide to listen to the teaching of man over the Word of God. He does not say, "I want to go to hell." This is said every time he denies the call of God to be saved. This is said every time he does not do what the creator put him here to do. Our only purpose in life is to glorify God. He is our maker. If we choose not to honor and live according to the master, we cast our souls into hell.

To not fall into the lures and traps of Satan, man needs to get saved and stay saved. He needs to grow from a newborn babe in Christ into a man of God. If you want to live a joyous and blessed life, keep your eyes on Jesus. Keep your faith in His Word and put your trust in the spirit. As long as you follow God, Satan cannot get his hooks in you. That old serpent may bite, but his poison has no effect.

Always keep in mind that God is our master. Once He saves us, He wants to use us for His glory. We must be led of His spirit. We must reach out to the fellow man. We must teach and show the lost way of the cross. We must spread the gospel of the good news, that Christ died for our sins. He loves us, and He wants to save us. He came from the grave to go and prepare a place just for us. He is coming to call us and take us to that eternal Kingdom.

One preacher said it well. He preached on the glory and blessings in doing God's work. Working for God is not like a job; there are no set hours. You get no days off, and yet it is not tiring. It is a pure pleasure and honor to serve God. He went on to say, "Look at it this way: you do not have to wait for a payday. You are rewarded daily, sometimes hourly. Each effort has its rewards. Remember, God rewards you every time you do something in His name.

"It does not matter whether it is giving money, giving time, studying, singing, teaching, praying, witnessing, etc. You cannot outdo God. The more you give or do for Him, the more you receive from Him. He is a gracious and giving God. He loves us and takes care of us.

"Finally, when the labor is over, when God calls His family home, when our work down here is finished, we will spend eternity in the fullness of His love. We are rewarded for our efforts here. But the great payday will be when we inherit the Kingdom of heaven, when time no longer moves, and when we bask in the wonders and glory of a place made by God the Father for His family to dwell."

The preacher went on to say, "If you are of God, you will love to worship and serve. You will study and learn all you can. You will want to do that which glorifies Him. That is how you show your faith---by your works. You show your works by your fruits. You cannot have one without the other. They go hand in hand. You cannot please God with good works without faith, and you cannot have faith without good works (James 2:18--20). If you want to be rewarded, if you want to bear good fruits, you have to have good roots. You must be planted firmly in the doctrine of Christ. Your roots must be watered by the blood of His salvation. You cannot be of God if you are not born again. You cannot please God if He does not know you as a child, born unto Him through the plan of salvation. Without being of His spirit through your faith, your works are in vain. NO good deeds regardless of what they are, no matter how much you do or try to do; if you do not put your faith in Him, it will not get you into heaven.

You cannot earn, pay, or sneak your way into heaven. You must go in the same as me, and I must go in the same way as everyone else. There is only one way in. Jesus says, "I am the door. No one enters except through me" (John 10:8). Dave added, "You better listen to the Word. Be born again! So, if you want to get to heaven, let us get started. The way is bought and paid for. The path is clear."

So let us get fired up. Praise God! We need to shout the victory and fight the battle, for with Jesus, the war is won! Christians, do not sit idle and let the devil defeat you. Do not let him cheat you out of one blessing. I say, march on, Christian soldiers! Stand and be counted. Hold high the gospel of King Jesus, always remembering the days are short, so fight the fight and keep the faith, for soon, it will be all over.

Then children, we can lie down and rest by the river of life. We can walk hand in hand with sweet Jesus. We will never feel pain, sorrow, sickness, hunger, or death ever again. We will have life and peace everlasting. We will be in the loving care and sweet embrace of our beautiful Savior, for we will be in God's glorious Kingdom, a place made by His love and grace for all who accept the born-again experience through His Son. Amen!

The brother said, "Oh, what a happy time that will be, when all God's children take their flight home, when all is put in order, and we reign forever in the presence of our Lord and Savior. You fare is paid. Jesus is the ticket. Please, in the name of God, do not be left out! Be of the number when all the saints of God are called and go marching home."

That was such a good message. It was short but to the point. That is the way of God. Nothing is hidden, and nothing held back, just the same simple truth. It does not take a degree to learn of God. You do not need lawyers to lay out the plan of salvation. You do not need the government to approve it. You do not need to rely on man. You just need to trust God. Accept His Word and believe in the death, burial, and resurrection of His Son. Those are the three steps to heaven, and if you take them, you will be saved.

Times were a changing. The Christian world and the world of man were in a state of confusion. It seemed that nobody knew what to do or which way to turn. Not many would listen to God. Nobody knew which way was right. Man was drifting far from the teachings of Christ, and at the same time, churches were pulling away from the true Word. They were beginning to get self-righteous, arguing over all sorts of things. They were getting power hungry and more interested in building up big bank accounts than in serving God and feeding His flock.

Why, there is even a world council of churches set up. This council tells the churches who will listen and what to and what not to preach on. It even decides who and what will be accepted by the churches. This is not needed. God set up the church. Christ is the head, and He set up bishops, preachers, deacons, elders and teachers to keep order. God gives us the teachings of Christ and the instruction of the apostles and His doctrine to run the church. We do not need to adapt the ways of man. We do not need to alter from God's plan. Here again, man has put himself in front of God.

We think that a large membership or a lot of worldly possessions make a good church. Some churches go along with the idea of man and accept the ways of man, even though those ways are not of God. Churches are teaching and believing all sorts of things. It is hard to believe that they ignore and neglect the Words of Christ. After all, He is the head of the church. It was founded on Him. He is the cornerstone, and He built the church, and yet they thought they knew best.

Some churches thought you had to go to their church in order to be saved. Others differed on basic teaching, such as baptism.

Baptism was being taught two or three different ways, yet Christ was only baptized one way. It was not for the remission of His sins, for He had none! In fact, if water could wash away sin, why did Christ have to die? Why, even in the Old Testament, blood was used, not water. God's Word even says that baptism is not the laying away of the fifth of the flesh (1 Peter 3:21). The Word shows that baptism represents the death, burial, and resurrection of Christ. So why does man see it in different ways? Because he does not accept the Word of God, that is why.

The plan of salvation teaches you to first repent and then to be baptized. It says to believe and then to be baptized. This is the Word . . . You cannot change it. To deny the Word is to deny the Son of God as your Savior. Who are you to tell God you want to do it your way?

It is not just baptism that the churches differ on. They differ on the divine power of healing, the gift of the Holy Spirit, the way to worship, and who to pray to and/or through. Why, some churches even differ on how to be saved. Some do not even believe in the spiritual conception of Christ. The list goes on and one. The fact is that man has screwed up everything he has gotten his hands on or stuck his nose in. However, God will not let this happen to His church. His people will not believe a lie. They trust solely in His Word.

There was a preacher I heard who said, "I thank God for the gospel-preaching, Bible-believing, soul-winning churches that hold up high the banner of salvation through Christ Jesus, for they are the family of God. They find peace in Him, and He finds pleasure in them. They are the body of Christ . . . His church."

The reverend added, "Finding God is easy. His plan is simple. Salvation is free. That is why man cannot accept it and does not want it. He wants to alter it. Change it. Make it hard to obtain. Then he can say, 'Look what I did. Look what I earned.' Well, it isn't that way. You cannot work for it. You cannot buy it. Christ bought and paid for it when He died on the cross. You will humble yourself before God. You will ask for it and receive it by your faith and through His merciful grace or will you not be saved. But do not feel left out, for God has something else for you. It is called His wrath."

Reverend James went on to preach. "Quit making the Word and ways of God so hard. Quit putting man's knowledge into the teachings of God. Do not listen to any other doctrine. That is what Jesus says. Do not listen to false teachings. Be led of the spirit. Christ says the just shall live by faith. You are not to seek the ways of man. Seek to please God. Do not follow the hand- me-down religion or the traditions of man. Man will take a little of this and a little of that, then mix in a little bit of God's Word, and then having you turning in circles or doing flips to be saved when all it takes is just a little talk with Jesus."

That is why there are so many different denominations and cults today. Satan will cause man to believe anything just to keep him from the truth. That is what Jesus tells us. That is what the Apostle Paul warned us of. Read it for yourself. Do not take my word for it. I am just a man. I could be just making this up, but by the Holy Spirit of God, you know that I am not. This is a message anointed of God, and it is for you. You must deal with it. What will you do?

Will the false doctrine, with all the different teachings, you must rely on God's spirit. It will show you the way if you let it. His Son will lead you if you let Him. You must first open your heart, and He will come in. He will open your eyes to the truth. You must put your faith to work by trusting in God and relying upon His Word.

God does not say one thing and mean another. He is the author of confusion (1 Corinthians 14:33). He did not and does not set up different ways for different people. He did not and does not favor a certain denomination. His plan was set up by Him for Him. His Kingdom is His. It is for His family. His Son was given that you could be born into His family. He alone decides who enters therein. He made the way. His Word shows us that way. That is why it is so important to put your faith in, stand on, and live by the Holy Word of God.

The Apostle Paul in his letters to the early churches told them to study the Word of God, show thyself approved of God, one who can rightly divide the Word of truth. By doing this, you can grow daily. You grow stronger in faith by hearing the Word of God. You also grow closer to God and Him to you.

Man must see the Word of God is the answer to all his questions. It will solve all the problems he has brought on himself because of man's rejection to the ways and Words of

God. He faces murder, rape, child abuse, robbery, suicide, lost morals of family and youths, jealousy, greed, lust, hunger, war, and even death itself. Then the hellfire of God's judgment.

All these and many others are brought on by man simply because of his unwillingness to accept the Word of God. Listen, none of these was in God's plan for man. However, these are the result of sin. They go hand in hand, yet we look to man and his knowledge for help instead of God, even though it is because of man's ignorance to God's Word and His trust in his own wisdom that brought forth this terrible mess we are in. But we know best right? Ha ha.

Remember, regardless of your knowledge or beliefs or actions, the Word of God will stand. It has stood the test of time. It will stand in your judgment. It will stand throughout the ages of eternity. God's Word and His will will be fulfilled. You had better prepare for it. They day of reckoning is closer, closer than you think. There is a way. There will come a day. There is a price to pay. No matter what you think or say, God will have His way.

Reverend James ended with that statement, ended with a good solid message. A few of Dave's friends told him the reverend sure knew how to make a point and get it across. Brother Dave answered, "No, he knows how to listen to God. God knows what you need to hear. He anoints His men. He gives them the message. The preachers go to His Word in prayer. Then the message is given. God uses His men to get His point across."

Now is the time to hear God's Word. Sermons like this one are being sent out the world over. God is giving everyone a chance to be saved. I just hope and pray man listens. Nothing else can save your soul. Nothing else can take you out of sin. Nothing else can place you in the safety of God's embrace. No man can save you.

You cannot save yourself. No man can take your sins away. Nothing you can do; no works, deeds, rituals, or payments can redeem you of your sins. You must hear and obey the Word of God.

You cannot join God's church when and how you want to. Paul wrote that God added to the church daily as He sees fit (Acts 2:47--48). That is why the churches need to wake up and get busy living by and preaching God's Word. There are so many lost souls to be reached, so many being led astray by man and sin. Churches need to realize they are not a church until Christ is the head. Amen.

Brother Dave was going on and on with his Christian work. He and the church he attended were busy at the Father's business. One evening he received a call from the pastor of a church located in Dave's hometown. Dave knew of the pastor and wanted to visit the church. The pastor told Dave he had informed the church about Dave being called to preach. The pastor called Dave and asked if he would come and preach at his church.

Of course, Dave was thrilled and answered, "I would love to! I will preach whenever I have the opportunity," and so the date and time was set. Brother Dave would hold the Sunday night service in two weeks. Even though Dave was glad the pastor had invited him to preach, he was also scared. He knew he had not been preaching long. He did not know how they would react to him; however, he knew he was called to preach, so he relied on God and accepted the invitation.

Brother Dave knew that anybody can speak about different things in the Bible. That is why so many get misled. People listen to a man speak because of who or what he is. Some people speak concerning God's Word because they decide they want to. Some people speak to push their ideas or traditions on man. That is not what a preacher is or should be. You cannot go to school to become a preacher. You cannot be elected to preach. You cannot say, "I want to be a preacher" and then go for it. You must be CALLED of God to preach, for He alone must anoint you to deliver His Holy Word.

Now do not take this the wrong way. After you are called, you can use any tools available to you, if you use these things for God's glory. But let us not forget the most important fact is that you must first be born again. You must accept Christ as your Savior. You must then be in total surrender to God's will, not to man, not to a church's doctrine, not to rituals or traditions, but to the mighty will of God. Plus, you must meet the standards set up by God's Word. If not, then God did not call you to preach.

If you look around, you will see many people speaking on stages on TV or even in so-called churches that are not of God's standards. They will have hell to pay. That is why there is so much confusion, so many denominations, and so much abuse of God's Word. Man is being deceived and led astray all in the good name of a church. While you are looking around at these speakers, you will also see man will allow himself to believe in anything. If not, these speakers would have no one to speak to, right?

If man, being so smart, would only see; if man did not support these false preachers; if man, being so intelligent, would read the Word of God himself, he would not believe in these false doctrines. These speakers would get tired of talking to themselves. They would have to shut up and get a real job. However, man DOES support them. He also believes in their lies and follows their teachings and sinful ways. How smart are we? Satan is having a field day. He loves it. He knows the majority of man wants to believe there is a God. He knows man wants to be right. Look, Satan himself fears God. He, just like man, knows of God. He also knows he is doomed for a devil's hell. See, knowing there is a God is not good enough. You must know God as your heavenly Father. Get this: Even Satan knows God is not your heavenly Father until you are reborn of His Son.

Satan knows you must be born again. He knows how you can be saved. He knows who can save you, but he sure is not going to tell you. In fact, he is going to cause you to believe a lie. He is going to use whoever and whatever he can. He is going to paint you a picture that you will like. He and all the false preachers, teachers, churches, and doctrines are all a smoke screen, rising from the fiery pits of hell, which if you could see through, you would be able to see the souls of men and women. People, just like you and me, were tormented by the flames of hell just because they went to their graves believing a lie. See, there is a truth to God's Word, and then there is everything else. It does not matter what you call it. If it is not of God, then it is not going to save your soul from the judgment of God's wrath.

That is why the first step is to be born again. Let God open your eyes to the truth. After all, it is His Word. Who knows it better than Him? Please do not be tricked, deceived, or misled. Satan is good at what he does. He will stop at nothing to rob you of your joy and steal your soul. The question is, will you let him? Are you letting him? Are you sure? Are you willing to pay the eternal price if you are wrong? Now ask yourself, "Do I just know OF God, or do I KNOW God through the salvation of Christ? Does the Holy Spirit dwell within me?"

Without receiving the Holy Spirit of Christ by the grace and mercy of God, through your faith in Him and His Word, you are depriving your soul of the many wonders and blessings of God. You deserve the best God has to offer. Christ died to give you that right. You are why He came, to save your soul if you let Him. If not, Satan will cause your soul to burn. The fact is if you are not saved, you are lost. All mankind is lost if they are not saved.

That is the importance of men being called of God to preach. Souls are dying being lost. People are falling prey to all kinds of false doctrines. It takes the preaching of God's Word, empowered and anointed by the Holy Ghost to bring man to the truth. That is why Brother Dave was waiting on the spirit to send him the message. God knows who will be at that service; Brother Dave does not. God knows the condition of the hearts and souls of those present; Brother Dave does not. God knows what needs to be said and how it has to be said; Brother Dave does not.

Neither does anyone else. God's Word needs to be preached according to His will, not to the will of man, not according to what pleases man, not according to what fits the customs and traditions of a church doctrine, but that which is pleasing to God. That is why He picks and chooses who will preach. Those who are called of God know they are held accountable for their preaching. True men of God rely solely on Him for their messages.

Brother Dave was getting ready for that Sunday night service. He had a message in mind; however, he was not sure this was what God had in mind. He got dressed and went to the church. He was greeted with love and felt very welcomed. The service began, and he felt the spirit of God. The songs and testimonies were given in praises to God.

Now came the time in the service for the bringing of God's Word. The pastor called Brother Dave to the pulpit. Dave felt scared and alone, yet he knew he would be standing on holy ground. He was standing before God as a man chosen of God. He was to feed the flock of Christ. He was to instruct the church that Christ built, the church of God's holy family who needed to hear God's Word, for in it was their strength and blessings.

Brother Dave, along with all those who are ordained of God, stand before God and man each time they step up to a pulpit. They stand with the burden of pleasing God. They must be under and subject to His spirit, for they must not only enlighten and inspire the children of God, but they must also allow God to use them with His Word to reach the souls of the lost. They must allow God to speak the Words through them that will cut to the hearts of those who know Him not, which will bring their souls to repentance. Yes, you see, this is a holy place.

That is why Brother Dave wanted to be sure of his sermon. He started by leading the church in prayer, asking and relying on God to deliver, which He did. However, it was not the thought Dave had in mind. But he obeyed the spirit. He began preaching on the thought "Let not your heart be troubled." His point would be "It will assure peace with God."

Brother Dave began. "If you are not at peace with God, your heart had better be troubled, for as you can see, this world is in terrible shape. Do not turn away from what is going on around you. Let it put fear and trembling into your heart. Do not close your eyes and think it is all a dream, or it is going to get better. It is not! In fact, it is going to get a lot worse. If we do not cry out for the mercy of God and His divine intervention, all will perish and fall into the pits of hell."

"The world has tried everything. They have put their hope in governments, looking for solutions to their many problems." Brother Dave went on to say, "They have looked to the courts, to doctors and scientists, for answers, all to which was of no avail. They helped in one area: creating different problems somewhere else.

"Here is the main problem. Man, because of the distance he keeps from the teaching of God, allows sin to dominate his life. Sin causes all sorts of problems. When these man-made problems arise, man relies on himself to fix them, not knowing that he being man is the problem. See, he cannot make things better. He has all sorts of motives, all of which are caused by sin.

"Here is the solution: trust and rely on God. Now do not take it the wrong way. Governments, doctors, lawyers, and even science are important to the well-being of man, if they too are of God. If not, again, they direct us in the ways of man. However, God will lead us according to His wisdom and mercy, not caring who can get rich, not using the solutions to become powerful, not trying to make a name for himself, just looking for the life and happiness of all, the rich and poor alike, having no respect of fortune or fame.

"However, we have a second problem. Man will not listen to God. Satan has entered into his subconscious, which causes us to believe we can do it ourselves. Look, we did not get in the mess we are in because we wanted to. We did not follow lust, greed, and our pride because we think of it as the best way. Man from the beginning of time has wanted to do right, but he has not. Because he could not. Because Satan has corrupted his mind.

"The Apostle Paul writes on this subject. He says he has the will to do good but does not. He does not want to do bad but does what he wants not to do (Romans 7:15--18). In other words, Satan can cause you to believe you are doing right, and the end thereof is death. Satan can cause you to do wrong even when you know it is wrong. When you know you should do good, Satan will give you a reason not to do it. Nothing has changed. Man thinks he knows best because Satan tells him so. So, if we do know best, then why do we not listen to what God has to say?

"Here is why. Satan will not let you. But do not give up hope, for God is here. He, not you, are the only power over Satan. You cannot do right or be right as long as you hear and listen to the serpent. Remember, you do not have to decide to follow the evil ways of Satan. Without God in your life, Satan is your leader. Yet God is ready to be your leader. He is ready and willing to help us. All we have to do is trust in Him and turn our lives over to His guidance. Don't you think it is about time to give God a try? We have tried everything else.

"God has not gone anywhere. He is right here waiting to save us. He even sent His beloved Son to bring us to Him. Our hope lies in God. Our way of righteousness is in His Word. Our salvation lies in His Son, for God is love. He is mercy and grace. He has all power and wisdom. Yet we ignore Him and seek our own ways, which is not ours but Satan's." Brother Dave then brought up some very good points. He said, "Do you think Eve would have taken of the forbidden fruit if she was not told to? Do you think the Israelites would have gone against God, who parted the waters and freed them from slavery if they were not led to? Do you think Pilate, knowing that Christ had healed the sick and raised the dead, wanted to kill him? NO! He tried not to, but he was told to. Do you think you deny and reject the salvation of Christ because you want to? Do you think you will go to hell because you want to? NO! The same power that caused the downfall of man is causing you to distrust God and go astray. "Why would you believe a lie? Man faces terrible problems all because of sin. With God, there is no sin. The short-term pleasures of sin bring more problems and even death. Yet something is telling you the pleasures of man are better for us than the pleasures of God. Something is telling you there is no pleasure in serving God, yet God gives unto His people everlasting pleasures. His storehouse is never empty. He gives joy and peace that cannot be measured. He fills hearts with love and gladness. So why would you believe a lie?

"Here is one fact: you better believe. I should say here is one fact you WILL believe. Life with Christ is far better than death without Christ, for when that glorious day of our Lord comes, Satan can lie to you no more. The truth will be revealed. All of man's thoughts, theories, ideas, and doctrines will be done away with when judgment stands at your door."

Brother Dave's sermon did not last long. He just preached what God gave him. After he had finished, he turned the service over to the home pastor who immediately gave an altar call. Two souls came who surrendered their lives to God. All in all, it was a good service. The Word had blessed, and souls were touched. But on the downside, there were others who were lost, souls who did not decide to ask God for their redemption. The sad part is that they may never have another chance. They may go to their graves believing a lie. But as their soul slips into the pits of hell, they will know and see the truth.

Well, another week had passed. Everything was going on as before. People were dying, and babies were being born. People continued to make plans, some of which included God, and some which did not. Some planned to worship God in spirit and truth, while others would just go to a church. Dave invited some friends to come to his church for Sunday service. He enjoyed visiting other churches, and he enjoyed having visitors to his church. It is so good to fellowship with and worship with God's family.

The brother and his family, which Brother Dave had invited, wanted to hear the new pastor. They had heard he was really on fire for God. The service started well. The power and blessings of God were abundant. The pastor did not wait very long, for he too was being led of the spirit. He took the pulpit when God said it was time for HIS Word.

He started by praising God. He also thanked God for all His love, mercy, and grace. He asked the church to pray for him and all the men of God who were called to preach. He said, "Pray that God gives them the anointed power to preach the gospel of Christ, that they may glorify the name of Almighty God." You could see the spirit beginning to move as he spoke. It did not take long before he moved right into his eye-opening sermon.

His sermon was "In God We Trust, or Do We?" He began. "This country was founded on that motto. That is why we have prospered so well. It is not because of knowledge or wealth. It is because we put God first. In fact, one of the first schools for higher learning was set up to teach the Word of God. It was not nothing to see Bibles being read both in school and at home. We even started school with a prayer to God.

"Boy, have we come a long way from that. The question is, how much further do we dare to go? Well, man will go as far as God will let him. Man says, 'We have got the rope, so let us go hang ourselves. Let us destroy everything God stands for. He will love us anyway. Let us ignore the warnings of the end of time. This is our world. We can do what we want. God owes us that!' That is the mentality of man and the wisdom of a fool.

"Look into the Word. The beginning is recorded, and so is the end. It tells us the steps that will take place. Man will fall away from the teachings of God. The love of many will wax cold. Man will allow Satan in the form of pride, lust, and greed to lure him away from and out of the grace of God. Not only can we read about it in God's Word. We can see it. Just open your eyes, and take a good look. It is recorded in the book. It is coming to pass. Yet we still do not believe.

"It used to be God was talked about in schools, in the public, and in government. But it was decided that this might offend someone or someone's false doctrines. I wonder who was at the head of that decision. Well, too bad. Maybe it is about time we stop worrying about offending people who are not of God. Maybe if they hear and see the power and wisdom of God, they too would believe. Look, church, if we do not tell them, then who will? We are the only tool God has.

"I wonder if they would be offended if Christ Himself asked them to keep His Word in their heart. Teach your children to pray. Read the Bible to them. Their souls will be in your hands. I wonder if they would still be offended when they face God's wrath. I wonder how offended God is. He sees His Word thrown away. Man has come up with so many doctrines, so many types of churches. It must make God very offended.

"Satan knows it does. That is why he misleads man. He causes man to do anything for self-gain, worldly respect, and to obtain power. The devil is happy when he causes man to mock, abuse, and deny God's Holy Word, which allows Satan to have more and more power over man. As each day passes, the world drifts further and further away from the grace and love of God. It drifts closer and closer to the Day of Judgment and the outpouring of God's wrath. No matter what lie you believe, God will get even. Satan himself will also face the eternal lake of fire. "Man, and Satan have teamed up to destroy this world, but God's people spend time in prayer for their lost friends and loved ones. God has allowed time to go on. He daily blesses His people and calls to the lost souls. But He is about to bring this world to an end. He is sick and tired of the arrangement man has made with Satan. He is fed up with all of the lies. It sickens Him to see the mockery of His Son. Man has pushed all the wrong buttons.

Man, and sin have pushed God to His limit. His revenge will be hell to pay!

"Because of our teamwork with Satan, our prisons and jails are overflowing. They fill up as soon as they are built all because man has lost his Godly morals. Crimes run rampant in our streets and even in our homes. The government itself, the very people we elect to make the laws and lead us, are full of crime and sin. How can we win? Well, you are not going to win playing on that team.

"You are losing, and time is running out. Your coach is calling all the wrong plays. But do you change coaches? NO! You just try anything he calls. You cheat and break all the rules. You trust him even though he is costing you the victory. However, this time when the clock runs out, you will NOT be going to Disneyland.

"Team Satan is causing our government to cheat us and abuse us all for their self-gain. They turn their backs on wrongdoings, such as price gouging, unsafe construction of buildings and power plants, not caring for our safety and well-being. They seek riches and power, which they use for self-gain and sin. They have replaced their love of God and for fellow man with their sinful lusts of sex, money, and greed. Yet they claim they are trying to better our way of life. We are losing and do not even know it. If we do, we must not care. We are not changing.

“We have not stopped the flow of drugs into America and into our homes because Satan uses this tool of sin. He allows some to get rich while it kills others. It warps the minds of adults and our own children. It destroys homes and families. It causes crimes of pain and death, but the fact is it has not been stopped because man does not want to stop it. We choose to follow sin.

“Man listens to Coach Satan. People fought all the way to the supreme court to have prayer taken out of public schools, and the devil says, 'Thank you!' We stood by and let a group of ungodly Antichrist lawyers force a judge to tell us that prayers to the Almighty God might offend an ungodly person. It might offend another kind of doctrine. Even our courts have teamed up with Satan.

“Satan thanks you for this. Now he replaces prayer in school with drugs. Yet we do not have half the right to remove drugs as we did prayer. This group of lawyers has also caused the court to go along with homosexuality even though that is a sin. We have okayed ourselves to kill and mutilate the life and bodies of babies in the mother's womb, all for the betterment of mankind. How can we believe such a lie?

“How can we think it is better to teach our kids about sex than about God? Why do we lie to our children? Sex is not to be used as form of sin. God intended sex for a married couple, not for the pleasures of sin and lust. If we must have sex education, teach it from the Word of God. After all, He is the One who gave us the tools for sex and tells us how it should be used. It is for the union of a man and a woman, both to create life and to allow them to show and express their love to each other. Any other use or form is sin. Not preference but ungodly sin.

Now Team Satan is telling us how to raise and correct us children. He uses his teammates called doctors, judges, lawyers, and others to mandate laws against God's Word. God tells children how they should behave. His Word tells us what to do if they do not. So why do we listen to man? Why do we make up lies and then believe them?

It is not our call to change or make up the laws of God. We do not have that power, nor do we have that right. Satan just leads, or should I say misleads, you to think that you do. Satan wants you to believe a lie. He does not want to go to hell alone. He wants you with him. He uses man to mock and abuse God's Word, to keep man from the truth and power therein. He does this and is able to do this because we let him. Why do we let him? Because without the power and salvation found in God's Word, we cannot stop him.

So, if you are tired of being misused, abused, and lied to, change teams! Jesus is trying to recruit you. If you want to be on the winning team, let your name be written by the blood of Christ in the Book of Life. He is trying to sign you to an eternal contract, one full of joyful bliss and one that will protect you from the pitfall of sin. Plus, it will deliver you from the punishment of God's angry wrath in the endless times of eternity. As a bonus, you will inherit the glorious Kingdom set up by His love, mercy, and grace, a heavenly Kingdom built for His team. Oh! What a place!

It does not matter if you believe or disbelieve. It will not matter if you accept or deny. God will prove Himself and His Word. Each and every one of us, regardless of race, religion, sex, or age, will all be judged by the Word of God. So, you had better find out where you stand now. Do not wait until you are burning in the pits of hell just to discover that "I could have," "I should have," or "O God, I wish I would have."

Open your heart and mind to the ways and wonders of God. Trust in His Words. Man can find the answers and solutions to all his questions and problems. God tells all and leaves nothing undone. He, unlike Satan, tells you the outcome of your evil ways, for only then you can make the right choice. You owe it to yourself to know all the facts.

In His Word, the facts of life are found. God shows us how man will reject His teachings, how he will be led astray to believe that he can make up his own rules. All the sins of man are covered in God's Word. There is nothing going on today that God did not warn us of. It is recorded. It is coming true more and more each day, and yet we still deny and disbelieve.

I wonder what kind of ideas the so-called brains of this world will come up with next. In fact, I am afraid to find out. What are we going to teach our children? What kind of disgraceful life will we show them to follow before we wise up? How far down the path of ungodliness will we lead them? Will we ever see how wrong we are? Will we ever turn to God and teach our children the love and mercies of God? Will you?

It is a horrible thought to think, but if we do not wake up, we are dragging our precious children right along with us into the flames of hell. What pain and hurt will be added to the great suffering of our souls as they burn in the eternal fires of damnation? For one of your children to cry out "Mom (or Dad), why didn't you warn me? Why didn't you tell me about God?"

The pastor preached a long sermon, and you could feel the power of God in every word. Brother Dave's friend told him that he and his family really loved the message. "We sure got a lot from it. Preaching like this," he added, "will cause people to really think about their way of life. It will cause them to see how the ways of this world, I mean, the teamwork of man and sin, are tearing down the morals and minds of us all to the point of accepting the filth and grime of sin over the joys and mercies of God."

He went on to say, "Oh, how we need the Words and ways of

God brought to life. Oh, how we need to call on the name of sweet Jesus to save from our sins. We need to turn and trust God before it is too late. No one should go to hell."

"No one has to," Brother Dave replied. Then he said, "Even if a person chooses to, why would they want to drag their families with them? Man must choose whom he will follow. He must choose heaven or hell. So why will he not ensure that his children have the same option? Man's duty to his family is to at least tell them about the salvation of Christ."

Brother Dave went on to add, "Mommies and daddies owe it to their children to warn them of hell and to tell them of heaven.

Children should not go to hell just because their parents are. Read them God's Word, at least let them hear the truth. Man is foolish to let Satan use him to rob his children of their souls. I wonder what parents will say when they see their children slide into that fiery pit of a grave."

With the world being in the shape it is in, you must acknowledge one important fact: this country, America, is the best there is. Yes, I have mentioned about a lot of faults and crimes in the life of humankind. However, the USA is far better than the rest of the countries. That is because of our ancestors and their trust in God.

It is also because there are still a lot of born-again Christians living in the USA. It is also due to the fact the Word of God is freely preached. God has blessed America simply because of those who worship and serve Him. God's people cry out daily in their praises and prayers, knowing God hears their humble cries. The children of God ask Him to save them from this sinful world. They trust in His Word, and because of their undying faith, America is still the land of the free. But so many have turned a deaf ear to the preaching of God's Word. Sin, false doctrines, Antichrist movements, and the lust and greed of man are quickly destroying the very foundation of our land.

I know that we have lost lives in conflicts and wars. I also know the people of God have spent endless nights on their knees pleading with God to save our soldiers and our country. Why? Because we know to trust in God. In fact, that is our national motto: "In God We Trust." But do we trust in God as much today as we once did? No, we do not.

That is why we are in perilous times. We have come to the point of trusting in and on everything and anything coming or going. Not only as a nation do, we NOT trust in God, but also many do not even accept that there is a God. Some people claim they have their own gods. In fact, it seems that no one knows what is right any more. We are so mixed up in our man-made doctrines and traditions we refuse to accept the Son of God as our Savior, just like the people did in the past. It is as if we are daring God to show the truth and power in His Word.

Does God have to render judgment and His wrath to prove that you are going to hell? Will it take the great day of the Lord when He takes His Christians to their heavenly home for you to accept Him as the Savior? I sure hope not for your sake. If so, I sure pity your soul.

How many more murders? How many more wars? How many more children have to be raped, abused, and starved to death? How many more man-made religions? How much more enjoyment will Satan have as he robs our family, friends, and loved ones of their souls? How much more acceptance of sin will be shoved in our faces before we get the message? What will it take for you to wake up? Wise up and stand up for the gospel and salvation of Christ.

The message is recorded. The warnings of these terrible sinful times are spelled out. The message of redemption is recorded. The plan of salvation is spelled out. Christ was sent here to save us from ourselves. Christ tells us of things that will take place, which are the sings of the end of time and God's judgment (Matt.

24:3--31). Yet even though we read about the nearness of that final day, even though we hear it preached, even as we watch them being fulfilled, there is no great movement of change. People still refuse to follow the ways and Words of God.

Christ also tells us you are born, then you will die, and then the judgment (Hebrew 9:27). Nothing has been able to change that. NOTHING will ever change that. You will die. You will face the wrath of God if you die unprepared to meet thy God.

How dangerous man loves to live. Do not live your life as if God is bluffing. Do not think of Him as a liar or a myth. Do not let His vengeance be what you receive of Him. Do not put yourself in that position. The price is far too great to pay.

Turn to God. Read His Word. Learn of the sings of the end, then watch daily as all things come to pass, proving more and more the truth in and the power of His Word. Do not denounce the judgment or the mighty wrath recorded. Trust in the divine scriptures of God's Holy Word. Get ready to be called of Christ as He comes for the holy family of God. Prepare to inherit and enjoy the many wonders and glory of God's Holy Kingdom.

Do not be the one who is left behind. Do not be misled, deceived, or cheated. You do not want to miss out on that wonderful and glorious day of our Lord. You do not want to see the souls of God's people being called from their graves and called up to be with Jesus, leaving you behind. Do not be the one hiding under the rocks from the face of our Lord, for they will beg to die. But DEATH will be no more! For from His throne in glory to the souls of disbelief, His wrath will begin to pour (Revelation 6:14--17).

Do not gamble with God. He does not bluff. He has already shown you, His hand. You have no chance. You will lose. In fact, you have already lost, for your rejection of Christ is the damnation of your soul. This is God's hand to call. He is trump. There are no wild cards! Do not be left holding the joker. Now it is time to pay up!

The power of God's glory, the agony of His wrath, plus the need of salvation were being preached everywhere, not just in the churches Brother Dave attended or knew of but in every church where Christ was the foundation, the builder, and the head. The true churches preach Jesus in the power of the Holy Spirit. People the world over were being warned of the danger and damnation that lie ahead for all who are not in the will of God.

But just as the Word of God states, only few will receive and accept the plan of salvation, which in itself proves the truth in His Word. The prophets of old told God's people they would not accept the Son of God as their Savior. Then when He came to bring all unto repentance, they mocked Him, tortured Him, and nailed Him on a cross, just as His apostles wrote. As the final day approaches, more and more people continue to reject God's only Son.

However, they cannot crucify Him again, for the King of Kings and Lord of Lords lives forever. Today man tries to get rid of the gospel of Christ by denying and disbelieving. We mock His power and teachings by allowing sin to harden our hearts. Man uses the ignorance of his knowledge to try and alter or disprove the plan of

God. Man, today tries to put His spirit to death, but there is no power on earth or in heaven that can measure up to the almighty power and glory of the Lord Jesus Christ. Amen.

Even as each day passes and brings us ever so much closer to the day of God's judgment, life and death go on as before and will continue to do so until God says enough is enough. Soon, He will give the angels the command to sound the trumpet. The day of the Lord is at hand, and then Christ will appear in all His glory to receive unto Him those born again of His blood. They will be called up to live with Him forever. Then the wrath, just as God's Word says, will be poured out on the souls of all who rejected His beloved Son.

All the powers of this world, all the greatest minds in this world put together, and all the power that Satan possesses or can conjure up cannot stop man from receiving his just reward. No plan and no law can alter or change the Word of God. God will keep His Word. He says this world will end and that man will be judged according to His Word. It will come to pass. If not today, look for it tomorrow or the next day. Sooner or later, you will see the power of God's Word being fulfilled.

Yes, God will put an end to this world. He will finally put an end to the sin and iniquity of man, for those whose sins are not made white by the blood of Christ will fall into everlasting punishment. Yes, those not of God will inherit an everlasting home of hell, just as God has promised, f or it was promised and prepared for the father of sin and his followers. The eternal lake of fire is the final destination for the devil and the souls of those who for whatever reason rejected the Word and ways of God. There is no alternative to the fact. God will have His day. It will last throughout the endless ages. Your souls will have hell to pay. Even now in the latter days, Christ has not given up on you. His begging and pleading spirit cry out to you and all mankind. He is calling for your souls to come, repent, and receive Him as your eternal Savior. Still, man ignores the call, or he has drifted so far in sin that he does not hear the call. Maybe he is too wrapped up in his own way of life that he does not even know he is being called.

It could be that you (or man) have heard the call, but Satan has interrupted it. He has caused you to answer by using your money or good deeds. He might be having you answer by using man-made doctrines or self-righteousness to please God. Look around you. Satan has man believing all sorts of false doctrines. He will mislead and deceive. He will give you a false security in believing a lie. He will cause you to follow man by allowing you to think man knows what is best for man.

However, none of these answers to Christ's call of salvation, for there is no name given in heaven or of man or of this world whereby you must be saved. NO money, NO fame, NO good deeds, and NO church can purchase what Christ died to pay for. Only His blood can cleanse your soul from sin. Only by receiving Him can you be born again. Only His spirit can give you power over sin and Satan. Why, even Satan himself knows the power, glory, and truth of God's Word. He is also smart enough to keep you from finding it out, but only if you let him.

As the day of your judgment swiftly draws so near, either by your death or the coming of Christ, there are still those who could care less about the Word and ways of God. They live as if life was a big party. Their biggest thrill is being high from drinking or drugs, having sinful lust, or gaining the wealth of this world and yet not allowing themselves to experience the blissful joys of a life with the Lord.

Some (I should say many) will die never knowing they were cheated out of the most thrilling and happy life ever imagined. In your wildest dreams, your mind cannot conjure up the many wonders and joys God bestows on His children. There are no words to describe the mercy, love, and grace of God toward His people.

You are being cheated and robbed, and you do not even realize it. You are being deceived to believe the ways of sin are more enjoyable than the ways of God. Do not allow Satan to mislead you any longer. Look, this life is temporary. The ways of sin will not last very long. If you live to be seventy-five years old, if you live it doing the ways of man, is it worth spending the needless ages of eternity in hell? Is what you are doing worth losing your soul over?

On the other hand, the joys and blessings of God are never ending. You get the best only He can offer. Plus, you get them here and in the endless time of the hereafter. Isn't this the real deal? Plus, God's sweet peace, joys, blessings, and endless mercies are free. You do not have to pay God to make you feel good . . . It is free!

The joys of sin are just a means for Satan to deceive you. He builds them up in your head to the point where you choose them to be more important than your own soul. Then he makes you pay for them. Yes! You pay him to steal your soul from God's grace. You pay for the joys of sin with money and then your life. But it does not stop there. You must also pay God for your sinful ways. Oh, maybe Satan did not tell you this part, but it will also cost you your soul.

You should not listen to man or to Satan. They both lie. Trust God. He is incapable of lying. He tells us Satan will use anything or anyone to keep us from the truth. We do not believe it, and yet we allow Satan and his ways to do the very thing God said he would. In other words, God says this is going to happen. We do not believe it. It happens. Then Satan tells us that it did not happen. On the other hand, Satan leads us to believe that God's Word is not true, and yet it comes true day by day. People are being saved; God is blessing and using His people just as He said he would. He answers their prayers and sees to their needs, just as He said He would.

The world is getting worse and worse. Sins, crimes, wars, floods, earthquakes, love of man to his self, false doctrines, man- made religions, Antichrist movements, and deaths are on every corner, just as God said. Satan tells us or causes us to believe this is not happening, but it is! You can see it. Why? Because God said so.

That alone ought to show you something, does it?

There is something we all must face, like it or no, believe it or not. There will come a time when all will stand before God. You must and you will see the truth, power, and judgment of His Word. If not now, it will be later. You must choose to either live for God or die without His mercy. Either way, you will receive justice for your decisions.

Make the right choice. Do not fall prey to the devil's trap. Do not get caught up or hung up in or on the ways of man and sin. Look up and call upon the name of our Lord and master. Live for and serve our most loving and merciful Savior. Trust and believe in His Holy Word. Your time grows shorter by each tick of the clock. Soon, it will be time for the great day of our Lord. Don't you want to be ready? Well, it is up to you. Will you believe in Him now of after it is too late? Will you accept Christ as your Savior and receive your heavenly home? Or will you choose to live by your own wants and desires and receive what God's judgment has in store for you?

The next week brought an invitation to Brother Dave. He was asked to preach on Sunday by a church in his hometown. That service turned out to be a gift of God right from the start. The testimonies and songs were praise unto God. You could feel the power of the spirit as people lifted the name of Jesus, praising him to the highest. Brother Dave had already gotten so much out of the service that it was hard to believe that it had just begun.

Then he was called to preach. Brother Dave began with tears in his eyes. He dwelled on thought of heaven. He started by saying, "This is just an example of just how wonderful heaven will be. This is just a touch of the glorious blessings we will behold, for our natural bodies can only endure so much of what God has in store. Yes, church, the best is yet to come, for one day, we will receive our heavenly bodies. Only then can we receive the fullness of His love, joy, and grace, which is not known of man or of this world.

"Oh, how I long for that day that I get to enter into God's Holy Kingdom. I want so bad to see the sweet face of Jesus. I want to feel His loving arms around me as I thank Him for His saving grace. I want to stroll on the streets of gold. I want to sit down by the river of life, the one that flows from God's throne. Oh, what a day that will be when in heaven my soul will be!"

Brother Dave then asked, "Don't you want to go there too? I want to see you there. I want everybody to go with me. That is why

I preach. That is why I am here. I want to teach you about Jesus, for He wants to make sure you get there.

"He died to save us. He came out of the grave to return to the Father. This was done to send His spirit, that through it, we would live as an example to the world. We have received the gift of the Holy Ghost, that through its power, we must be a witness unto all. We must teach and preach the Word of God. We must reach the loss of this dying world. We must use every tool available. We must spread the good news. Jesus came to save you."

Pastor Dave went on to say, "In some cases, we use missions, radio, and even TV to spread God's Word. However, the sad part is God is not the only one who uses these. The devil also has men on TV, radio, and in missionary fields. Yes, Satan himself uses the power of broadcasting to spread his lies. He tricks, deceives, and misleads. Then man does his evil works. He has his hand in everything and his mind on you. That is why we must trust in God and hold onto His unchanging hand.

"I have heard men preach the wonderful gospel of Christ. I have heard the true Word of God. But I have also heard the devil's doctrine, which appears to be of man's knowledge. It came from the pits of hell. Do not get caught up in the smoke screen. There is only one Savior---the Lord Jesus Christ, the Son of the Almighty God. There is only one faith and one baptism. There is none other.

"I have heard the doctrine of a two-part salvation. 'Be saved and then receive the next part, being the Holy Ghost.' Some say gifts of the spirit, some say being sanctified. I have heard doctrines of reincarnation, Antichrist, voodooism, satanic worship, how to pray to this saint or that saint. Why, you should handle snakes, some on getting saved and getting rich, some accepting homosexuality, and the list goes on and on.

"That is why it is so important to study and learn about the Word of God. Let His spirit shows you the truth. Know what is of God and what is not of God. Do not ever take my word or any men for the living word. Search the Holy Scriptures with the anointing and power of Christ's Holy Spirit. After all, it will be by His Word that you are judged (John 12:48).

"Do not look at church doctrines, rituals, or traditions. Do not look at man-made religion. Do not rely on the foolish wisdom of man to teach you. Do not trust a college to help. Do not expect lawyers or the government to lead you to the Word. That is why this world is in the shape it is in. Everybody has their own opinion. It seems that some know more and better ways than others, and they all know more than God.

"Some of these so-called doctrines take things out of the Bible and misuse them. Look, not every apostle did the things that Paul did. Not every Christian was an apostle. Not everyone was a deacon or elder. Not everyone is called to preach. People are used of God as He sees fit. There are many members in the body of Christ. Each has its own function and importance. There are not big 'Is' and little 'Us.' We all are saved and called of God to do His work. That is to win the souls of the lost and to feed His flock.

"You must know enough about God's Word to know what you are reading about. You must know in what time frame you are reading. You must know in what time, who you are reading about, and who did these orders and power pertain to. You must remember at a time Christ was here on earth with man. They were led by His powers and the teachings of His Words. They saw firsthand some face-to-face as He lived among them, as He brought us out of the period of the law into the salvation of grace.

"Christ set up the church. He being the cornerstone, the foundation being, thou art truly the Son of the living God, and God placed Him as the head of it. While doing so, Christ was able to heal the sick and caused blinded eyes to be opened. He even raised the dead. He still can raise the dead, but does He? He gave powers to the apostles to finish His Word, which they did. They set up the offices and duties of the church.

"In the writings to the early churches, you will find them: the who, who would be used to hold the office; the what, what offices were needed; the where, where in the order of rule they would be placed; the when, when would you be qualified to receive the call of office or be ordained; and the how, how to carry out the duties of the office. You see the offices of bishop, leader, pastor, deacon, elder, preacher, and teacher.

"You will not find the office of pope, father, rabbi being called of God. You will not find the setup of different denominations, just letters to those churches who pushed themselves up for pride, self-gain, or power. Christ completed all He was sent here to do. He did everything the prophets of old wrote He would do. That is why He cried, 'It is finished.'

"However, He left us with His teaching, His salvation, His church, and two promises, one being the Comforter, the Holy Ghost, and the other is His final coming and the end of time. Now Christ is with the Father; the Holy Ghost has arrived. You do not have to wait on it. He kept His promise.

"It dwells within the hearts of all those who are His. In enables us to ward off the temptation of sin and the ways of man. It does just what Christ said it would do. It empowers us to be a witness of Him and His salvation. If it had not arrived, if it did not dwell within you, then Satan would snatch you right back into sin. Remember, God gives you the Holy Spirit through your acceptance of Christ. It gives you power over Satan and sin. No man can give it, pray it, or deliver it to you. It is a gift of God.

"Remember, church, search the scriptures. You will find your place. God used certain men to do certain jobs. They were given certain powers to get certain things done as He saw fit. He too will use you in His way for His glory if you let him, if you are not pushed up with pride, power, and self-gain. I am not Paul, Peter, or John. I cannot do the things God had them to do; however, I have a job to do that they cannot. God is using me to reach out to you.

So do not pull out a few scriptures to make you into something you are not. We are all just sinners saved by grace through faith in Christ. We all must work to win souls and build up as we hold up the holy name of Jesus."

Pastor Dave finished by preaching on Christ's salvation and the Christians' need to love, honor, and serve Him. He said, "We should pray for a true miracle of God. We need it to take place at every service. The salvation of a soul is a soul being picked up by the loving arms of Christ, pulled out of the snares and traps of sin. He is put on the path of righteousness, the one that leads you through this life and onto the Holy Kingdom of God. Now you tell me, what is more important or rewarding than that? It even causes the angels to rejoice."

He said, "Do not accept just any doctrine. Do not try to see how close you can come to heaven on your way to hell. The result is still the same. You lose. You have no say in the matter. You must hear, accept, believe, and obey the divine Words of our Savior. Do not trust or ask anyone except God to tell you what is right, for Satan or man will jump at the chance to throw you off track. Satan knows he must get you before you find God. Believe me, he does his job very well."

The church praised God for the source and the preaching. It truly was uplifting and a spiritual blessing. Brother Dave started toward home after the service. He put in a tape of Reverend Hart. It was called "The Powers of Satan." Even though Reverend

Hart was of a different denomination, Brother Dave knew of his spirit, knew he was a man of God. Brother Dave also knew that denominations are a man-made thing. They do not mean a thing as long as the doctrine is of God.

The sermon started at the beginning. Satan who once was an angel of music tried to buck and compare himself to God. He was kicked out of heaven, along with the angels who followed after him. He uses earth as his footstool now. He then caused Adam and Eve to sin. He caused them to lose their home. They were kicked out of Eden and punished. He then caused Cain to kill Abel who was kicked away from his home into the wilderness.

He then caused man to totally turn away from God in the days of Noah, which caused God to destroy the world with a great flood. Noah found mercy with God, and he and his family were saved. God placed them in the safety of an ark and sealed the door shut. The ark had one door that God closed and an upper window.

No one could see in or out. No one could get in or out. God did not want the saved ones seeing the tormented lost.

No one could open the door except God. The saved could not hear the cries of the lost as their hearts and souls cried out. They begged and pleaded for mercy as God poured out His wrath. They wanted to be saved, but it was too late. God did not hear them. Judgment was passed.

So shall it be in the end of time. Before God has had enough of man's disbelief and rejection, you still have a chance to be saved. It is now. However, when judgment is passed, God will not hear your cries of pain. Your begging for mercy will be in vain. Do not be left out. Hell will be hotter than the waters are deep. Get in the shelter of God's saving grace. Do not doubt the wrath of God, for He will put you in your place.

Satan then caused the children of God to lose their promised land. He caused them to betray and reject God's Word. He will do the same for you. You will lose the promised land if you listen to the ways and words of him and man. You will die lost only to wake up in the fiery pits of hell.

Satan then caused man to turn on the Son of God. He used the religious leaders to reject and betray their Savior. He is still doing that today. He causes man to reject and deny the very One who came to save them. Jesus is our ark of safety. He will take you in. You can be saved from the almighty wrath of God, but you must come unto Him now, before the door of salvation is sealed off. Jesus is the door. He stands with open arms. He is calling for you to come in. Find peace with God. Find shelter for your soul. The storm clouds are raging, the warnings are being given, and the judgment is at hand.

"Look out!" Reverend Hart cried. "Here comes the devil. He is loose and at it again. He is going to and for, devouring whomever he may. Be careful! Satan is deceiving and the master of disguises.

"Watch out!" he said. "He will come to you in all sorts of forms. He may come as lust of the flesh, sinful sex. He may be in the form of money. Your love for it will cause you to fall prey. He may appear as a so-called man of God, who doing deeds and offering false pleasure and safety will pull the wool over your eyes."

Do not feel at ease if you cannot hear him. He will MAKE you hear him. He will send you a thought and try to use it to confuse or mislead you. Thoughts like *God's Word is not real; You are smart enough to know what is right and wrong; I am not going to give up the things I enjoy; What about my friends? There has got to be another way; I am not going to act like those people; Who is this man to tell me what to do? There is no God. He is just in your mind.* And he goes on and on; the thoughts do not stop. But you do not have to listen to them or react to them.

Satan will do or say anything to keep you away or turn you away from God. Then he laughs at you and God because he has tricked you into giving him your soul. The biggest lies he uses are "Oh, do not worry. God is too good to make you burn. All you have to do is try to be good, help people, do not steal or cheat. Do not commit crimes." God will remember you. Please do not get caught up in the devil's ministry. He will cause you to burn in hell.

Now do not doubt the power of Satan or of the devices he uses. If you are not careful, he will give you exactly what you want or what you think you want. He will control you with riches, fame, degrees of knowledge, and power. Yes, even religion. You cannot defeat him on your own. No one can. That is why you need Jesus. Look, Satan will even let you think you have got him beat just to entrap you. Just so, you will not call on God for help. Now you say you do not believe that can happen? Then you are already one of his victims, for you are lost and do not even know it. He has you in his control. He has robbed you of your soul. If you want proof, allow God to come into your life. His spirit brings you to the truth. His Son brings you to the victory. His world brings you into the safety of His Kingdom.

Here are how Satan has misled us: A man takes a gun or knife and kills his wife and children. Why? A man brutally rapes a five-year-old child. Why? A teenager goes down the road and shoots just anybody. Why? Well, one thing I do know is that these things were not done by God's people. No, you will not find a born-again Christian committing any crime, nor will you find God approving crimes in His Word. So, if this not of God, then of who? We both know that answer.

Here is the truth. We have educated ourselves on this matter. We have come up with there is something wrong with him. Yes, there sure is. We have decided he is sick. I would agree. He is sick all right. He is sick on sin. Satan has mentally deranged him. He controls his body, soul, and mind. These are all acts of the devil and his rage: rapes, acts of homosexual activity, killings, holdups, thefts, and child abuse. These are not a sickness. These are out-and-out sin. Drugs and drunks are not a sickness; they are just sin.

Now we have sicknesses that come from and are a result of these sins, like venereal disease, addictions, HIV, and mental scars with depression. However, the sicknesses did not cause the act. The acts of sin caused the sicknesses. God did not create anyone to do these acts. There is, however, a driving force behind these acts. Man needs to wake up and stop making up excuses. Sin is sin!

If man would accept Christ as his Lord and Savior, if man would put his trust in the Word of God, then these acts and all crimes would be no longer a part of the life and times of man. Satan would not have a foothold on us. We would have peace and happiness, just as God intended. Satan could not use man and woman to sell their bodies for sexual pleasures. No one would buy or sell drugs. No nude movies. No adult bookstores. No crime in government. These are all against God's Word. So why do we accept them? Why do we put up with them? Why do we make up excuses for them? Why not listen to God?

Reverend Hart ended with this note: "Listen, if you get caught in the act of a crime, then you are found guilty. The judge then sentences you because man-made laws state you will be punished for acts of wrongdoing. Now if you get caught and if found guilty, you have to pay for what you did. Now whose fault is it? Whom can you blame?

"You cannot blame God. He told you to be saved. He gives you the Holy Spirit to overcome your wrongdoings. He tells you what not to do. He tells you what will happen if you do. There is no alibi, plea bargaining, or excuse. Everyone is guilty. But Jesus can grant you a reprieve. He alone can set you free with His salvation. You will have a full pardon. However, you must remain in His grace. You must obey His teaching. Do not worry. It is not hard. His spirit will help and direct you. If you are a born-again Christian, then your sins are under His blood. You will not face the angry punishment of God's wrath. Amen."

The reverend's last statement was "Be careful. Watch and pray. May the grace and mercy of God always be with you." Brother Dave thought to himself, *Boy, what a message.* He wanted his friends to hear this sermon. Brother Dave thanked God for Reverend Hart and his words. It is great to hear men of God preach in the anointed power of His spirit. He could not help but think so many men pouring their heart and soul into messages like this, and still, so many lost.

The preaching was on fire. The Word of God was being brought out with power. True men of God were giving all they had just to show and warn man of the nearest of the coming of Christ and God's judgment. Yet people ignored and turned a deaf ear to the pleading of God's anointed preachers.

But you must realize the call for judgment can come to you before Christ comes. See, it can come in the form of death. You may tie your shoes when you get dressed in the morning, but the undertaker could untie them that night. Where will your soul be?

Then again, you could ignore the call of God for your last time. The spirit may never touch your soul again. God could get fed up with your rebellious pride. How many times will you get to tell God "No" before He gets tired of calling your soul to repent? Every time you tell God "No," you pass judgment on yourself. You do not stand a chance, and you give God no choice.

Yet while each day passes and draws closer to the day of our Lord, life goes on as before with man being born daily. People are dying by one means or another. Some are getting richer, while others are so poor they are starving and have no homes. Crime is growing, while the good times are slowing, for you see, time stands still for no one. That is until the keeper of time puts an end to it all.

Brother Dave and many others were enjoying the many blessings of God. They were trying to please Him by growing stronger daily. They were trying to serve Him and grow closer by the power of His Word and their obedience to His Holy Spirit. God saw their efforts and blessed them.

Souls were being saved. The children of God were praising His holy name. People were witnessing and testifying of God's love, grace, and mercy. It did not matter what was going on in the world. God was pouring His spirit out to His people. Even in the bad and sin-filled times, the children of God had peace and joy, for they were found to be at the Father's business.

The work and joy of God is very rewarding. God takes care of those who are His. He removes fear, eases heartaches, and takes their burdens upon Himself. He gives them shelter from life's terrible storms just because He loves them, just because they accepted the love and salvation of His Son.

There is no way to tell the unsaved world of the power and glory in serving the sweet Savior. They would not and cannot understand the way, power, glory, and blessing of the Almighty God are not meant for the world. It cannot be explained to them. God's wisdom and power can only be received through the spirit. It is only meant for those who accept the Son of God as their personal Savior. That is the way it is because God says so.

But the fact is it is meant for you and for all, if you hearken to His call. See, Jesus died for all of us. He wants everyone to receive everything God has to offer. Yes, Jesus wants to save you. He wants you to inherit the many treasures of God. He wants you to tell others of the love and blessings God has in store for those who are born again.

God needs His people to share His Words and mercy with the lost and dying world. Man needs to know that now is the time for salvation because His love and mercy does not go beyond death. It is not extended into judgment. It is not available at your call. You must accept it while the spirit draws, for you see, this is not Burger King . . . You cannot have it your way.

You cannot be saved when and how you want. You can only be saved when Jesus is knocking at your heart's door. You better answer His call unto repentance. You better ask Him to come into your life while you can still hear His knock. Do not turn Him away. Hell is a price you do not want to pay. No man can come unto me except the father draw him (John 6:44).

Another Sunday was at hand. Reverend Evans was starting service at another church. When it came time for him to preach, he was not prepared. He had one, but the text he had been led to use was no longer in his heart. God had changed the sermon. The reverend was in doubt what to preach. He decided to wait on God, so he began to testify. He started telling how much he loved and worshipped God.

He then began to tear up. He told the congregation, "My heart is so full of God's spirit right now. I am being blessed. But not to preach. I cannot get this memory out of my head, so I feel I must share it with you. After all, God does know best. I may preach a little later, but for now, this is what He wants you to hear. I just pray it can be used for His glory."

The preacher began to tell of a girl. The little girl was ten years old. "Some of you remember her. Well, she used to come here for Sunday school and church. She almost always came alone, either on the church bus or she was dropped off." The preacher said, "You might remember praying for her. We sure had a lot of prayer requests for you. You see, she was eaten up at that very young age with cancer.

"She used to come as often as she could. She always prayed for her mom and dad and always told how she loved God. But then she could not come very much. She was very sick and weak. The cancer was eating her alive. She had already gone through more than a child should have to bear. However, she kept her faith in

God. And always had good things to say.

"At this time surgery had already been performed on her head. She had lost all of her hair. She had to have some of her leg removed. The cancer was spreading. Her health was failing. Now there was no surgery left. There was no hope. She had little time left. Everyone knew death was at hand. However, she knew her life was in God's hands.

"Church, we too should know and accept the fact that our life is in God's hands. We too are at death's door. We just do not know the how or when. We just do not think about it. We too could die at any time. This body must and will die, either by some form of sickness and accident or some form of sin. It may be God will lay this body down when Christ passes judgment, and time is no more.

"It is amazing how the grace and mercy of God embraced this child. It enabled her to know and accept what lay ahead. We too need a touch of that grace. We need to realize where we fit in God's plan. This child faced death but not alone, for God had put a comfort in her soul. He would be with her and shelter her from the bitter sting of death. She was blessed, for she was a child of God.

"She was only a child in age, but God had made her a saint. She received strength we can only admire. She had grown close and drew near to God. Oh, if we only had the faith of a child! If only we would let God bring us up in the ways of a saint. We too could face whatever comes our way through the power and grace of God's Holy Spirit.

"Well, I received a call late one night. I was asked to go to the hospital. It was a call I knew was coming, but I did not want to go. Sue was dying. The doctor said she does not have much time left. I prayed, 'Please, God, let me get to her before you call her home. Please, Lord, let me pray with her one more time. Lord, O God, I know she is yours. I know she does not need my prayers, but Lord, I need hers. She is such a strength and blessing. She means so much to me, dear Lord. If it be in thy will, let me bid her my good-bye. Let me assure her we will meet again. If not, Lord, call her in peace. Be with her, God. She loves You and needs not to suffer. Amen.

"I arrived at the hospital and was met by the doctor. 'Preacher,' he said, 'there is nothing more I can do. She will not be with us much longer.' Tears began to roll down his face when he said she would not make it until the morning. I too had tears in my eyes when I asked him, "Do her parents know?' The doctor replied,

'They have been here all evening. They know she is failing, but I cannot tell them their little angel is soon to be with the Lord.'

'Preacher, this child is so full of love and tender joy yet so strong in the spirit. She has touched so many with love and strength. She has given us so much joy and inspiration. I cannot tell them her life is over. My heart is so heavy. I want to do something . . . anything. Yet I know there is nothing left to do. God has made the final call.'

"I told the doctor that I would tell them. I then cried out to God. I prayed for His strength and grace to be with me. Surely, thou strength and grace are sufficient for Sue to face death. It is sufficient for me to face her parents. O God, be with me, Lord. Guide my approach and my words. Send a touch of divine mercy to her family. Help me, O Lord, to hold up and be as strong as this thy child. Please, God, do not let them see how much I hurt. Help me to see this parting as a sweet sorrow, O Lord, not as a good-bye but as an I will see you again. In the holy name of Jesus. Amen.

"As I approached Sue's room with the doctor, I saw her parents. They were in the hall outside her room. They were embraced in tears. Pain and hurt were on their face. Just then, I felt an awareness in my soul. I knew God was here. My prayer was answered. Praise His holy name. When they looked up, they saw me and the doctor. They knew then what they did not want to know. No one had a choice. It was time for her to be at peace. They had to face the dreadful fact that it was time for Sue to go home.

"I told them what they did not want to hear, but God showed them there was nothing to fear. Sue would be going to God's home. He now would make her whole. She would be in no more pain. She would suffer no more. Her tears would only be tears of joy. She was going to be at peace and forever in the presence of the Lord. I said, 'Let us pray. Let us ask God to be with us. He can help us through this sorrow.' And so, we prayed together as we held hands and knelt before God.

"I then opened the door. As we entered Sue's room, I saw this sweet, sweet child. I almost broke down. She was lying there with a faint smile on her face as she ever so slightly reached out her hand. It was more than I could bear alone. My soul cried, 'God be with me! Give me your strength. I need help!' The least I could do was to hold up and be as brave as she was. Then I went nearer to her bed.

"As I reached for her hand, she turned her little head my way. A chill ran down my back. I could almost see death in her face. God held back my tears. My lips did not want to move, but God supplied me with strength to speak. I asked, 'Sue, how are you doing? Do you feel okay?' She replied, 'Oh, Brother Evans, He does not let me feel much of anything. I am just fine. I am in good hands now.'

"It seemed I had to swallow my heart as I heard her speak. Then she asked how her parents were. They came around the bed so she could see them. She looked up at us with more love than I ever dreamed possible. Through God's power, I was able to put on a slight smile, even though I could feel the cold hand of death creeping up to take this precious gem. Her face was so pleasant. Yet we knew that she knew.

"Her parents were melting in sorrow. They could hardly stand at that moment. Sue tightened the grip on my hand. She began to speak in the voice of a heavenly angel. She said, 'Preacher, keep on preaching. Tell everybody about Jesus. God, please help my mommy and daddy.' She formed her lips in a kissing position and then said, 'I love you, Mommy and Daddy.' With that said, she slowly closed her eyes and softly whispered, 'Jesus is taking me home.'

"I will not go into detail after that point. I will just say that she was gone, gone on to be with the Lord."

The church was in tears. What a story! What a testimony this child left behind! Reverend Evans went on to say that this was the most blessed sight of death he had ever witnessed. "What power and grace were bestowed by God to that precious child. Can you imagine lying there facing death and not a selfish word or thought? Her last wish was for help, not for herself but for her mom and dad. Her last request to a preacher was not prayer for herself. It was for Jesus to be preached. What a way to say good- bye. We should all pray for what she had left.

“Church, this is just one memory I have. There are hundreds, even thousands, like it in some way all over the world, for you see, death in Christ does not have to be tragic. It is only tragic and heartbreaking for the living. Jesus can ease the pain. He can give strength and peace. He conquered death. He can remove its sting.

“Preachers and Christians, the world over has witnessed such things as this. Those who have accepted Christ, they have His Holy Word of promise. He will always be with them all the way, not the end but through the end. He promises, 'I will never leave you comfortless. You will never have more to come upon you than you can bear.' He also lets your soul know death is not a good-bye but a welcome home. Amen.

“Church, there are plenty of doctors and nurses who have witnessed death in many forms. Some like this, while others are filled with such mind-boggling terror that it turns their stomach. Many of them have changed their minds and hearts about the powers and ways of God, which just goes to show He is still in command. Praise His holy name!

“Listen to me, church, death comes to everyone. People of all faiths die. All kinds of so-called religious people die. Even those who claim they do not believe in God; they too will die when God says so. It does not matter if you do not know Him. Before He sends death to your door, you will cry out for His mercy. You will not want to face Him as you draw your last breath, for then, the truth is at hand. God is God.

“Do not expect mercy as your soul slips into the fiery pits of hell. Do not expect that someone can pray you out of God's angry wrath. That is not the way it was, and that is not the way it is. That is not going to be the way it will be. You are saved when you answer the drawing of the spirit through your faith in the death, burial, and resurrection of Christ. Do not believe a lie. You cannot be saved just because you are dying.

"I will leave that subject with this thought," Reverend Evans added. "Read God's Word. Then know the truth. When Noah went into the ark, did God save any of those who were drowning in the flood? No! When God sent fire and brimstone upon Sodom and Gomorrah, were any lives spared or saved? No! After Judas rejected Christ, did he get saved? No! Now ask yourself, do you think God is going to change the plan of salvation, His Words and promises, and the judgment of the saved and unsaved just for you? I think not. Did God extend mercy to the man in hell when he cried out in agony? No! Then tell me, why do you think you are so special?

"Enough on that. Let me share an incident that took place at a hospital. It involved a preacher friend of mine and both doctors and nurses. This one is quite different. A scream rang out for a doctor. It came from a man's room. The man was dying, and he was in pain. But he was fighting to hang on. A nurse ran into the room, and she paged for a doctor. Two doctors on staff came into the room.

"The man yelled at the doctor, 'Get my family in here! I want my sons. Go get my sons!' The family who had just stepped out to get some coffee at the hall lobby heard the commotion. So, the two sons and wife rushed back into the room, at which time they found him screaming out in pain.

"The oldest son could not stand to hear the crying screams of his dad. He asked the doctor, 'Can't you do something? Can't you give him something for the pain?' The doctor answered, 'Son, your father has been given all that he can take for his pain. He should not be feeling this kind of pain. There is nothing more that we can give him.'

"Just then, the man let out the most blood-curdling scream ever heard. It set chills through the room. The boy's dad then yelled for his sons to grab a hold of his arms and pull him up in his bed. 'Oh, please help me! Help me!' he cried. He said, 'Pull me up! Pull me up! My feet are sliding into hell! I can feel the torments of the fire!' The boys cried out and hung onto their father as he passed away.

"The shock and terror in that room were amazing. Everyone was terrified and stunned. This was a most horrible sight. Even the hospital staff cried out for God to have mercy but to no avail, for you see, judgment had been rendered. Even the strongest medication known to man cannot quench the torments of God's wrath. Remember, church, God's Word is true. He is in command."

He then asked, "How would you like to have one of those sons? Just think what a gruesome thought to have to listen to a loved one cry out for help to no avail. Just as the door of death closes, and they see their soul's destiny. Worse yet, think of what you would put your family through if you were passing from this life and facing God's punishment. Do not be deceived. 'Do not believe a lie because this could be you!'"

Now listen, it is easy to make up stories; however, these were not made up. They are true. If you want to hear more, then talk to some more preachers. Better yet, talk to some doctors and nurses. You will find death and the fear of life after death can and does cause and create shocking scenes, scenes you do not want to see or, worse of all, take part in. Remember this: God is in charge. He will put you in your place. If you do not change and give God a chance, you will leave Him no choice.

The message of these two stories packed such a punch. There was not much need for an ordinary sermon. What else could be said? The lessons in these episodes summed it up very well. All in two facts: God does take care of His people. His punishment is as real as heaven. See, it does not matter what you think about God's Word. You will face death and the judgment.

No one can do it for you or with you. You alone must answer for your belief in or your rejection of God's Son. Nothing or no one else can save you. You will forget your idea, doctrine, and pride at death's door, for God opens your eyes to the truth. When you see what your soul must face in eternity, you will know, accept, and truly believe that it was true. That it is true. God is God. His Word is truth, and He is in charge.

Remember, God allows you the chance to choose your soul's destiny. It is your choice. He also gives you power through Christ to change. You will either accept His Word or live by it, or you reject and defy it. It is up to you and you alone. You must decide. "Will I face the glory of God's Kingdom, or will I face the pain and torments of His mighty wrath? Will I have Christ to lead me through death's door, or will I go out kicking and screaming? Will I ignore the salvation of God now then try and blame God as my soul slips into hell?

You owe it to yourself to give it some thought. Man needs to think long and hard on the subject. Even now, while God is using this service to reach and win souls, the clock is slowly ticking away. Each tick brings us closer to the day of your death or the great day of our Lord. It is God's call which day comes your way. But do you dare to face God without accepting His son? That is your call.

Reverend Evans closed with this: "The Word of God tells us we all need and must be saved. He then tells us how to be saved. The Word goes on to tell us of the glorious blessings and rewards for those who are saved. Then last but not least, the Word tells us there is our pain and torments for those who are not saved. There is nothing else God can do except call you unto repentance. Then it is your move. You decide what is in store for you. Please choose wisely. There is hell to pay."

Now was a beautiful time. Spring was setting in, flowers were beginning to bloom, and the air smelled so fresh. God had allowed another season to start. He was giving man a little more time to be saved. Praise God! Some took advantage of the allotted time; however, most just went on with their sinful ways of life. They did not put much thought into the Words or plan of God. They just went on about their business as if time would last forever.

Brother Howard and Brother Dave had heard about a lawyer who had given up a good practice and was now preaching the Word of God. He would be holding service in a small town not far from theirs. They decided to attend one of the meetings because they had heard about his preaching and wanted to meet him.

They planned to get to the church early enough to meet and talk with the lawyer/preacher, Reverend Tom. They arrived and were introduced to the reverend. What a blessing it was to visit and have fellowship with another man of God It did not matter that they came from different lifestyles, a different town, or a different church. They were of the same spirit and on common ground. They were all born again.

Reverend Tom was a very educated man. He had been with a successful law firm, yet he was very humble and spiritual to speak with. He wanted to know about Brothers Howard and Dave's ministries as much as they wanted to hear about his. After a little chit-chat about life, God's grace, and the winning of souls, Reverend Tom began to tell them how he was not a preacher and a part-time Christian lawyer. For now, he let God send him to churches to preach and trusted God to send him cases or clients to represent.

He told us, "I could not stay in the lawyer business after being saved. I did not like all the side deals and manipulation of justice. After being called to preach, I could not stay with the law firm. I had to serve God. I wanted to win souls. I had to tell people about true justice, righteousness, and judgment you see because God's law is fair and final. There is only one judge, and He wrote the book.

"Our justice system is much different. Now our laws are good and fair. The lawyers and judges tear it apart. They use it any way they want to, as long as it gets them what they want. We let the guilty go free because of the underhanded tactics and misuse of the truth and sadly have people in prison because their lawyers were not good enough at playing the game.

"Lawyers are built up by getting a killer, a rapist, or a drug lord to go free, anyway they can. You can know that your client is guilty, but your job is to use every trick of the law, any loophole you can to get them off. This is done daily all in the name of justice. We use side deals, plea bargains, hiding the truth just to put criminals back on the streets to commit more crime. I ask you, where is the justice?

"Now do not get me wrong. There are good truthful lawyers and judges who represent the law the best they can. But they are just human like the rest of us. They also make mistakes. Plus, they cannot stand up against the misuses of the law and truth. You see, it does not matter what the truth is. It is what you are made to believe it is.

"Now apply the same rules and misuses of the truth to the doctrine of Christ, to the churches, and the preachers. However, praise God's holy name, the good ones can stand forever against deceivers, mockers, and misusers, for we are powered by the anointing of God. The Holy Spirit rules our lives and preaches the truth of God's Word, the righteousness of His laws, and the just of His judgment.

"It was not my knowledge that showed me these things. It was not a college that showed me the problem or the solution. It was the wisdom of God through the divine guidance of the Holy Spirit, which brought me out of darkness and into the light. I have the truth in my heart and soul. I was given the problems of man and the solution. I met the God of the universe, the master of truth, the Lord of the law, and the writer of justice. I met the judge of judgment. Praise and glory to His name!"

Reverend Tom was putting it on the line. He said, "The problem with man is man. Man has drifted so far away from God and his teaching. Man has no respect for God's laws or his own laws of man. What man needs to solve the problems is the solution, the Redeemer who brings salvation. We need Jesus. We must seek Jesus. We do not need new doctrines, nor do we do need to conform to the ways of man. We need to be transformed into the likeness of Christ. We need to be born again. Brothers, we need Jesus!"

He then said, "That is why I am living and serving God. That is why I am preaching His Word. Man needs to know there is a judgment coming. Humankind will be judged by the Word of God without respect of race, riches, or age, for all will stand before and answer to God. Then all will receive their just reward.

If God finds you guilty of rejecting Christ, if you are found guilty of following the ways of man and sin, you will be sentenced and punished by the wrath of God."

Brother Howard butted in. "Thank you for that sermon. Now it is time to go inside. You have got to preach again." The three of them laughed and praised God. They had a good time with their fellowship, and now it was time to go to church. The three of them entered the church, smiling. As they took their seats, the service began.

As Brother Tom was called to the pulpit, he stopped at a table where he picked a bunch of newspapers. He asked the church to turn to Matthew chapter 24, then he prayed and began to preach. Reverend Tom started to read God's Word about the sings of the end of time, but first, he gave us spiritual food from the Word.

"Church," he said, "God is truth. Without God, there is no truth. The truth is man is lost. God tells us all you must be born again or face His wrath. He then warns us and tells us of an end of time when final judgment is rendered, a time of His total and awesome destruction of the world, of the endless time for eternity. God does not tell us of the exact time our world will end, but He does give us events that must and will take place before that great and glorious day of our Lord. With that, let us go into God's Word."

He began by preaching verse by verse and sign by sign, and then he read the headlines from the newspapers. Covering event by event, he preached and brought to light the truth of God's Word. People were astonished at the facts. God's Word is being fulfilled right under our noses, and yet man still ignores the signs of the time.

He brought out the fact that our bodies give us signs of sickness and even death, and then we seek help. We try to take care of the problem. A doctor reads the signs and tries to make it better by telling us what to do or what medicine will cure the problem.

He also showed us how we read the weather to know what is coming our way. We can tell when storms are approaching. We can tell of a drought, flood, or tornado that is at hand. We warn people what to do to escape the danger of other bad weather or how to prepare for it.

We all know that sickness will come. We know that death will come to us all. We know storms will come. We know disasters will come. We read the signs, and yet we cannot stop it. We just do whatever we can to prepare ourselves for it. So why do we not do the same for the signs of the final coming of Christ? Why do we not read and acknowledge the signs of time? Why do we not do whatever we can? Why do we not prepare to meet Almighty God?

If you do not listen to the weatherman, you will not know the storm is coming. If you do not listen to the doctor, you will not know how to take care of yourself. But if you do not listen to the warnings of God's Word, you will not know you are heading toward hell! If you do not listen, it does not change what is coming. If you do not believe what you hear, it does not stop what is coming. I just mean you will not be ready when it comes.

You cannot prepare for death after you die. You cannot seek shelter from the storm after you are swept up in it. More importantly, you cannot be saved from the judgment and wrath of God after you wake up in the fiery pits of hell. He then said, "Here is your sign!"

Reverend Tom went on with sign after sign, verse by verse, and proof by proof, removing all doubt. The end is quickly approaching. No way could you ignore the fulfillment of God's Word. No way could you ignore this man of God who was led of the spirit. This message came right from God's throne. The master had given fair warning. Anyone who will can read the signs. God gave His Son that whomsoever calls on His name can be saved. Do not put it off! Time stands still for nobody. While there is still time, mercy is extended. While His saving grace is abounded, get ready because here comes the judge.

Brother Dave and Brother Howard both thanked God for that message. What enlightenment! What a powerful witness and glory to God! What a soul-winning tool to use God's Word and man's media to show the signs of His Word are truth. Just look around; Satan cannot deceive you and man cannot mislead you if you open your eyes to the sings of time. Amen.

Readers, you must know the truth. I know some do not want to, but you must face the facts. God's Word is truth. Everything is and will take place just as God says. Oh, I pray, Lord, help us to see the errors of our ways. Shield and redeem us from sin. O Lord God, save us with thy grace.

Well, not much is changing. Time is rolling along, and life goes on. Sin is on the rise and continuously eats away at man, while those born again keep busy preaching and teaching the gospel and salvation of Christ. In fact, that is why God allowed time to roll on. The church was on fire. They were trying to reach out to the lost and dying world. God honored their labor and extended time and His mercy, for it is not His will for any to perish. But it is His will for time to end. I pray you heed the warning.

People were making plans, some for the future, either not knowing or not caring the end was at hand. Most of the world was ignoring the crime, pain, and strife. They were trying to find a little piece of life they could enjoy. Man was busy at trying to make his life better and easier for himself but to no avail. Life became more hectic and dangerous than ever. Little does man know that living without God adds to the problem, not to the solution.

Man has created a real mess because he has depended upon man. Satan is having a field day for man, and his church has drifted further away from the teachings and blessings of God than ever in this world's history. People were giving their souls to Satan in trade for just a moment of false hope or peace, while other souls were being traded for a few minutes of sinful pleasure. But God's people did not give up. They kept the faith and stayed in the fight.

The tribulations were so great. Sin was in so much control, that it was only by the power and grace of God that the saved were able to endure. They had no fear, for as long as they loved and served God, they knew He would be nearby. It used to be hard to get people to admit they needed to be saved, but now it is even harder to get them into a true gospel-preaching church. Satan has offered so many false doctrines, so many man-made doctrines, so many false gods that the truth was being hid.

Oh, but praise God! There were still some in search of the truth. There was still some crying out for God's mercy. Yes, even in these perilous times, God was still saving souls. His Word was still reaching out to and calling the hearts of man. Christ was still knocking on heart's doors. He was still pleading to lost souls, just as He is pleading for you to "come unto me." Do not let Satan deafen your ears! Do not presume you know what is best. Listen to the sweet call of the Savior.

Times are growing worse. Even Satan knows it is because of sin, and yet man calls it progress. There is little love to be found. People have lost their morals, and sin is literally ruling the hearts and minds of man. We are accepting anything coming or going, from killing unwanted babies, divorcing for any reason, and homosexuality to include homosexuals adopting and raising children to worshipping the devils, vampirism, and man caring more about the rights of criminals than that of the victims, from claiming that God respects all types of religion to there is no God or hell.

Why, the non-born-again churches are growing by leaps and bounds, while the churches in God's grace are growing by one or two at a time. Even that in itself ought to prove to you that man will believe anything the devil puts before him. It does not matter what form it comes; it can be called progress, man's knowledge, self-righteousness, pride, or greed. It is all the devil! It is a lie and a mockery to God. It is just another trick to divert you from the truth. Do not fall into his trap. You will be sorry.

If you do not rely upon God, do not worry. Satan and his helpers will be right there. You may not want to admit it, but something is keeping you from asking God to save your soul from the pits of hell. I ask you, what is it that will keep you from facing the judgment and wrath of God? You better be sure, for Satan is good at what he does. Know this: if you think anything other than being born again through the blood and spirit of Christ will redeem your soul from the wrath of hell, then Satan is better that you gave him credit for. He has already robbed you of your soul.

That is why in these last days, instead of people taking heed to the warnings and call of God, they have taken to the ways and short-lived pleasures of sin, just as man did in the days of Noah. Man was warned then also, and they too ignored it. God shut them out! They perished just as God said they would, and you will too, for He says, "If you do not become a born-again believer, then you are condemned already" (John 3:18 and 36). You have no choice because you have given God no choice.

Man is so wrapped up in his sin instead of teaching his children the wonderful blessings of serving a loving God, instead of our elders living in joy and as an example, our children are watching their brothers and sisters and peers smoke dope, get drunk, or engage in the lust of sex. Why, they even watch their parents indulge in these tools of sin. We teach our children it is okay to lie, cheat, or even use others for self-gain. We have accepted profanity as part of our language. We let them watch filth and sex on TV. We are telling them that it is okay for a man to have sex with another man.

It is bad enough when an adult decides to reject the Word and ways of Christ. It is bad enough when an adult elects to spend eternity in the pits of hell, but why would an adult want to drag their children along with them? Our children are growing up feeling at home in a life of sin, having no hope because they are being kept dumb to the mercy and grace of God. Why should it be left up to someone else to tell your children how to be saved and how to live a Christian life, or how they can escape the wrath of God's judgment and inherit His glorious Kingdom? I ask you, is this the love of a parent or the deception of a devil?

The least we can do is to teach our children about God, even if we do not accept it. We should see to it that they go to a solid Bible-preaching church even if we do not. They need to learn what God has in store, of the blessings of His reward and the punishment for rejection. They have that right, and we owe it to them. It is the most important part of being a parent. Believe this if nothing else: God will hold you as a parent responsible for blinding your children to the light, which is Christ, the Son of God.

Listen, the devil should have to work hard to rob our children from the grace and glory of God. They should not be placed in His grip. They should grow up basking in the goodness of God's love. God should not have to beg and plead for them to come unto the salvation of their souls. We should be raising them up knowing when God calls you to answer with a yes. But no, we do not want them to know that God will call and save their soul. We want them to be just like us, foolish and hell-bound.

You think that you are a good parent. You send your kids to school, and you teach them how to get the best of this life, and yet you put them on life's path that leads them to hell. How can you sleep knowing you could be the one who caused the damnation of your own child? What will you say to your child when you are both cast into the lake of fire? What will you say when your child, engulfed in flames, asks, "Why, Daddy? Why, Momma?"? But you do not have to be quick to answer. After all, you will have the endless age of forever to explain . . .

But I pray for your child. I pray that God touches our children. Let them hear and hearken unto the sweet precious call for their souls to repent. I pray, Lord, please bring them in before Satan or through their parents that their tender ears become dear to your call. Amen. Do not worry. God will touch them and call them unto salvation. He will not cast them into hell without offering them salvation. He promises to extend His saving grace to everyone. That is His will, regardless of what you taught them to think or to believe. But because of what you have taught them; they may decide to be just like you.

Man needs to learn and teach the Words and ways of God. Man must receive the wisdom and knowledge of God so he can know and be ready for what is to come. Man needs to be able to discern the spirits to see which are good and of God. He needs to know and understand the powers of Satan's deception. Satan knows how God works, and he uses this against you. He knows when God comes calling that he could lose his grip on your soul, so he floods your mind with deceit, skepticism, and falsehoods. You must also want to hear from God. If you do not listen, your call could go unheard.

A call from God comes in many ways. He knows what you need. It could come to you in a dream. It could come to you in the form of guilt or by hearing His Words preached. God can use others to reach you or an experience as He did in this case. A woman (we will call her Linda) told me about an incident that took place in her life. It happened like this:

Linda was married and had a little boy named Paul. Paul was five years old and, being like most boys, was full of pep and vigor. He was always getting into something. Now Linda or her husband did not practice or teach religion. Neither of them went to church except for a wedding or a funeral. However, this did not make them bad people. In fact, according to man, they were a good and moral family. They just did not know about Jesus, nor did they know about the Words of God. They also did know they were about to learn a thing or two. Remember, this is a true story.

There are millions upon millions of stories on how God reached out and touched someone. This is just the one He laid upon my heart to relate to you. If you would just talk with Christians, they could tell you enough stories to fill shelves of books on how God touched someone. There is no end to His saving grace. In fact, you could have a story of your own of how God touched you while you are reading and relating to portions of this book. Wouldn't that be wonderful! Praise His holy name. I know that this book could be your story, your touch, or your call from God. No, I do not have ESP; I just know God. I know when you dwell upon things of a Godly nature, God speaks ever so gentle to your soul. Can you hear Him?

Well, back to the story. One night Paul's dad was at a bar. He was not doing anything he should not be doing, just having a few beers with friends. Linda was very worried. Paul had taken sick and begun to run a high fever. She knew something was wrong. He did not want to play or eat, which meant he was getting sick. Linda checked his temperature. It was 103 degrees. Paul was acting weak and began to get drowsy. Linda had to do something.

She gave him the normal medicine for fever, but it was not working. She put cold compresses on his little forehead and tried to get him to drink fluids, but nothing seemed to help her little Paul. She was getting a little frantic, as most mothers would, so she called the bar. She had to get a hold of her husband. (We will call him Dan.) Dan got on the phone and listened as his wife said,

"You have got to come home. The baby is sick with a fever. He needs to go to the hospital." Dan said, "I am on my way."

While Linda was waiting for her husband, her son went to sleep. She knew with his high temperature she should not let him sleep. She tried to wake him, but he did not respond. He was very hot and began to talk deliriously. She was worried, and even though it had only been minutes she called her husband, Linda was scared about her son's health. Why wasn't he here? The bar was about twenty minutes from home, but that did not matter . . . He should be here. She was just not thinking about anything except getting her son to a doctor.

At that moment, Linda heard the baby call out to her. It was in a week and shaky voice. "Mommy, Mommy, come on. Mommy, come on!" And then he went limp. He said nothing more. Linda let out a scared "Oh my god! Oh my god! Please help me!" She ran to the phone and called 911. She was on the phone when she heard her husband pulling up. Linda told the 911 operator, "I'm sorry, my husband is home. We will take the baby to the hospital ourselves." Linda thanked the operator and hung up the phone. Upon doing so, she grabbed the baby and headed for the door.

Paul opened his eyes and then shut them again. When they got into the car, Dan asked no questions. He headed to the hospital. Linda could sense or was just hoping that Paul's temperature was dropping. She checked it, and she was right; it was down to 100 degrees. She told her husband so he would slow down.

When they got to the hospital, there was a slight wait. The baby was acting better; although he was restless, he tried to sleep. Upon exam, it was found that the baby had a bad infection; however, his temperature had returned to normal. The doctor said, "A high fever is normal with an ear infection. I have given him some medicine, and the nurse will give you a prescription for drops and medicine. He may be tired and want to sleep. Your son will be just fine."

When they got home, Linda got Paul ready for bed. As she put him down, he began to cry. As she tried to keep him from crying, he began to sob. "Oh, Mommy, why wouldn't you come?" He was trying to talk so hard between sobbing and crying. He asked her again, "Why wouldn't you come?" Linda did not understand, so she asked him, "Paul, what you are you talking about? I was right here with you all the time. Mommy doesn't know what you mean."

Paul continued sobbing as he tried to answer. Linda picked him and held him as close to her as she could. She tried to calm him, and again, he looked up at her and asked, "Mommy, why didn't you hear me? Why didn't you come?" Linda, not knowing what to think, asked, "Baby, I didn't go anywhere. Where did you want me to come?" The baby had calmed down quite a bit, and yet there was something strange in his little voice.

"Mommy, I was with Jesus." Linda gasped! Her heart was in her throat. She could not believe what she was hearing. Her baby, her son, went on to say, "Jesus took me walking in place with a whole lot of flowers. It was pretty too. I was going away, and I kept yelling for you, but you never came. Why didn't you come with Jesus and me?" Linda could not answer her child's question, even if she wanted to or knew how to. She was in shock. She could not believe what her son was telling her. She could not answer for another reason, but her son did not give her time to answer.

He went on to say, "I told Jesus, 'I want my mommy.' Jesus said, 'Your mommy cannot come. She doesn't love me, but I can let you go back to her.' Mommy," he asked, "Jesus is so nice. Why don't you love Him?" Just then, Dan came running into the room. "Honey," he said, "what in the world is going on?" Linda told her son, "I do love Jesus." She then told him to go to sleep, and they would talk about it in the morning.

Dan could not wait. As soon as the door to Paul's room was hut, he said, "Okay. Let's have it. What in heaven's name is going on?" Linda held her husband as she told him what had taken place. They both wept and thanked God that their son was all right. They did not know what or how, but they knew something had happened.

In the days following, they talked about God and church. In fact, they started reading the Bible a little, but as in so many cases, that soon passed. Their son was doing fine, and slowly everyone returned to and went right back with the way of life. Something (Satan) convinced them that Paul had just had a dream. He must have seen something on TV or heard one of those TV preachers. That was all it was. Sure. Sure.

What else must God do? How much more can we expect? Just what will it take for man to turn to God and His blessings of love? What are you waiting for? Will you wait until it is too late? Will you be deprived of a heavenly home? Will you discredit His Word in hopes of preventing its fulfillment? Will you neglect or reject the call of God and then have to face God when you finally face His judgment? Do you think your friends, church, pope, priest, bishop, pastor, or family can do anything as you stand at the judgment seat of Christ?

Well, what is your decision? Will you wait, or reject, or ignore His call? It is your choice. Please do not let anyone make it for you. Do not listen to those thoughts of *You do not need it. It is silly. You are not going to go to hell. What will your friends say? Your family? You will not have any life.* If there is nothing to this decision, then why is there a force against it? After two thousand years, why has man not been able to destroy the name of Jesus? If man is so big and smart, why is he not able to prevent hate, greed, crime, and death?

I will tell you why. Because man is not in charge. Man is too busy doing what the devil wants him to do---mock and reject the Word and call of God. Now look, man knows he should not beat his wife or rape and have sex with children. Why does he? We know we should not hide the truth to let a guilty man go free, but we do. Why? We knew it was not right to deprive the Native Americans of their freedom, their land, and their very way of life. We murdered their women and their children. Why?

Why do we make excuses for our sin? The Bible tells us if you have not chosen to serve God, then you serve Satan. If you do not choose to believe in the salvation of Christ, then you are already condemned. If this is not true, they why do we not stop what we are doing and live in peace and harmony? Why do we not love all humankind and live happily ever after? Because we cannot. Because the Word of God is true. If you do not have Jesus in your heart and soul, then you have sin that comes from Satan, which brings forth death, which will cause you to stand and face the judgment.

And yet to this day, man cannot figure this out for himself. Why? Because our power and so-called knowledge cannot and does not stand up to or compare to the power and deception of Satan. We think we can change or stop the will of Almighty God, the God whom Satan himself fears. My God, who cast him out of heaven and prepared a hell to cast him and those who tag along after his sinful ways. What Satan himself fears, and we do not? What God Himself tells us to fear, and we did not? What Satan tells us not to fear, and we will not? Go figure. Who is your boss? Paul's mom is just like all of us. We make excuses for the truth and accept a lie. Linda did not see the light, and to this day, she is unsaved. She still looks back on the episode and explains it away as a bad dream. Can you imagine that? After God used her baby boy to tell her of Christ's love and beauty, even after He gave her child back to her, after her own child said that Jesus told me you did not love Him, how could she not see that she was lost? How could she ignore and disbelieve what she saw and heard? Well, he did not do it by herself.

You say that this could not happen? Then you too believe a lie because this did happen. God touches and calls to man in many different ways. He calls to you so you can choose to be saved. Unlike Satan, God does not cause you to do His bidding. He gives you a choice to be saved. You must choose Him over sin. You must be born again by His spirit, so please hear and answer yes to His call. Do not wait until judgment and then on His mercy call, for He will not hear nor will He answer. You will be lost, and into hell, your body will fall.

As time ticked ever so swiftly toward the day of "no time," the nonbelievers seemed to think the world was actually getting better. Actually, Satan was giving them a snow job and a good one too. He had pulled out all the stops and was using anyone and anything he could to trick and deceive man. Which one are you, the one being used or abused? Without Christ, you are either a deceiver or a deceived. If you think not, if you think you are doing just what you want, then tell God to leave you alone, and if you must go to hell, then so be it. If this is not what you want, then ask God to make Satan leave you alone so that you can make up your own mind.

Satan knows that the hands of God's clock is about to stop. He knows it will not be long until his soul, spirit, and powers are cast into the eternal lake of fire, so he is busy doing all he can as quick as he can to rob man of his soul, for Satan both fears and knows the coming of Christ is to be soon.

Let me, at this time, obey God. This is important, or the spirit of God would not have laid it on my heart. Satan has powers to come into your soul. You alone cannot stop him. Let us look at the Bible as a history book. Let us look at the events that are recorded by eyewitnesses. Let us not consider spiritual matters but just the recorded facts.

If you read the Bible and did not know that it was written by holy men as inspired by God, not reading about salvation, rebirth, the setup of the church, or heavenly matters, then let us say that the Bible only told stories and events of what was seen and heard by the natural man, not saved or unsaved by all man. If the Bible was not of Godly men, then men would believe it.

If we were taught about the Bible events by man at school and at home, we would accept it. We believe that Hitler had power over people. He caused people to follow him and to believe in him. We accept that kings, mobsters, and outlaws have power over people. If you were in the mafia, what the kingpin said would be law. We even accept that there is power over man, and as long as it is not Godly power, we will believe it. We accept that some people have seen and can talk to spirits.

Let us assume that Jesus's name was Johnny and that Johnny has ESP. He was able to talk to those of the spirit world. He had a lot of backers and followers who have seen his word. Now Johnny comes to a man who was in bad shape. He went into a trance and said, "This man has an uncommon spirit. He needs to let it out. If you want, I can try to reach the spirit." Then Johnny chants and calls out the spirit, and it comes forth. Johnny tells the crowds,

"The spirit knows me. He came out. I told him to go away, but do not mention my name to the other spirits."

The man felt a lot better. In fact, he leaped with joy, and the crowd cheered. Everybody knew that Johnny had ESP. Well, to Johnny's surprise, when the spirit ghost (or whatever it was) came forth, people saw a mist, a puff of cloud or something. They saw it, and they wrote about it. We would believe it, don't you agree?

Then what does it matter that Johnny was Christ Jesus, the Son of God? The power He had was not ESP; it was God. The uncommon spirit was not uncommon; it was the devil. The man was not just in bad shape; he was a raving mad man, going about stealing, terrorizing, and even stealing. The spirit did not come out because he was asked to. He had no choice, for God had given His Son power over all things, Satan included. The spirit did not know just of this person; Satan knew Him well.

In fact, he knew Him and the Father. He also knew of the awesome power of the spirit, for it was that power that defeated him in heaven. It was that power that cast him out and that same power that defeated him at Mt. Olive, when he went up against Jesus. It is the same power that will also cast him in the pits of hell. Yes, he knew who Jesus was. That is why he got out of His presence.

Both stories are true. The events are true. People witnessed them and wrote them down. Only the names and reasons were changed. But now, because we know it was of God, we do not accept it because it deals with the Son and the salvation of man's soul. Something causes us to have doubts and disbelief. Why doesn't Satan want you to know what he knows? Why will he not allow you to seek the advice of God?

Because he wants to use you to get revenge on God. He wants you to deny and reject God's call unto repentance. He wants to force God to cast your soul into hell, even though He loves you, even though He sent His Son to die and redeem you. Satan wants to laugh as he snatches your soul out of God's grace and into his wrath. He does not want to be in hell alone. That is why!

Satan is good at what he does best. He knows how to use our minds, knowledge, pride, and the fact that we do not know Jesus. Many of us know of Him, but that is not good enough. Satan knows without the spirit being in you, you have no power over him. Without being born again, you cannot understand the truth, power, or wisdom in God's Word. Without the salvation of Christ, you are easy pickings. In fact, he does not have to do anything to some, but as soon as you seek the truth, he goes to work. Instead of answering when Jesus calls to your soul to come forth, he wants you to flee from His presence. Will you? Why?

Satan had thrown up a smoke screen. There was talk of peace and progress. The government and media were playing right along. We were being led to believe that worldwide peace was at hand. What a joke! Nowhere in history has man lived in peace and harmony with man, nor will we ever. Man cannot be at peace unless he has peace with God. Man cannot have no enemies and he love for all mankind without the love of God in his heart. This is a fact that cannot be disputed. Do you want proof? Then open your eyes, and do not be blinded by the smoke of lies.

Stop accepting the excuses, and look at the problems. Make your own list. What is the crime, trouble, and dispute you see? You are not stupid. Use your God-given horse sense. Do you see love and peace on the rise or sin and crime? Have we made progress? Are our children safe? Are our love and respect for man making our streets safe?

Do we have more people in a true church on Sunday than we do in our prisons and jails? Do we all serve and worship the same Almighty God? Are people running to get saved, or are they running after false prophets and doctrines, just as the Word of God said? Does man exhibit the love of God or the lust of money, possessions, or sex? Is this truly progress? Is this the betterment of man or the fulfillment of the sings of the coming of Christ?

You see, you do not have to accept or believe God's Word to make it so. He will do that with or without you. He does not need your support to bring this world to an end. He does not need your help to judge the sin of man. Jesus does not need you to execute the will of God. Just stand back and watch. You will see. God loves you. He sent Jesus to die for you, but His love will not cause Him to lie. No one will escape, alter, or stop the execution of judgment.

Do not fall prey to the snares of sin. Do not listen to the falsehoods of man. Do not get so wrapped in worldly ways that you cannot see the writing on the wall. Do not get so busy in the times and stress of this short life as to not prepare for the eternal life. Make sure you know what you are doing and where you are going. Do not be deprived of God's Glory Land or be deceived about His place of wrath. Make sure you get the one you want, for once you get there, it is forever. Amen.

Man was trying his very best to make this world a better place.

He was trying to better his life, beautify the earth, and conserve what it had to offer. Yet he would not allow or ask the One who could make life perfect. God is ready and more than able to pour His blessings and wondrous power and wisdom upon man. All we have to do is to turn to Him. Put our trust and faith in Christ, then all things could be the way they were meant to be. Mankind could be a winner with God. Why does anyone want to be on a losing team?

The odds are stacked against us. We have proven that we are not good in a pinch. We throw so many low blows that our gain is plagued with penalties. We do not pay attention to the coach's signals. We are not team players. We are getting beat and going down for the count. God is ready to throw in the towel. He is calling the game, and the season is about the end. God is moving His team into the winner's circle. Will He keep you, or will He let you go? Will you be safe or cast out? Have you signed your contract with Christ, the agent of God, or have you traded your soul to the devil? When the game is over and God goes to hand out the awards, whose team will you be on?

Unfortunately, man has decided to go against God. He would play against the odds and take his chances. He would use his own game plan. That is the way Satan is. He lets you do whatever you want as long as you play to lose. And lose you will, for Satan is causing you to take a nose dive right into hell. Remember, Satan does not care about you. He does not care about winning. His game plan is to cause you to lose your soul.

And yet man thought that he was getting ahead. He was gaining in his mind. He was getting smarter in man's knowledge while growing further from the wisdom of God and the truth. He was getting a hand on restoring and reserving his way of life. Man was busy at trying to ensure himself of a longer and better lifestyle. Man had gained a sense of false hope, but that is okay with Satan. You can do just as you want, as long as you stay on is team, just as long as you lose. Remember that with sin, you must lose. With sin, you WILL lose.

The fact is that by not playing by God's rules, man's endeavors are for naught. Man's lack of the Word and plan of God was causing the fulfillment of His will. Man was causing the destruction and damnation of his life and soul that he cherished so much. Man could not see what God can do for us, what we cannot do for ourselves. If we cherish Him, the creator and giver of life, He will give us life eternal. He will cherish our love and save our souls. He will make you a winner forever. Remember, God plays for keeps, but it is His rules, His game. He calls the shots. But who puts the ball in your court? Who will you play for? Do not pinch in a clinch. Do not drop the ball. You are playing for your soul.

God is watching as time runs out. He is calling for you to come unto Him, while there is time for His mercy and grace to be received, for the last tick of time will bring all to an end. Man's ways, thoughts, theories, doctrines, and beliefs will be put to rest, for our life as we know it and this place on which we live will be destroyed. Now the game has changed. He takes the ball into His court, and it is time for Him to put things in order, according to His Word.

God has called for Christ to come and to take the born-again team to the holy courtyard of heaven, there to bask in the wondrous glories of God's Kingdom, the place prepared just for those who chose to serve the blessed Son of God.

Which also brings forth the call of judgment and justice for all those who chose not to be a part of God's family, those who did not accept God's Word, those who denied His call to salvation, and those who rejected His beloved Son. All stand before God. As He rejects them because He had no part of Him in this life, He has no part of them in the life hereafter. Their soul is lost and cast into the place prepared for unbelievers and deceivers, a lace called hell, a fiery furnace, a lake of fire, a place of eternal punishment for the souls of the damned, the condemned, and the unsaved.

This life will be over. Everything will be destroyed so that eternity can begin, so that the souls of the saved can live without the presence of sin. Heaven is real, and so is hell. Make no mistake. Time is running out, but you still have the opportunity to be saved. God wants you to walk through those pearly gates. He wants to give your soul eternal peace and happiness. He does not want you to inherit the wrath of His judgment.

Satan was very busy. He had to be. The troublesome crimes of man were skyrocketing. He had to lie and deceive many. He tried to hide the drunkards lying in our streets, the drug addicts who robbed, stole, and even sold themselves for sex just for a fix. He tried to hide the fact that half of crime and trouble are caused by these two mind-killing, soul-imprisoning devices of sin.

Satan tried to camouflage the fact that most of the other crimes and troubles we face are because of our obsession with the pure lust of money and sex. How we kill and cheat for money, how we rape and abuse each other for sexual pleasure. He does not want us to see how we are demoralizing our minds and bodies as we yield to the desire of sin.

But Satan is not working alone. He has help . . . our help. That's right! We are helping Satan destroy ourselves. He does not have to hide all the miseries of sin; we have shut our eyes to them. We even made excuses for them: what we saw and knew, what we could not handle, what we ignored. That neither stopped it nor caused it to go away. It just helped us to get through another day. Not believing something does not make it go away. Rejecting the truth does not alter or change the fact. That is why man is in the mess he is in. He is being played for a fool. He is being deceived and led down the path of sin to the pits of hell, and yet he holds onto the devil's hand with his self-righteousness, unwilling to see the sorrow and destruction of sin.

Ignoring what sin brings does not alter or change the result. Neither does it alter nor change the Word or plan of God by ignoring it. Man can see the result of sin if he would just look. We are living proof to the Word of God, if we could just see what is going on. The fulfillment of God's Word is at hand. We cannot prevent it or escape it, so why ignore or reject it? Call sin righteousness, unwilling, and let God be the God He is.

Let Him bring your soul unto salvation and your vision into the light. Do not be blinded by that voice in the back of your mind. Do not listen to the excuses and explanations of man. The Word of God is being fulfilled as you read. The hand of God is about the stop the hands of time. You have got to understand. God told us sin brought death, and it did. He tells us what sin will cause. It has. He tells us we will face His judgment, and sin will promise us you can be saved if you want, do you?

God's Word is true. It has stood the test of time. It will stand in and through the endless ages of time. Its truth is coming true every day. You are the one about to fall. You are the one who will say, "I should have listened to God's call." While it is not too late, please let God be your God. Do not be enslaved to the desires of sin. Do not let the deception of sin hold you captive. Do not be imprisoned by the lies and ways of man. Let the Word of God set you free.

Let the salvation of God's Son give you back your life and soul. Know the truth, and accept the will and plan of God. Know that you are at peace with Him. Be able to look forward to and rejoice in His coming. Let not His appearance trouble your heart or put fear in your soul. You can be a child of God and His pleasures of glory to you He will bestow. Praise and glory to His name.

Even though we were in perilous times, each day brought new hope. It also brought with it more time. Yes, time and hope were given to the believers and nonbelievers alike, yet the purpose as different. Some took advantage of it, but most did not.

To the nonbelievers, it gave them another day to eat, drink, and be merry. A little more time to scam and cheat themselves into riches, power, and fame, while others use it to work on the problems of man. Another day to try and figure out what life is all about yet not looking to the One who gave them another day. To Satan, he used it to draw another soul down the road of sin, another day to spread his lies and doctrines. He used every day as if it were to be his last, used them to rob man of his soul and inheritance to the Kingdom of God. He used every minute to pull man further away from God's mercy and grace. He refused to let man reach out to outstretched waiting arms of Christ, for unlike an, he knew his days were numbered.

But praise God, all was not in vain, for some nonbelievers became believers. Some were being saved because the believers were using each and every day to spread the gospel of Christ. Each day found them busy at God's work. Each day gave them hope of winning a lost soul to the saving grace of God. It gave them another day to worship and praise the heavenly Father. They used each day to thank Him for His loving mercies and blessings of kindness, for they too knew the great and glorious day of the Lord was at hand.

How you use each approaching new dawn is very important. You are important and special to God. Each day allows you another chance to make God your choice. You are someone special. Christ loved and died for you to have a way to redeem your soul. Therefore, your decision is important. While this day gives him another opportunity to reach out to your soul, to knock one more time at your heart's door, do not turn Him away. Do not let the sun set, bringing to an end this day, while your soul is lost and you live in sin, for the dawning of the new day may awaken you to the realization of the truth. This is the beginning of the end. God has spoken. Time now has stopped, and eternity is about to begin.

Please, in the name of our Lord and Savior, use what time God has given you to seek Him and call out to Him. Make your peace with God. Be at ease with His coming. Prepare to meet thy maker proclaiming the bloodshed salvation of Christ. Know that you are sheltered from the agonizing torments of God's wrath. Be you forever safe in the loving arms of Jesus. Amen.

Read the next chapter very closely. Ask God to shut out the ways and ideas of this world. Ask Him to allow you to read with an open mind and heart, for the next day very well might be the last day. No one knows for sure the exact time, and no one knows what will bring forth God's order. "My Son, go get our children." Everyone knows that God will give the order. The power of Satan cannot withstand the call. If Satan must bow to the order and power of God, where does that leave you?

Not if, but when Satan takes his place in God's plan, where will you fit in? What will be your excuse? How will you handle the rejection of God for your rejection of Christ saving your soul? Will you deny or disbelieve when God puts you in your place? Will you be able to be convinced there is no hell or that God will not punish you as you are engulfed in the flames and torments of its fury?

If not, use your time wisely. The Word of God and His promise of judgment will unfold. His pouring out of His wrath and the rescuing of the saved are facts. You do not have the power or ability to wish it away. The Word of God is true. Everything else is a lie. All, I mean every place, person, and everything, will fail and give way to the Word of God. Your only choice is when you will reckon with His truth. So instead of crying out to the rocks to hide you from His power and wrath, cry out now for His mercy and grace to save your soul. If time allows you to draw your next breath, you have time to be saved (Revelation 6:14--17).

The breath you now inhale may be your last. If not, rest assured that you will draw your last breath of this life. Will the dawning of a new day bring your death or the beginning or our new life? Who gives you the promise of your next breath? Who can promise you there will even be another dawning? Man cannot give your life after death. All our knowledge and so- called wisdom cannot cause or stop a new day's dawning. We are powerless over such matters.

He holds your every breath. He controls the day's dawning. It is He who sent His Son to save your soul. It is the same He who tells us after death there is the judgment. He who tells us we must be born again. The same He who tells us His wrath and torments will be poured out on those who are not born again. Be not deceived that the same God who brought you into this world is the same God who will take you out!

Do not try to make God out to be a fool. Do not pass Him off as just a thing or phase made up by man. Do not believe that life began without a call to order. It had to have a beginning. That beginner is also the ender. Do not call God a liar or think that He is bluffing. The same God who allowed Jesus to suffer, bleed, and die for our wretched souls, the same God who so loved the world, sent us a means of salvation (John 3:16).

He is the same God who will get even and get revenge upon those who mock the One who died for us and reject their soul's redemption. He shed His blood, and by your denial of so great of a salvation, you hurt and anger the Almighty God. If you face God without the blood of Jesus atoning our sins, the same God will be true to His Word. He will cast your soul into the fiery pits of hell without blinking an eye.

When will God call for the end? When will He put things in order? It could be today, tonight, or maybe next week. One thing is for sure; it will come. God will keep His Word to the saved and the unsaved, for He is God over all. He is the God who will take the call. When the call comes, where will it find you? The destination of our soul is still in your hands. While time allows, choose. Make the ways of God your choice. If not, you opt to let God decide. Without Christ pleading for your case, you give God no choice and your soul no chance.

At this time like all others, man was busy at his business. Some were going to work, while others were on their way home. In other parts of the world, some were getting high on drugs or alcohol or both. There were some watching or indulging in sex acts of all sorts, while others chased after and worshipped false gods or prophets. People were begging for their lives as criminal acts ran wild.

Throughout the world, just like today, people were being murdered. There were battles and wars being fought on every front for every reason. Whether it was racial, greed, power struggles, or religions, man could not get along with his fellow man.

Praise be to God, some were still preaching, praying, singing, and shouting! They were proclaiming their sweet victory in Jesus. Yes, in other words, this day or night seemed as yesterday or a day last week. There was not much new occurring, just the same ol' same ol'. However, that meant a little more time for God's people to bring the Word to the lost and dying world. Just another tick of God's clock.

Yes, it is true that God's clock is winding down. It does not need our okay. God controls time and the destiny of man. Regardless of teachings, beliefs, or traditions of doctrine, the Word of God was and is coming true minute by minute. Each passing day brings us closer to its fulfillment. Do not let it catch you off guard. Watch and pray is the warning. I will come again and receive you . . . That is the promise. Every knee shall bow, and every tongue shall confess that thou art the son God . . . That is reality. The end is at hand is the fact (Romans 14:10--12).

Brother Dave woke up on his own. It was time for him to rise and shine. His alarm did not go off like it should have, so he turned on the radio and checked to see if he had pushed the alarm button, but no music came on, only static, the emergency signal. He turned to another station, and it was the same thing. Finally, a man came over the radio with a tragic new report. An awful event had occurred.

He stated his name and station letter and then reported, "I know it is still dark here, but in other parts of the world, it is supposed to be daytime. The report just came over the wire that it is dark the world over. My god! The sun is not shining anywhere. The wire lines are tied up, and the reports are coming in from all around the world. My god! My god! What is happening? The sun refuses to give forth any light. I cannot believe what I am reading. The world is in total darkness.

"We have contacted some of the best minds known to man. We have here on a phone line one of the most renowned professors of astrology. He will try to enlighten us as to what is going on. Sir, how could this be? And what are we facing?" The professor answered, "I have no explanation for this. It is tragic, and I am scared at what might have happened." He went on, "We could be facing a very dangerous situation. It could be that the earth, due to some unknown reason or orbital mishap, has fallen or been drawn out of its orbit, thus being shielded from the sun."

The radio announcer asked, "What in this world or in space could cause this to take place? Please tell us something." The professor, being one of the most knowledgeable men of this field, had to answer, "I have been on the phone with NASA and radar stations worldwide. I have spoken with my colleagues and with space scientists in three countries. But I must be frank. We can come up with no logical reason as to what has happened, nor can we say what caused it. It has to be something we are not aware of."

Right then, Brother Dave was aware of God's Word. Man may be unaware, but God's Word tells of the signs of the coming of the end. Could this be? As Brother Dave's mind pondered on God's Word (Matthew 24:3--31; Mark 13:3--133; 1 Thessalonians

4:16--17; 1 Corinthians 15:52--58), like so many believers, Brother Dave fell to his knees, shouting praises to God. His wife heard the noise and came running, as she too heard the newscast. She threw her arms around Brother Dave's neck as they began to rejoice in the name of the Lord. It was time.

Their children awakened by the noise began to cry. He and his wife went to comfort them. Reverend Dave told them, "Boys, do not be afraid. Daddy is here. You do not have to worry. Everything is and will be just fine, for you see boys, what Daddy has been telling people to prepare for and what Mommy and Daddy have been working for has now coming to pass. Things will be okay. Now God has taken charge. We are in His hands. Praise Jesus!"

As more and more people began to wake up, as more and more heard and saw what had happened, the sounds rang out from house to house. You could hear screams crying and people yelling for help. You could hear people sobbing in fear. Some were begging. "God, O God! Please help us! God, do not let this happen! Oh, my Lord, have mercy on us!" Yet others were singing and praising God; they too knew it was time. Brother Dave glanced at his watch. It has stopped, and so had the clock on the wall.

He then went to the window. The streets were full of people and cars. They were trying to get anywhere and everywhere. It was madness. Then he began to cry tears of joy. He looked up and saw how dark it was. The stars were gone. The moon that shone last night was no longer in sight. Not a cloud was in sight. Nothing was hiding them; they were simply gone.

He shouted, "The moon and stars have fallen from heaven just like God said they would!" Above his shouts of glory, you could hear cars crashing. People were going amok. Cars were running into one another, into buildings and trees. People were going nuts, trying to get away from what was happening. The cries of pain and fear rang out. Screams of pleas and terror filled the air. The town, the country, the whole world was in a state of all-out panic.

At that moment, an announcer came over the radio. "Now hear this: we have a message from the president of the United States of America. My fellow Americans, there is no reason for alarm. Please do not bring any danger and panic upon yourself. Please, you must remain calm. I repeat, do not panic. There is no need to be afraid. We are in no immediate danger. You must help yourself and your country. Help us. We must maintain order. We will get through this.

"We do have a major problem. Believe me, we know and realize the effect and condition that is at hand, but this no means a disaster. Even though the whole world is in darkness, we can go on. We have been assured by scientists worldwide that our earth is still in its regular orbit. We are not in any harm whatsoever. We have an unnatural problem. We will have to make some adjustments, but our lives can and will go on. Everyone must do what he or she can until we can find out what caused this to happen and correct it.

"I, as president of the United States, do hereby declared the US to be ordered into total martial law. This order is in effect now, and it is for the entire nation. Martial law has been ordered through the world. This is done for the safety of all the people. Nothing will be tolerated. If you break the order, you will be shot. No one is going to take advantage of this situation. You will be safe. By order of the president, the policing agents have been ordered to shoot to kill.

"Everyone is to now turn on all the lights in your home, offices, lants, factories, and stores. Every light in America is to be turned on immediately. Nothing else that uses electricity is to be used except for refrigerators, freezers, and life-saving machines. You are allowed to have one radio, and that is it.

"I have already ordered all armed forces to report back to the US. All police, firemen, National Guard, coast guard, military reserves, and Red Cross are to report to your headquarters. You will be met there by the military armed forces. You will help enforce the martial law as ordered. The troops are aboard and will assist you upon their return. All military and civil equipment and resources will be used to protect and serve its citizens. Americans, I say to you again, this nation is under martial law."

The president went on to say, "This message is being taped. It will play on all radio stations every thirty minutes. It will be played over the public address systems each hour. It will also be printed on all channels of the TV stations. This will be done until we have more information.

"We are at no outside danger. This is a worldwide dilemma. The rules of all nations have ordered martial law and order. We are all in this together. We are all in agreement. All forces and resources will be used. Every street and alley will be monitored and patrolled. This will not turn into a disaster or a time of riots and crime. Rest assured you will be safe."

The message from the president seemed to bring a calmness to the people, yet panic and fear was still in charge. The sights around churches were shocking. People were fighting to get in. They were lying and kneeling all over, begging God for help. Some stood and demand of God. "Give us back our sun!"

Even at this darkest hour, even though the writing was now on the wall, people were still more concerned with maintaining their normal way of life. Man was more wrapped up in destiny of his world than he was for the destiny of his soul. Man, still thought he was in control.

There were many who now saw the light through the darkness of this day. Cries of "God, save us!" could be heard everywhere. They were begging for their souls and lives. They were so afraid of what was to come. But was it to no avail? Just as God had shut the door to the safety and shelter of the ark, had He shut the door of mercy and grace? Just as it was too late for their cries of panic and fear, is it too late at this point?

Satan was really busy now. He had a lot to do and so little time left. There were some who blamed God and the Christians. Brother Dave was told, "This is your fault. All you people who kept saying, 'I want to go to heaven,' you brought this on us. You and your God. But it will not work. We will get through this. Then what will you use to scare us with?" Everyone had their opinion as to what was happening. Everyone blamed someone.

The hardening of the hearts of some caused them to turn against the Christians. They threatened them and scorned them, but God touched them. He dried their tears and assured their safety. It was hard for the Christians to understand how man could be foolish enough to think this was just a mishap. This was no accident. This was an order by God.

The hearts of God's people were ever so heavy. Just the thought of their unsaved family, friends, and loved ones broke them down. They were so concerned for the lost world, and yet the world hated them. In fact, it was not safe for them to be on the streets. They could not go to the stores to shop. They could not visit their loved ones. They could not even go to their own children or to church.

Yet they remained true and strong. They refused to be counted with those of the world just to be able to fit in. New laws and orders were passed. Not only was it a darkened sky, but the darkness also fell on the eyes and hearts of man. Christians now were being abused. They were treated as outcasts. Yet they held into the promises and Word of God.

As they began to feel the pain of the times, as now they feared for their safety, as the world pressured them to go along with their plan, as man had settled in on dealing with the problem at hand, ignoring what was truly at hand.

God spoke to His people. The Holy Ghost delivered the message to their souls. "Let not your hearts be troubled nor have fear, for in my Father's house are many mansions. I went to prepare place for you. I will also come again, that where I am you may be also." Oh, what peace fills their soul as they were embraced by the love and mercy of God.

Then just as quickly as the darkness fell upon the world, the blackened sky split open with a tremendous crack of thunder. "My god!" was the cry as giant bolts of lightning passed through the sky and smacked against the earth. The lightning bolts had such force the earth shook and trembled. The brightness of their light lit up the world.

My god, my god! What a sight! The earth was lit up brighter than ever before. The darkness was gone. People were rejoicing that there was light. The whole world was in the brightness of the light, so bright, in fact, they thought it blinded them from the shape and form of the sun, and yet there was no sun.

The instant had a mind-boggling effect on man. He was overwhelmed. Mankind the world over began jumping and shouting with great joy. They had every reason to celebrate. They had been in darkness, and now they saw the light. But did they see the LIGHT?

The children of God were rejoicing, for they knew they would soon be with their Lord and Savior. They just knew they could not wait. They leaped for joy. They sang and shouted praises unto God. Their hearts pounded out of their chests. Their longing expectations could not be contained. Heaven was near.

Many of them fell to their knees and cried out, "My Lord! My

Lord! Here I am!" Some fell with their faces to the ground and worshipped the coming of the risen Son of God. Others shouted praises to Almighty God. They were full of blessings and praise to

God the Father. They were engulfed by the Holy Spirit. The thrill was too much to bear. They cried out, "Jesus is coming! Praise God, Jesus is coming! The Holy One! My Lord, my precious Savior! He is coming! Praise God, oh, praise God! Oh, thank you God, thank you for Jesus! Thank you for saving my soul. Hallelujah! Glory to God! I am going home!"

The air was filled with praises and songs of joy. You could hear "Oh, my God, thank you, thank you. Jesus, my sweet Jesus, is coming to take us home!" They shouted the world over. They wanted to make sure their praises of love, joy, and worship reached all the way to God's throne. They praised Him with all they had: heart, body, soul, and mind. They were overtaken by the thrill of the Holy Spirit. They wanted God to know they loved Him, worshipped His very presence, and were so grateful and thankful for His wondrous love, mercy, and grace.

Words could not explain what was in their hearts, but that did not stop them. They continued to express the joy of their souls. Praises of Him and thanks to Him were being sung out. Songs of victory through the blessed blood of Jesus could be heard through the shouts. The sights and sounds had to be pleasing to the ears of God. His people were rejoicing. They were awaiting and welcoming the coming of His Son.

But for those who had not accepted the salvation of Christ did not accept He might be coming. In fact, they ignored the celebration of the born again, for they had their own reason to celebrate. They had light. The sun had been put back into place. The darkness was over. The panic, danger, and fear were over. Their worries and minds could be put at ease. Things surely looked brighter now.

Then at that instant, the great trumpet of God sounded. The blare of His trumpet was deafening to the ear. The whole world heard it and took notice.

Then, lo and behold, there was the Lord Jesus Christ, the Son of God, the Redeemer of souls. Yes, praise God! There He was. There for all to see stood the Lord of Lords. The most holy One was in full sight. There was the "I AM." There was King Jesus, enhanced with the powers and wondrous aura of God, standing upon a cloud of glory.

His blissfulness and beauty were breathtaking. The magnitude of His very presence could be felt the world over. He had returned to fulfill the Holy Word of God. God had made the call, and Christ had come to take His children home.

Yes, this is the rapture. This is the ending of man's time and the beginning of God's endless time of eternity, for you see, Jesus is the final phase of God's plan. There is no more doubt. All mankind could see the righteous truth and divine power of God's Word. Behold for judgment is at hand.

When the great trumpet of God sounded, the sights and events of God's plan began to unfold right before the eyes of man. The world over lost its breath. Some knees buckled. The call had come. God was waiting for the deliverance of His people. Christ Jesus had come to receive those who slept and those who were alive and watching for His coming.

The call was both thrilling and chilling to the soul. It went to the uttermost parts of the earth. The call went out to the depth of the seas and to the locks of the graves, for time had ended, and death had been defeated. Death was no more. Those who had slept who had accepted Christ and did knowing Him as their Savior were awakened. The graves under the sea and of dirt and stone had to give them up.

As the call came, the graves burst open. As they obeyed the Son of God, all was given up. The blessed children of God began to come forth. Bodies and souls were reunited as they began rising, shouting, and singing praises unto their Lord King Jesus. At that same instant, at that same call, at the twinkling of an eye, the living children of God were also called.

They were changed as they received their heavenly bodies, bodies that were whole without sickness or pain, who knew no death. Bodies who hungered not for food or drink but for the food God, to feed on the love of God and drink from the waters of eternal life, they too heard and answered their heavenly call. Their souls were given the charge to rise.

Then all of God's people, all members of the Savior's church, every soul that had been born again, either dead or alive, were leaving. They were called up and began to rise. They were headed for a meeting in the air. Oh, praise God! They were rising to meet the Lamb of God on His cloud of glory.

There to ever be with their Savior as He leads them through those pearly gates of heaven on streets of purest gold, there to live and forever be sheltered in the most holy presence of God the Father, the Son, and the Holy Ghost, leaving behind all memory of those who were left to face God's wrath.

God's people came forth, shouting the victory and singing praises, for they were on their way home. They did not look back nor could they. There was nothing back there for them. They were about to embark on the shores of glory. All eyes and hopes were up ahead. They were going to inherit God's glorious Kingdom. This was the first of many joys. This was the first timeless moment of their forever and ever. Amen.

Oh, the sights! They were so glorifying and so beautiful. There were cries of danger and pain and yet cries of joy and happiness. People were pleading and begging for mercy, while others sang praises unto Jesus for His mercy. There was so much going on all at the instant, and yet all was in order, for all was in the plan and in the divine order of God.

Nothing was left out. No one could escape, even those who or whatsoever reason had not accepted Christ or had rejected His Words. They too received new bodies, for time, death, and sin were no more to be. All was subject to the call of judgment. Those left behind received their eternal bodies, and yet theirs could feel pain, sorrow, and woes. Their memories were not erased. They knew every time they had told Jesus "No."

As the non-born again were left behind, they screamed out and fell on bended knees, now confessing. "O God! Oh, my Jesus Christ! He is your Son and the Redeemer of souls!" They cried out for His saving grace and begged and pleaded for His mercy. But it was all in vain, for as it is written. "Every knee shall bend, every tongue shall confess. It is also written you must be born again or face the wrath of judgment (Romans 14:11--12; John 3:3).

Those left behind, all those who missed out on the call to glory, they were shocked, amazed, and terrified. Yes, reality of the truth and power of God had set in. Mankind the world over began to run from Him. They tried to hide from the sign and very presence of the Lord Jesus Christ, but as is written, they could not. The horrible fact was disbelief had stopped. The plan and Word of God were known to all humanity.

There was no doubt now. The lost and condemned world reached up toward heaven; their longing cries were in despair. They wanted God's grace. They needed His mercy, but their moans of pain and their groans of agony were not heard because along with the children of God, mercy, and grace, they too were gone. All that was left was the torture and unmerciful punishment of His wrath.

Oh, what fear fell on the hearts and souls of man. They knew they had been wrong. They had been deceived all the while. They begged for another chance. They now were scared and trembled at the very thought of rejecting the Son of God. Seeing Him in all His power and glory made them forget the ways of sin. Man could not convince himself any longer. Satan could not lie and is lead. The safe deliverance of God's people to their promised home in glory was now coming to pass.

Now everyone wanted to accept Christ. Everyone wanted to answer to His call to rise. No one wanted to be left behind, but because the Word of God said, "I will raise them up," also said, "I will pour out my vengeance and wrath on them who had not been saved" (John 3:36). The same Word of God that brought salvation and redemption now brings damnation and torture.

The very sight of Jesus as He stood in honor and full glory, the sight of the bodies of God's children coming forth out of darkened graves, the sight of friends and loved ones being called up to meet the Holy Lamb of God in the air did not convince man of the truth of God's Word. His power could not be denied. No one now ignored, nor did they rely upon their thoughts or ideas. For they had to stand by and watch with ears of envy as God called His born-again home. Oh, the hurt they beheld as the very ones they had mocked and laughed at were now being led according the Word of God, by the Son of God, to the Kingdom of God as promised. To witness this was unbearable. The awful feeling of rejection as they cried out was more than they could stand.

Some shouted out to their loved ones, and others yelled at the preachers. They cried, "Please don't leave me! Take me with you! I believe now!" Some shouted to Reverend Dave and Reverend Evans, "Tell Jesus I wanted to believe. I was going to!" But their pleas could not be heard. The unsaved were left. The Words of God, the many calls of the Savior, were etched in their broken hearts. The sighs and the reality of the rapture were burned in their minds. That alone would shock man to death.

Yet death would not come. The misery and the pain, the memories and the torture, would last forever, for all had received their eternal bodies. Now all had to face and endure or enjoy God's eternal judgment. Man had been forewarned. All had been called unto repentance. Now was the fulfillment of the Word.

Yes, seeing the children of God being called to glory, knowing that you too could have answered His call but for whatever reason you chose not to, now you were left behind. This alone brought tears and fear to their hearts and souls. They now knew this was just the beginning of their sorrows, for this was the first moment of their eternal destiny.

When Christ made His call to His people to come forth, all graves opened in obedience to the Lord. Watery graves rolled back to obey the call. Just think where the graves are of every born-again Christian who has ever died all had to open. They could not hold the saints any longer. They had to let go. Death was no more. The dead in Christ now lived and was offered up at His call.

Can you mentally take thought as to what was going on? Roads and highways, which now cover up old graves, burst open. Roads everywhere split apart to yield up those of Christ buried beneath them. Think, if you can stand the thought, make a picture in your mind of the horror and fear as those not of Christ had to face. These are not just words. This, my friend, is reality. This was the day of our Lord.

Watching graves open, watching the bodies come forth in answering to His call, was too much to handle. But those left had no choice. They had to face the truth and witness the fulfillment of the Word. This was just one order. There was more to come. All had to be fulfilled. This was the deliverance of the church, a blessed event for its members but the beginning of woes for the unsaved.

Yes, cemeteries the world over heard the call. All who died with Christ came out of their graves to live with Christ. Think about the graves lying beneath the tall buildings, homes, and factories of man. Now really think; let the thought and reality sink in.

All graves, regardless of what was on top of them, burst open, in glory and honor to obey King Jesus. Every grave everywhere obeyed the Word.

There were buildings, offices, hospitals, and schools the world over that had graves beneath them that split apart to give up the bodies of the saints who were dead in Christ. This caused the buildings to crumble. Mass skyscrapers were torn apart. The screams of pain and fear filled the air. These buildings came crashing to the ground, smashing cars, trucks, and trains. Big hunks of cement and iron fell like rain, causing traffic to crash into one another and into crowds of people who were trying to escape the falling buildings.

Oh, it was awful! People were being smashed by buildings and run over by cars and buses. Human bodies were ripped apart and thrown about as all of life would end. Yet death did not come to them. There was no escape! They could feel the pain of death as floors and sides of buildings fell, crushing every bone in their bodies. They could feel the hurt when buildings began to explode, sending beams of steel and iron-like spears through the air. People were staked to the ground like slabs of meat, and yet death was gone! There was nothing to ease the pain, the hurt, or the torture. It would be forever.

There was no safe place. People were being burned and buried alive, but there was not death, no quenching of the pain. No way to hide, nowhere to run. All was being destroyed except for the souls of the unsaved. They would suffer forever. Their torment would last through eternity, for they must endure the fullness of His mighty wrath. It was His day of glory. He was giving the orders, and all was subject to Him.

The escape from His wrath was gone. The deliverance of judgment had come. The unsaved were doomed. They had no choices. No one to blame but themselves. They had a chance to escape. They had many a chance to be saved. Now they cannot change. The time to choose Jesus as your Savior is over. Everything else is a liar. There is no help or hope for you now. This world faces total destruction, and mankind faces the pits of hell!

Yes, destruction had begun. Everything built by man was tumbling down. Their way of life was coming down around them. There was nowhere to flee. The crying screams, the busting glass, and the explosions of gas pumps rang throughout. Why, even the iron rods and steel beams, the telephone poles, and the radio towers, the very things we used to improve our way of life, were being hurled through the air like toothpicks. The tall towers were flying through the sky like spears, while bodies were being slashed and cut open, smashed and on fire. Yet there was no death.

The awful spine-chilling cries and the horrible sights and sounds were beyond the realm of human thought. People were begging to die just to end the pain, begging for mercy just to ease their suffering. But there was no use. Those who chose not to be born again were having to endure more than everything dreamed or deemed possible. Why, the bloody screams of pain and torture alone more than the mortal fear could bear.

Your heart would burst with sorrow at the blood-curdling screams. Your eyes could not bear to see, and your mind cannot envision the horrendous sights. This body could not last one moment in such torture. Yet no one found peace. They were facing and would have to endure God's wrath for the rejection of His Son. Oh, how grand and glorious is God and His Kingdom, but oh, how dreadful and tormenting is His wrath. You must always remember, God is just in His judgment. He is true to His Word. If you forget, there is a hell to pay.

Payment was due. Now it is time to pay up. Their bodies had to be changed into eternal ones, thus enabling them to suffer and endure their everlasting condemnation, the same condemnation you were foretold of and forewarned. Now it was upon them. They did not take heed to the warning then. They did not cry out to be saved then. But they sure are now.

Man was in a panic. The hurt was unbearable. He was running, crying, and screaming, but he had nowhere to go. Man's cars, trucks, and buses were trying to dodge the falling buildings and open graves, only to crash into one another. Hills were split apart; there were rockslides and avalanches that crushed and buried man alive. But this never brought death, just pain. Nor did it shelter or hide them from the wrath and revenge of God.

Man was trampling one another, running over family and friends. His feet were stomping on the heads and bodies of those who had fallen. People were falling into and being pinned in the very graves that gave up the children of God. Broken and busted bodies were tossed around like paper. The fear mounted, and their pain was excruciating. It was very chaotic. Every man was for himself. Nobody stopped to help Mom, Dad, or anyone because there was no help for anyone. This was just the beginning.

Can you imagine? Just think this all took place while the children of God were called up to meet Jesus. The thoughts of the sights and sounds would drive you insane. It seems unbearable. Impossible. But it is reality. Everything found in God's Word will come to pass. The call had come. The world was facing total demise and destruction as man faced the judgment and either their reward or their punishment, according to the Word of God. Amen.

Yes, this was the rapture, the taking of those born again of Christ and washed in His blood. This separated and left behind those who had rejected so great a salvation, and still, this was not all. There was more to come, and come it did. It brought with it more hurt and sorrow, even though the intensity of pain and suffering is far beyond the logic or comprehension of man; more does were added there also.

When the Lord called to His Christians, graves were opened. The water yielded its dead, and those living were taken up to be with the Lord. Some of those who through salvation got to go up and were taken up were pilots. It did not matter. When they heard the call, the saved pilots and passengers were taken away, leaving the airplanes to fly by itself. Can you see the faces of those left behind? They were in pure panic! Who would land the plane? Who would stop other planes from crashing into them? How could they find the airport? You talk about fear!

Why, some even had family or a friend seated next to them who got the call to go and meet Jesus in the air. As they watched them being called away, they were left behind. Their cries of fear and mercy mingled with those coming up from the ground and filled the skies. They cried out as planes ran out of fuel, crashing into the ground. Some had no way of finding an airport and crashed into mountains, exploding upon impact. People screamed and fainted. They knew they were going to die. But death was no more.

Instead, upon impact, they were awakened by the pain of death. They knew they should be dead. The terrible pain of their bodies smashed in the ground was real. "Oh, what is wrong? My body is burning from the explosion. How can this be? God, let me die! Please, Lord, do not let me suffer like this. Just let me die!" But there was no end to their sorrows. Death and mercy had been removed.

The call found some while they were sleeping. They woke up and rose. Others were awakened by their departure and the voice of Christ Himself. Some wives and husbands cried out to God as they tried to hold onto their departing mates as they left behind the beds where they slept. Those left behind now wanted to go where they did not want to go before. They wanted to go and meet Jesus. They knew what this meant. They knew they should have answered when Jesus called out to them before. Now they could not. Now they begged and cried out to Him, for they knew what was in store; however, the answer was no.

Some parents ran and cried out in torment as they watched their babies taken from their cribs, for the call went out to all, to those born again and to those who were still innocent and pure in heart. No one was left or missed who belonged to God. God's children sang out in praises. Oh, what a wondrous sight as the beautiful souls and bodies of the children of God floated through the air.

Oh, what gladness they be held. They were full of love and peace as they went to meet the Savior. The heart and souls were filled with joy as the moaning and groaning of pain, despair, and agony of those left behind was filtered out. And yet the sight of them leaving did not please those who were left behind, for it brought them to the painstaking truth. They were lost and doomed forever.

Families worldwide were torn apart. Some were traveling in cars and trains. Some were just at home, while others were practicing some mind of faith or another. However, those who had accepted Jesus and put their faith in God's Word were called away. These good, loving families were separated, never to meet again. Maybe it was dear Mom or Dad. In some families, it was the children because they chose to love and follow the teaching of Christ.

Oh, how their souls cried out! Hurt must have torn hearts apart as they stood by and watched their loved ones being taken from them. How hard it was just to endure the rapture's separation. Hands reached out for and even held onto that old sweet mother as she left. Maybe it was grandma or grandpa. To some, it was a beloved brother or sister who floated angelically to the Kingdom of God, leaving them behind.

Just that scene would be more than we could stand, watching that precious loved one leave, leaving behind that burning memory of them, telling us about Jesus and His salvation. It was shattering having to think of the times Jesus called to your soul. Knowing you did not have to be left behind was punishment in itself. But the worst was still to come, and come it did. There would be no end to the woes, no easement of the pain, and no rest for their tormented soul.

Accidents were taking place every second. People trying to run and hide, seeking safety, were struck down by driverless cars. Buses whose drivers were called up were both hit and ran over crowds of people. The pain was intense; the sights were mind- boggling. But there was no end; no death for this moment would last forever. There was no disbelief of the power or truth in God's Word and plan and no escaping it either. There were no disbelievers now.

The very things that made life a little more enjoyable were now causing unbelievable pain and destruction. People were being pinned between two colliding cars, the pressure at impact so great that their heads, fingers, and toes would have to burst open. Yet the pain was relentless and woes unmerciful. Still, death did not come.

The sight of human bodies engulfed in flames, running and screaming, trying to quench the pain, the sight of babies being taken from the arms of moms and dads; oh, how they pleaded for their soul. "Please, Lord! Oh, my God! I beg you, let me come too! I am sorry, Lord! Please take me with my baby!" What sorrow, what soul-aching pain it was for them to be left behind, seeing their sweet precious child in the arms of the Savior. The sight of pain and terror could be seen on pregnant women as their bodies tore open at the sound of His call to enable that unborn child to return back to God.

You cannot begin to think of the pain, sorrow, and woe of God's wrath. This mortal mind would disintegrate at the very first glimpse of God's power and glory. Yet those left behind watched as friends and loved ones were tormented together. The sights would kill us to witness. It was happening to everybody. Payment was due, and they were paying dearly.

Their thoughts were short, their pain was great, and their souls were in torment. And still, it was not over. They still faced the eternal lake of fire. Nothing could help them; nothing that man had depended upon or put his hopes in could give him hope now. None of man's teaching or ways even entered their minds. Their thoughts were on the pain and misery of their souls. There was nothing to help them, no one to come to their aid. They were lost and doomed forever, headed for a devil's torment.

The burning memory of being misled and deceived kindled the fire in their hearts. They had allowed their souls to be traded for the pleasures of this world and gave up the treasures of heaven. Their souls had been robbed by the sins of man and then held hostage until the judgment. Satan used them and abused them with drugs, sex, and false doctrines. But now, nothing else mattered. They cried to God begging for mercy, praying to Him for death, wanting an end to their pain and suffering.

Their minds did not ponder the thought of what they used to do or be. They did not have thoughts of their world and what it offered, for their world and everything in it and on it was being destroyed right before their very eyes. Now their minds were on all the times they had heard about Jesus---how He would save them from God's wrath, how He would come for them. They thought of all the times and chances they had to redeem their souls, but because they did not want to accept the gift of salvation, God now gave them the wrath of His judgment.

Many saw the torture of those who had taught false doctrines of hope. Big, religious, upright, and wealthy men drawled and moaned for the pain and destruction to stop. Churches that used to be a safe haven for souls now were crushing the body and spirits of souls.

Man was running aimlessly, trying to avoid the pain and torment. Then one ran across one of his older children. Their child was in awful pain. They were pinned and being crushed by a slab cement. Think of the sight of your child being in so much pain and pressure, their eyes about to pop out of their sockets. Think of the added hurt as you hear the scream beyond the realm of man's mind. "My god, Daddy! Why didn't you tell me? Mommy! Mommy! For God's sake, why didn't you warn me?" What could they say? What would YOU say?

There is nothing to be said. There is nothing that anyone can do. Everything man had or made was being destroyed. Even the earth on which he lived had to obey God's Word. The crashing planes falling like flies, the tumbling buildings and the explosions that shook the earth so violently, the cries coming from the lost souls made it tremble that much more. It caused dams to break and the earth to quake. God had spoken, and His will was to be.

Their cries were devastating and mournful as they rang out. Their sorrows and torments were unspeakable. The earth shook and trembled with destruction. The lost cried out in such pain and with so much velocity that the whole universe was upset. The earth had plunged out of its orbit and was drawing ever so swiftly, closer and closer to the sun. Or was the sun shaken into a downward plunge to the earth? What did it matter? The result was still the same.

The scorching rays of heat were causing the earth to get very hot. The waters began to dry up. Everything was hot and burning to the touch. If the bodies were not on fire with flames, they began to burn, to scorch in the intense heat rays. This just added another to their many lists of sorrows. Fear grew as the earth began to smolder and smoke.

Think of the shock of some who thought they would not be left behind as they faced the punishment of the doomed as they were smashed, crushed, and burned. They ran around, crying, "But, Lord, isn't I one of yours? Didn't I do good works? Didn't I give money and build huge churches? Look at the followers I had. Why, they worshipped me. They knelt and kissed my hands. I prayed for their sickness, and they were healed."

Others tried to blow their own horns. "Lord, didn't we give our lives to the church? Didn't we help the sick and poor? Didn't we take Holy Communion every week? We traveled and sang. We raised money for charity. We ran and supported orphans." These cries rang out louder and louder. They were in a frantic. The pain was increasing, and the heat was unbearable. They yelled and begged for mercy.

Souls screamed at Jesus but to no avail. They tried to tell Him, "I belong to a church. Oh my god! Stop this pain! Lord, I was baptized as a child. I even confessed my sins to the man at the church." Some pleaded for mercy because they told people to be good. Some cried, "Lord, didn't I learn to preach? Didn't I have my own church? My god, my god! Not me, Lord! I should go with you, Lord! I did my best. I'm not a nobody! Please, Lord, please! Come back for me!"

The answer rang back from heaven. The Lord said in a thunderous voice, "Depart from me, you workers of iniquity. I never knew you (Matthew 7:21--25). What you did, you did for yourself. You wanted the praises of man. Satan swayed you with deceit and tradition. You use only the words that got you a large following. You mistook the spirit and powers of Satan as mine. You did not let me come into your heart. You put YOU in front of ME. No, you are NOT one of mine."

What a rude awakening from those who had followed false preachers and false doctrines. What a pity it was to hear them cry out in pain as they cursed the religious leaders who led them astray. All this time they thought they were right, but they had believed a lie. Now that lie would haunt them over and over, for the truth was revealed.

No disbelieving. No trusting on their knowledge. No misleading lies were being told. Everybody was worried about the torment and punishment of their soul. The only thing being said was "God, help me!" They begged the Lord to ease the pain, to quench the burning fires. "Let me die, Lord!" Pleading for mercy and begging for grace was their only concern. Why, the devil himself had to shut up.

He could not do his dirty deeds any longer, for you see, his time was also up. The truth was known to all. God's Word was being fulfilled word by word. Satan himself knew that he faced eternal damnation. He also knew this time would come, and even he could not stop it. He knew how much God loved man. So, to hurt God, Satan robbed man of his soul. He used sin to blind man of the salvation of Christ. But now all could see, all knew firsthand, for they all faced the power of God's wrath.

There were a lot of people left behind who belonged to a lot of different churches. But Christ had taken His church to heaven. They wailed in pain and tried to hide from facing the mighty wrath, but they too were found to be lost. Just because they were some kinds of a church member did not ease the pain. Their color, size, denomination, and power were cast aside. It did not comfort their soul. Everyone was the same, lost and in pain. There was no way out. The lake of fire was their final destiny.

As the wrath was pouring out on those left behind, and the pain and torture escalated, so did the sun's rays. The earth kept drawing closer and closer to the sun each moment. Trees began to scorch; the ground itself was like hot coals to man's feet. Water was now all dried up. No livestock, pets, or animals had survived. The trees and grass were burned up. The earth was like fire.

I cannot express, and there are no words to describe. It's humanly impossible to think of the suffering of burned, crushed, and mutilated bodies being tormented and punished to death without dying. The picture is not a pretty one, and this is not the end.

The earth and sun were getting closer and closer to each other. Everything on the face of this world had been demolished and now was melting away. The broken bodies of man now burning either from the memory of seeing Jesus leaving them behind or from the fires of gas and oil or from the direct heat of the sun. Nevertheless, all was being destroyed and melting away.

Man, still crying out to God, could not hardly walk. The ground was setting their feet on fire, their bodies throbbing in pain, their souls and heart torn apart. They had been mangled to no end. Soon, nothing would be left. Man, and his world were burning up and melting away. They cried out again, "God! God! Have mercy! Please, please, ease our pain!"

Then all at once, the earth shook. God answered their cries, but it was not to ease their pain. It was to bring about the end. Now came time to put all things into place, thus fulfilling the final chapter and promise of His Word.

God Himself reached down with all His power and glory. He lifted hell and all its inhabitants, being those who died without Christ whose souls were burning it its fiery flames. He also gathered together all those on the earth facing the torture and the torments of being left out of the rapture.

Then . . . the end. Just as the heavens and earth of our world burned up and vanished, God plunged hell and the souls therein along with Satan and his spirits together with the lost souls of the living into the eternal lake of fire, there to be forever! There to endure and suffer the teeth-gnashing pain and agony of its flames.

Oh, what a terrible ending it was, having God cast you into a lake of fire, having your body engulfed in eternal flames, feeling the pain, smelling the burning of your own flesh, watching as you see your mom burn, listening as you hear one of your children crying out in torment.

Your heart wept for them, but you also had to endure your own torment. Yes, you were sorry for them. You hurt for them because you could have warned them, but you did not. Now you both burn; God had spoken. It was done. Nothing but heaven and the lake of fire remained. Eternity would last forever.

God was pleased. His children were safe in their new home. All evil and every lost soul was in the fiery lake of fire forever. The two would never meet or mix ever again. There was no more sin. There was no more Satan. There were no more death and no more time. At last, God was in command, and everything went according to plan. Praise His holy name. Amen.

Now all those who came forth in answer to the Lord's call rose and went up with joy in their hearts, for they went to meet and be with the blessed Savior. As they left here, they went shouting and singing praises unto God, for their journey would take them to the grand and glorious Kingdom of God.

All the angels stood throughout heaven to receive those whose robes were washed white as snow by the blood of the Lamb. As they were welcomed, Jesus opened those pearly gates, which led to their God's "Holy City." The redeemed were granted entrance into His Kingdom by His Son just as He said, "Enter, thy good and faithful servants. Your battles are over. Come in and receive that which was promised to you and prepared just for you" (Matthew 25:21).

Oh, what divine and pure joy over swept their souls as they passed through those gates of pearl, to then stand on streets paved with pure gold, as they began to behold the wondrous sights and bask in the beauty of this most holy city of God, the place of comfort and rest for their soul, a place of blessed peace and full of glory, which would last forever. Yes, it was the city of

God, but it was also their heavenly home.

Upon entering, they fell at the feet of Jesus and kissed them in thanks and praise for the salvation of their souls. What a joy it was to know the trials and tribulations of this life were over. Oh, how glad they were to know they would now live forever in the presence of Almighty God, living with Jesus and being sheltered in the arms of God. Oh, what a place to be!

Think for a moment. Just let your mind go. Let your heart dwell on a place that was built by the hands of the Lord. A holy place. A place where you would never need or want for anything. A place of peace and divine grace. A place where you will be cared for and kept by the power, glory, and mercy of God the heavenly Father. Now know this place is real. It is heaven. A place full of love and happiness. An eternal place that gives you forever to enjoy.

Well, these thoughts do not give justice to the magnificence of its glory. There is no means known to man to describe or even tell us of its glorified wonders, for we are limited on words and by what our minds are able to comprehend, as well as by what our hearts can endure. God even tells us in His Words that we are not capable to go beyond the realm or thoughts of this world. Therefore, man's eyes have not seen, his ears have never heard, neither has it ever so much as entered into his mind the many wonders and glorious blessing laid up in store for God's children in their eternal home.

Just think how in this world would the all so mighty God with His powers and glory be expected to break down His greatness into mere words of man? That would enable us to visualize or relate to the great wonders and glory it is to inherit His Kingdom.

This is not possible. This would limit God to our expectations. God is much more than we could ever know. Our minds and bodies cannot endure just one thought or glimpse of the miracles and wonders to come. That is why we must be changed. God has to prepare us for His glory.

We must lay these bodies of sin and earthly statute down and must receive new whole immortal bodies. Only then will we be able to endure the glamour and enjoy the greatness of living forever in the Holy Kingdom. Only the bodies not knowing corruption, only bodies made of God full of His glory, would contain our spiritual being and last throughout the endless ages of eternity. So, the call came. We were changed and called up.

They became angels and saints of God through Christ Jesus. As they inherited their home in heaven, they began to enjoy and marvel at the wondrous glory of this city of God. Some went to and for. They met with many of the old prophets and saints. Others just walked about in amazement as they sang a new song of praise, a song only they could sing. "I have been washed in the precious blood of the Lamb."

What a thrill it was to meet the likes of David, Jacob, Moses, and Abraham: these Godly men of the Old Testament. It was great to sit and listen to them tell of their dealings and relationships with God.

It really meant a lot to be able to meet and hug the necks of Paul, John, and Peter, to be able to thank them for what they did for Jesus and how their lives molded ours, how their empowered teachings brought you closer and closer to the Savior. Yes, it was truly great knowing them as your brothers in Christ!

But the greatest gift of all was to be able to hold the nail-scarred hand of my Lord Jesus and then worship, praise, and thank Him for the saving of our souls. Just to be able to be in His presence was worth living a Christian life. Now we are blessed to live in the splendor of His glory forever. What a reward! Praise God in the highest! I want to be able to kiss the wounds that held my Jesus to that cross, which caused His divine blood to be shed for the redemption of our sins.

Songs of praise rang out as the children of God began to thank Him for His love, mercy, and grace. They began to see the many rights and joys unfold as they walked within those walls of jasper, along the banks of the river of life, just beyond the hills of glory. They began to praise the Holy Son of God, for He sat on the right hand of the throne of God. This was truly a wondrous sight to behold. This began their first moment in God's Holy eternal Kingdom.

Now their joy, peace, and heartwarming wonders had begun. People were reunited with brothers and sisters in Christ whom they had witnessed to or preached to. What a thrill it was to see a soul you led out of damnation or to see again that preacher who first told you about Jesus. Oh, how sweet and precious were those memories.

However, one function of their memory had to be altered. Some of their memory was erased or limited, for God knew man could not begin to fully enjoy the wonders of heaven if this memory kept reminding him of friends or loved ones who were left behind. No man could have peace knowing that because loved ones or friends had rejected Christ and now faced the painful torments of God's wrath.

So those parts of the memory and all the events or things that were bad, sad, or painful were erased. NO memory of sickness or death. NO thoughts of good-byes or hard times. God did this to enable His children to fully be at rest and in peace.

Now they were ready to spend eternity as God had intended. A blissful life of sweet peace and harmony. A life without egos or jealousies. A life full of grace and love. No pain or death. A life free from sin and corruption. A life that would go on forever without sickness or tears. Yes, this was truly heaven.

Just think about a child of God whose life on earth was ugly and painful. Their bodies were disfigured by one means or another. Then as Jesus called, they were changed. They got a new body, a glorious body free from defects. Their new bodies were the bodies of angels, beautiful to the sight. Yes, others were called who were blind, and yet they served Christ. Oh, how they too praised God, for as they were called up, they were given sight. God gave them new bodies and healed their blinded eyes. Now they could behold the beauty of heaven! How glorious would it be, to be blind and have your eyes touched by God's hand and have your first sight to be the beautiful face of sweet Jesus? Praise God!

What a relief it was to some as their wounds of pain and war, which marred the body and soul, vanished away by the power and love of God. How the blistered hands of hard work were smoothed away. Why, God even wiped the wrinkles and pain of old age away. Yes, even tired, worn-out bodies received joy and eternal rest. Well, praise the sweet name of Jesus for the happiness and joy of those who followed Him. This was just the beginning. The peace and wonders had just begun. Yes, the mighty grace of God had much more in store. Amen. Praise God! What a wonder and blessing it was to see the peace and rest of sickened bodies as they were made whole and pain free. Think of having your body eaten away with cancer or HIV. Think of those who were bedridden because of a stroke or injury. Their lives were limited. Oh, but not the love of Christ. They now praised Him! Their pain was relieved, and their bodies purified, all through the healing powers of our blessed Savior.

As the call to glory came, it also brought happiness to children around the world who had been saved. Some of them had spent their lives in a wheelchair, never being able to walk or run, never being able to be like other children. Now they leaped with joy as they ran down the streets of glory and played on the hills of life everlasting. Just let your mind ponder the acts of love, mercy, and grace the children of God were experiencing. It was glorious! People who were blind had their first visual sight to be the saints of God going up to be with Jesus. Those who had never walked had their first steps to be on the clouds of glory. Those not hearing any sounds heard the soft precious voice of Jesus as He said, "Come, my child. Suffer no more. Come sit by God's throne." People who hated their looks because of burns or abuse now smiled as they were made holy. This list of healings goes on and on. The joys and gladness go on and on as do the endless ages of bliss, the eternal Kingdom of God. Amen.

As you think of these acts of mercy and wonder, you only have a glimpse of glory. Your heart and soul would burst open with joy. You could not stand just the thoughts of the many glorious wonders in store for God's people. We as humans could not withstand the warmth, love, and passion bestowed upon the redeemed. The depth and degree are immeasurable to man. We are limited, and our minds and bodies are inferior. But not in glory. We become as Christ. We are able to receive all the father has to give.

Think for a moment if you can, without any distractions. Haven't you got a dear mom or dad How about a grandpa or grandma, a son or daughter, or maybe a brother or sister who died leaving behind their testimony of Jesus. Wouldn't it thrill you heart? Wouldn't it warm the most inner part of your soul to be able to be held in their arms again? These are not idle words but the promises of God to His people. This is heaven. This is the enactment of God's Holy Word. This is the everlasting land of joy, peace, happiness, and glory. This is your land if Christ is your Savior.

A place of no sin, no despair, and no sickness. The children of God had inherited the beautiful city of God, there to bask in its glory and to bestow all the wonders and power it beholds, never to see the last breath of life stolen from the soul by the sting of death. Praise God forever! Death had no more sting, and life has no more limits.

Oh, blessed is the Lamb of God, who by the power of God conquered death, hell, and grave. Oh, how sweet is the victory over this life, how precious is the salvation of souls, how grand and glorious is the reward. Yes, they sang the praises. They shouted the victory, for Jesus had enabled them to inherit all its grand and glory forever: the Kingdom of God.

Praises like this were ringing out. You could hear the shouts and cries of joy throughout the boundaries of heaven. For those washed in the blood of God's only begotten Son had received their promised land. They had entered into a land prepared by Jesus Christ himself. A land of sweet milk and pure honey. A restful home for the tired and weary. A peaceful land for the troubled soul. A rewarding place. A land where they could live and enjoy the many blessings of the Lord, with the best part being it had all just begun.

Yes, from the portals of heaven, praises glorifying His name will ring out and forever ring on. As his precious Christians receive their blessings of an eternal life, basking in the love and grace of God, their praises will ring out with such glory. They will echo throughout the lake of eternal fire.

They will serve as a reminder to the lost souls. The praises will trouble their minds and put sorrow in their hearts as they are reminded of the mercy, peace, and joy they could have and should have had, if they would have only taken heed to the Word and put their faith in Jesus. They would not have to receive and endure the tortuous and angry wrath of God's judgment. Praise God forever! Praise His holy name!

Now I know the rapture did not take place, for I am still here, and you are still reading what will take place. But even though we do not know WHEN, we do know it WILL take place. It did not take place as Brother Dave awoke that morning, but it may when you awake in the morning. It may be tomorrow or next week or even next year. But it will be.

I also know that I did not go into a lot of detail as to all that takes place at or in the end. You can read about those things in the book of Revelation. I just wanted you to know that no one escapes God's plan. In His plan is the taking up of His people and the judgment of those who are lost and left behind.

We all fit into God's plan. We all have a place in it. We all must know that the great day of our Lord is coming. You will receive your just reward. God will put things in order and put you in your place. So be ready for His coming, or get ready for His wrath.

Remember that you do have a choice. Christ saw to that. He gave up His home in glory to come to our aid. He could have called on heaven's angels when man put Him on the cross, but then man's soul would forever be lost. So He willingly laid upon the cross as rusty nails were driving into His hands, the same precious hands that had touched and healed the sick and raised the dead, the same hands that touched rocks and caused them to give water for the thirsty, the One who had done no wrong, the same One who called to heaven for bread, and it was given to feed the hungry. Jesus did not have to lay on the old rugged cross but praise God He did! He did so for me. Yes, because He loved us so. He gave His life that we would have life eternal (John 3:16).

Jesus paid the supreme sacrifice. He shed His holy blood for the remission of our sins. He alone is our Savior. He holds the keys of death, hell, and grave. He is the door to heaven. He is the mediator between man and God. He is the builder, founder, and the head of the church. He did for us what no one else could, for He is Jesus, the Son and glory of God!

Even though the call has not come, even though the trumpet has not sounded, you must give some thought to eternity, for the last tick of the clock may be the next tick you hear. What will be your destiny? Would you be one gathered to go and meet Jesus in the air? Or would you be left behind? I pray you become a Christian.

I pray you take heed to and listen to God's Word, for therein is he warning of damnation and torture of those who are lost and already condemned. Therein is also the promise of a heavenly home to those who are born again. A home of peace and joy. A home everlasting in victory. A place made just for you. A home that awaits you.

Would you not rather inherit the Kingdom of God where your soul would live forever? Where it would be blessed and kept by the love and grace God rather than have to face the pain and torment of God Almighty's wrath? Where you will suffer throughout the endless ages of eternity?

Now do you still think that it does not matter what you think or believe? You cannot think that God's Word will be altered or changed. You cannot believe God has to do it YOUR way, do you? God did not consult with you when He created life. He did not ask for your approval when He destroyed this earth with the great flood. Jesus did not ask you if He could bring salvation to man.

This means He does not need your approval or your help. When He takes charge, His Word will stand.

You will die your death when God calls for you. There is no way to prevent it. You will face judgment as ordered by the Word of God, regardless of what you think or believe. You will receive your just reward, whether you want it or not. Do not let Satan cause you to be fooled or to believe a lie. God has given His Word. He has made a promised. He will do exactly what He says.

Give some strong thought to those Words of God. Without respect of person, regardless of who or what you are, what you think or believe, or your knowledge or wealth, God says every knee shall bow. Every tongue shall confess that Jesus is the Son of God. Listen, these are not just some idle words. This is not a game. You can decide to put it off. You can decide to ignore it. But you will bow, and you will acknowledge God's Son.

The question is WHEN. I pray it will be when you ask Him to save your soul. When you accept Him as your Lord and Savior, so that you can await and look forward to His coming.

I hope it is not as your soul slips into the fiery pits of hell, for after death, there is no mercy. When you draw your last breath, as you close your eyes in death, you will know who Jesus is. You will cry out for Him to save you, but He will not hear your cries, for He knows not who you are.

I also hope you do not wait until you watch the born again go up to meet Jesus as He stands upon the clouds in full power and glory. I really pray that you do not wait until you are left behind before you bow and call upon His name, f or then, He will execute the fulfillment of judgment. You will know the power and glory of God's Son at that point. But at that point, at that moment, your eternity has begun, and God's wrath is upon you. You will want mercy, but you will run from the face of His Son.

Listen.

Listen as He speaks to your heart. You need to hear and answer the sweet call. Yes, the Lord now calls for you to come unto Him. He wants to save your soul. He died to redeem you of your sins.

Listen. Right at this moment, even as you are reading, He is dealing with your heart. He is calling you unto salvation. He is offering you God's Kingdom. Please, please do not turn Him away.

Do not let Satan deceive you. Do not be deprived of God's mercy and grace. Do not let the ideas or teachings of man turn you away from the glories of God. Call out the name of Jesus. Do not be defeated. You have victory through Christ the Lord.

I know the thoughts Satan is rushing through your head, but you must not let them overrule the tender loving call of the Savior. You must not ignore so great of a love as Christ as for you. Forget everything you have thought, been told, or read. Do not look for an alternative, for there is none. Just let your mind and heart ponder on the goodness and grace of God's Son. Heaven awaits you.

Heaven is one man's reward, just as hell is another. Heaven is for those of us who accept and live by the Word of God. Hell, and its torment is for those who choose not to believe in or accept God's Word. Do not be like the man who died and cried out in pain as his feet felt the flames of hell. Do not be like those who scratched and begged at the door of Noah's ark for mercy, for you will be one when Christ comes and calls for His redeemed who will be left behind.

Will you at least give God a chance? You have nothing to lose and heaven to gain. If the Word of God is not right, if it does not bless and bring peace to your souls, you can go back to your old ways. You have not hurt yourself or lost anything but time. But when God proves His Word to be true, look at what you have lost. Look at what it will cost your soul. The stakes are high. Are you willing to take that chance? You better be, for that is exactly the chance you are taking, and you are playing for keeps.

Know and remember that Satan wants you to believe that your way is right. He does not want you to give God a chance, so he helps man to discredit and downplay the power and the truth, for he knows the Word will free you of his entrapment and the wrath of judgment.

Will your name be written in the Lamb's Book of Life? When the last tick has tucked, when Christ comes, will He call for you, or will you be left behind as you beg and plead for another chance? You do not have to be left behind. Satan does not have to have control of your eternal destiny. There is nothing in this world worth losing your soul over. There is nothing you can do, be, or buy that even comes close to the joys and rewards of serving Christ. Do not be fooled by man or the things of this world. They cannot offer you what God promises you.

You need to forget about trying so hard to make life a little better and building for a tomorrow. Your life can never be better if it is based on the artificial pleasures of this world. You need to base your life on the joys of the Lord. You need to stop thinking of what tomorrow will bring because your tomorrow may never come. Where do you have a promise of tomorrow?

Your tomorrow may never come. You may not have until the rapture of God's children before you face God's wrath. This may be the day you lay this body down in death as your soul slips over the jagged walls and into the pits of hell. This may very well be the day the Lord sends the death angel to your door. This is not a drummed-up scare tactic; this is called REALITY. You know you are going to die; you just do not know when or how.

No one can give you a tomorrow except God, your creator. No one can give you salvation except God. You can only be saved when you hear the call from God, so even if you have a tomorrow, you better make sure you do not drift so far away that you cannot hear the spirit calling. You need to do a reality check.

First, you may be taking your last breath. Second, Jesus may come in the next moment.

Third, you may have told God "NO" for the last time.

That is the reality of life, and there is nothing you can do about it.

You had better put out those thoughts the devil is using to distract you from hearing and obeying the call of salvation. I know that he is trying to trick you. I also know that he is trying to deceive you. He used the same tactics on me just as he does on everyone. He does not have anything new to use, just his same ol', same ol'. You would think we would be wise to them by now. He likes to use the "Oh, what will your friends think?" Well, who cares! When you face the pits of hell, can your friends turn down the heat? He uses thoughts like *I will not be able to have any fun.* I ask you this: where is the fun in hell? *I like running around drinking, getting high, and having sex.* Good for you. Now just where and when do you suppose God will let you out of hell so you can run around? It does not matter what thoughts run through your head; it is all for the same purpose. Satan wants to keep you from going to heaven. He wants you to suffer with him. Listen, we have all heard these same thoughts. He has a lot of them to throw at you. I know it can get hard, for the closer you get to accepting Christ or God's Word, the harder Satan works.

He knows if you get a taste of the blessed spirit, you will no longer thirst for the evils of his. Here is a thought to ponder:

"I know my life can end any day, so why would I choose to do something that will lead me to hell? What does this world or man have to offer that I would choose to go to hell for?"

Food for thought: if you tell Jesus no today, you may be hell tomorrow. Was it or was it not worth it?

You need to put Satan and his spirits in check. He does not care anything about you. He will use family, friends, loved ones, money, power, and the lists go on. In other words, he will use whatever it takes to get to you. He does not try and lure you to go to hell. He is the reason for hell. He will cause your soul to burn. Do not listen to him.

Let Christ come and make His abode with you. He loves you more than anyone. No one has a greater love for than the Lamb of God. He died for you and now stands at your heart's door, pleading to you with those nailed-scarred hands, reaching out to save you, save you from that devil's hell where Satan awaits you. Just now as He calls, listen. He is pleading for you to come and make your peace with God. Please do not let this be the memory that haunts your soul as you forever burn in that eternal lake of fire. Do not reject the salvation of the Son of God, just to have to accept the pain and torture of God's angry wrath. Let Jesus come in and give unto you the blessings and wonders promised to God's children. Let Him prove to you that Satan is a liar.

I know you may not be a bad person; however, if you are not born again, you are lost and doomed to face the damnation of His judgment. Do not think that because you are a good and respected person that God will not let you or make you face all that pain and agony. That is the most used trick by Satan and man. God cannot lie; therefore, He will not change or alter your punishment just because you were a good and moral person.

If He would do this, He would have to go back on His Word. He would have to lie and cause Jesus to be a liar. He would have to have Jesus to die in vain. Why would He send His Son and then allow Him to die for our sins if sin could be erased by good deeds or good morals? Well, I hope you do not live in this fantasy. Satan will try to have you believe this and many other foolish ideas.

God's Word is true. It has stood the test of time, and it will stand throughout eternity. It will also stand in judgment as the judge of man. So, take it to heart and believe it when the Bible says that God gave us His Son to pay for our sins. God will save us by forgiving our sins through Jesus. God will take us to heaven when He sends Jesus for us. God will punish the nonbelievers by the pouring out of His wrath. God does not give us a choice to either accept His word or not. You must decide to make heaven your home. If you do, then you have chosen to go to hell. So be it. Please do not wait until His saving grace is gone before you realize the truth. Do not take the chance that there will be a tomorrow. Do not expect God to keep on calling and calling only to be pushed away and pushed away. Sooner or later, God is going to be fed up with the sinful mockery of His Words and of His Son.

Sooner or later, man will face His judgment.

Jesus has done all that He could. He bore our burdens and felt our pain. He gave His life so we can be born again, so please, for the sake of your soul, let Jesus unveil the truth, free you from your sin, and save your soul from damnation. Let Him prepare you to inherit that holy city of God. Do not push back the hand that reaches out to save and shelter you from God's eternal torments.

You know that He is calling and reaching for you right now.

That is why Satan is trying so hard to trick and deceive you. As Jesus is trying to draw you near, Satan is whispering, "Lay that book down. Let us go do something. You do not need to go read this crazy stuff. He is telling you this stuff that is not for you." Well, Satan IS a liar. This stuff is for you. It is for anyone who wishes to be saved from God's wrath and wants to inherit His Holy Kingdom.

I fully understand the pressure and the thoughts being used to pull you away from the joys and blessings of God, for I have walked on the same path. I felt the same way as you do. I too have been led away from accepting my salvation by the tricks of Satan. I fought the same battles as you now fight, the one between your heart and your soul against your flesh and mind.

Yes, I too worried what would my spouse think. What would she do if I choose to follow Christ? I also wondered about my friends and family. How they would react. I worried about my coworkers; how they would laugh and kid me. Satan was quick to remind me of all the things I would not be allowed to do anymore, of all the fun I would not be having. But then I knew that I did not want to die and go to hell. Yes, I know exactly what you are going through.

You see, I am the man in the beginning of this book. I am the one that Satan convinced and deceived. This is until I dreamed of my soul being engulfed by the flames of hell. I am the one who stood in church holding onto the pew. I was fighting my soul's desire to be saved. Yes, me and the devil fought NOT to answer as the sweet Savior called for my soul. So, you see, I know very well what you are going through.

How well I remember how hard it was as I tried to make up my mind. Satan would not let go. He kept trying to mislead and confuse me. I do know how hard it was to take that first step, but praise God! I did! And I have never been happier or the same since.

That first step was tough until I told Jesus, "Lord, I am coming." Then He was right there to bring me unto the throne of mercy and grace.

I will never forget how wonderful I felt as the bonds of sin were broken, and I accepted Christ as my Savior. I cannot tell you anything but that I had a personal touch from heaven that cannot be compared to anything. My soul was overflowing with joy and bliss as Jesus came into my heart. I cannot explain the love and peace I now have, nor can I tell you of all God's goodness, mercy, and grace. But I can tell you, without a shadow of a doubt, that the best is yet to come, for I know that my name is recorded in heaven. I also know I have a home prepared by Jesus Himself. I know He will lead me and keep me until the call comes from glory, and then He will open the gates and welcome me into that blessed holy city of God. No, I no longer have to worry about the things of this world, for I am just passing through. I am on my way to the streets of glory where I will live with King Jesus and God, my heavenly Father.

Yes, I do know what you are going through. I also know who you are dealing with, but praise God! I now know what a relationship with God can be. And I want you to know that yes, I am in this book. My name is David. But being in the Lamb's Book of Life is more important, and like mine, your name can be listed therein. Yes, you too can answer the call to glory if you answer your call to salvation.

If not, then your name will be added to the roll call of hell, for either heaven or hell is where you will spend the endless time of eternity, for with or without your belief or your approval, the Word of God will come to pass, so do not be shortchanged. Do not let Satan cause you to lose your soul. He is lying to you by clouding your judgment. Come and take part in the joys of salvation, and avoid the miseries of damnation.

Take time right now. Go back and think of the things that you have read. Then ask God to show you the right path of life. You will see then the things found in this book were written from me to you because I can and I am concerned for you. I do not want you to be naïve to the tactics of Satan and his spirits of sin.

I wanted you to know of my life, how I was misled into a false security, how there was so much pressure against me as I sought to find peace with God. As I sought God, I found the Words and ways of the Lord satisfying to my soul. Yet Satan still tried to deceive me. I wanted you to know that it was not until I found Jesus that my life was made whole.

I want you to see the desperate need we have for salvation. I hope to at least get you to think about facing God in judgment, whether it be at your death or the great day of the Lord. I just want you to realize how the seducing spirits of sin and Satan cause man to act carefree and to think foolishly.

If I have helped you in any way, then I am very glad. If I have not, then I am sorry, for I feel that I have let you down. But I know where help can be found. You can find it in the Word and love of God. I urge you to go into it. Read the promises God makes to those who believe in and accept the saving power of Christ.

Read about the many joys and blessings received by those who elect to serve the Lord. Let the Word of God give you the truth and knowledge of His coming. Be informed. Know the reaction to your action. See the glory and wonders of God as they unfold to those who are born again. See also the pain and torments of His wrath as it is unleashed upon all who deny or reject the call to be born again.

You need to read and understand about the powers of sin and Satan. You need to know of man's weakness against them. You need to see if you do not rely on the Lord, then you will be deceived and misled into the damnation of your soul. You also need to realize that churches, men and women, families, lust and greed will all be used against you.

Satan holds no boundaries. He will use, misuse, and corrupt anything that is not anchored in the blood of Jesus. He will gain your trust and rob you of your soul. He will cause you to put such an importance on things of this world, knowing that only these things that are of God will stand when this world is destroyed, that you would be willing to deny the Son of God.

Do not allow your soul to be deprived of Paradise. Not because of some man-made doctrine. Do not let man's knowledge make you naive enough to think that there is another or better way. Remember, anyone or anything proclaiming Jesus but denying the power and salvation thereof is not teaching the true Word, and it is not of God.

These are not my words or my ideas; this is the Word of God. You need to stop listening to the spirits used of sin. You need to read the Holy Word, for it was given to us by God. It will lead us to Christ, and it is the only thing that will take us to glory and the gates of heaven.

I want you to take a minute and think about death. I know you do not like to think about or even talk about dying. Well, guess what? Satan does not want you too either. Food for thought: we see people dying all the time. We know we will also die. For now, let us forget about the pain sometimes associated with death.

If death is just separation from this life into eternal rest.

If 90 percent of what is preached at funerals is true, like "they have gone on to a better place" or "they are better off now."

If we can die and come back as something or someone else, then why do fear dying? We do not like to discuss death as it pertains to us?

If death is better than this life, why would we not want to die? If it is a better place to go, then let us go! Why stay here? If we get to come back, then let us give it a shot. If we do not like that life, then we could do it again. If we know these things, then why are we so reluctant to die and so sad when someone we love dies.

Because we do not know. However, allowing ourselves to believe in these things is easier than facing the truth.

The truth being Jesus, says and who is better than He to know about life after death. He tells us after you are born, you have two appointments. The first is with death. The second is with the judgment. Both of which you will keep. We know and accept the first appointment. It is the second one that we do not want to acknowledge.

But if we accepted the Words of our Savior and prepared for the second appointment, we would have nothing to fear. It might be that it is not the unknown that causes us to fear and be uneasy about life after death but the hidden innermost thoughts of facing the judgment of God with an unbelieving heart.

You say you do not fear or believe in the judgment or in a heaven and a hell. What if you are wrong? That should make you uneasy about dying. That is why it is uneasy to talk about. That is why Satan does not want you to think about it. He knows what is coming. Man will die, and after death, he will receive the choice of judgment that he chose for the eternal destiny of his soul.

If this was not so, why does God send His spirit to draw you to repentance? Why are there forces to lure you from accepting God's Word as the truth? Look, man can accept anything he sets his mind to. He can cause himself to believe in whatever he wants. That is until it comes to God's Word and ways. You can decide to go anywhere and do anything you want, but not until you decide to seek Christ do you get influenced by spirits.

This has to mean something to you. You have got to realize and face reality. There is a hell. If you do not accept the Savior, you will find yourself in hell. You will be pressured and pressured to ignore and disbelieve, but Jesus died to give you victory. Do not be deprived of heaven. You deserve to be saved, and you have the right to redeem your soul. The blood of Jesus gives you that right.

Do not make it harder than it is. Just listen as Jesus calls you into salvation. Christ has done all the work. The hard part is over. There is nothing you have to do except to accept and believe. You do not have to buy it. You are not asked to work for it. There are no rituals to go through. You are saved by grace through faith. It is a gift of God brought to you by His loving Son, the Lord and Savior Jesus Christ.

I have got some good news and some bad news. Here is the good news. It is found in John 3:16. The good news is that He who believes in the Son of God has everlasting life. This means from the moment you accept Christ as your Savior; you do not have a "might" or a "could have" or a "maybe has." It says you DO have. That is a promise, and God gives you, His Word.

Here is the bad news. It is in the same verse. The first half is the good news. The last half is the bad news, which is that he who believes NOT is already condemned. That is to say God condemns your souls because you received not His only Son. There is no if, ands, or buts about it. So sayeth the Lord.

Think of the bad news in that verse. If you do not believe that you are already condemned, God has doomed your soul to face and endure the pain and suffering of His wrath. It does not ask for a reason, alibi, or excuse. It says that you are sentenced to an eternal life of torment and torture. That is how simple it is. There are no in between, no believing this part and not that, or a chance that God is going to alter His promises. It is either that you believe and received God's blessings or you do not believe and have to receive His wrath. It is your choice.

I remember lying down at night in fear, for I knew the thin string of life could be severed by the cold blade of death before I awoke. I also knew that it did not matter whether I believed or did not believe if the Word and promises of God were true. They would be proven to me as my soul began its eternal destiny into the flames of hell, which I did not believe in. That bothered me.

The last thing I wanted was for God to say, "I told you so."

That is why you need to listen to the Savior as He calls. If there was not anything to save you from, then why Jesus be calling to you, and why would Satan be telling you that it is not true? Please do not make God prove Himself to you. Take Him at His Word. Do not let this be your final denial. Do not reject His call, and do not turn and walk away, for the price for doing so is far too great to pay.

Remember, you are living your judgment with the passing of each day. You have received the good news as well as the bad news. Your court is in session. The trial is about over. The Word of God is both the judge and the jury. What will your sentence be? I pray you will be acquitted by the blood of the Lamb.

I pray in the name of Jesus as He touches your heart, as He begs for your soul that you let Jesus plead your case. Do not be found guilty in the crime of John 3:16, the denial and rejection of God's beloved Son. This crime carries with it a mandatory life sentence. Therefore, if God pronounces you guilty, you will face a never-ending life term of punishment. You will be imprisoned in the flames of hell and tortured throughout eternity.

You need to think of your soul and what God has in store. You really owe it to yourself to hear and take heed as the Lord knocks at your heart's door. Let the devil know that you are tired of being used and lied to. Let him know NOW that you will not be defeated or deprived. Christ died to give you a new birth. Now let Him give you the best God has to offer.

How can you turn your back on a love such as that? Why would you want to? How can you allow Satan or the things of this world deprive your own soul of a heavenly home? An eternal home built and blessed by all the power and glory of God. What would the profit be if you gained everything you wanted of this world but lost your soul (Mark 8:36)? Then I wonder in the end, what would you give if you could to save your soul? Right now, what would you turn your back on to avoid hell?

Seek Jesus, and you will have the sweet thrill of victory. You will never feel the agony of defeat. You do not want to be like those who will see the Word of God proven as His wrath is poured out over them. Accept the Word of God with your faith, not with its fulfillment. Amen.

It would be great. What a blessing it would be if someday after a while (or maybe tomorrow), we could meet in that grand and glorious Kingdom of God, there to sit by the beautiful river of life, the one that flows directly from God's own throne. We can join in and sing; we can offer up our praise for the immeasurable love, mercy, and grace bestowed upon our souls as God delivers the promise of His people. Praise be to God!

If this cannot be so, then we will have to bid each other farewell. However, here is my prayer that I leave with you. I pray for God to help you and show you the errors of your ways. I pray for you to see the truth and saving grace found in His Word. I ask God to let you see the devil for what he is. I hope that you will always know the love and mercy of God and not ever know the anger and revenge of His wrath.

I also thank God for the loving Savior those dwells in me. I thank Him for the opportunity to reach out to you, for I have a love for and carry a burden for your soul. I would love to see you saved. Jesus wants to, and He would love to save you, but it is up to you. You are the one who must ask to be saved or be the one who has to deal with being lost and damned.

If by now you have not taken the time to ask God for the salvation of your soul, if you have not asked Him for guidance and help, I pray that you have at least decided to find out more about the teachings and the gospel of Christ. I really hope you see your need to learn and obey the Words of God. I pray you will go into His Word or better yet into a good Bible-believing, Bible- preaching church.

Not a man-made, man-pleasing church but a true church, one where you can hear the Word of God as it is preached and empowered by the Holy Ghost. I do not mean the fall down on the floor, kicking and rolling, or the snake-holding, holier-than- thou Bible thumping, man-made spirit.

I mean the Holy Ghost of God. The Comforter who brings sweet Jesus into your soul. The Holy Ghost sent to guide and to strengthen. The holy Comforter who empowers us to be soul- winning witnesses to the love and saving grace of our Lord and Savior Jesus. That Holy Ghost.

The one who makes a change in our life. The one who gets rid of pride, hate, greed, and lust. The one who causes us to love everybody, even our enemies. The one who puts us in one faith and one accord to love, serve, and worship God our heavenly Father, through His Son. Amen. Praise God!

I sincerely ask God to let you know the difference between a man who wants to be a preacher, who studies and is taught to preach, or one who is "self-made," and a man called of God to preach, for only when you hear the Word through the power of the Spirit will it do wonders for the soul.

Know too if it is not by a man of God, if it is not empowered by the Holy Spirit, then you only hear the enticing words and ideas of man, which are one of the biggest deceiving tricks Satan uses against us. He can use this because we would rather listen to and believe in someone who tells us we are right and that we are doing good before we could accept someone who tells us we are bad and doing wrong.

In other words, Satan causes us to believe what we want to hear because it makes us look big and feel good. That is why there are so many churches, doctrines, and religions. We would rather believe a lie than to admit that we are wrong. We will accept anything Satan throws at us as long as we do not have to depend on someone else or say that we are sorry and ask for forgiveness.

I guess that is just the way we are. That is why so many people are going to hell.

That is also why it is so important to go to a church founded on, set up, and run according to the Holy Word of God. That is where we can be fed in spirit and grow in grace. It is where we are strengthened and given victory over the trials and tribulations of this sinful world, a place where we can gather to worship and praise in spirit and in truth.

If you find a church that reaches out the lost by preaching and teaching the bloodshed salvation of Christ rather than building up members, funds, or egos, then you can be sure it is of God. For His spirit will bless it and be in the midst of it. If you are not looking to be fooled, then you will not be.

You will know when God is in the presence of a service, for His spirit will touch the very souls of man. His Holy Spirit will bless those who are His. It will also call to and deal with the hearts of those whose souls are in need. It may be by the prayers of the righteous as they pray for you. It might be a song of love and praise. If not, then by the hearing His Word, for it is not His will that any should perish.

That is why He gives the power and truth of His Word, for in it we are given the why, the how, and the means of salvation. It teaches us the ways and lives that are pleasing unto God. The word gives us the many promises made to His people. It tells of their inheritance of His Holy Kingdom.

Then we learn of its power of freedom. How only it can draw and free a soul from the bonds of Satan and the ways of man. We are shown how it is like a two-edged sword. How it cuts out the heart of sin and stone at the same time, replacing it with a new heart, a heart filled with love and peace.

It also tells us of the importance of church. How we should not neglect the assembling of ourselves together for the worship of the Lord. How we should go even more often as we see the day of our Lord approaching. Then it goes on to warn us to just how fast that day could be at hand.

Regardless of what you think or believe, you must admit we are our own worst enemy. We try to explain away or ignore away what we do not want to believe, but you must know and realize the world cannot continue on in this shape much longer. Sin is dominating our lives and lifestyles.

There is no way you can read the newspaper or watch TV; there is no way you can read this book or even take a good look at what is going on around you without seeing the warnings of the end coming. Since the warnings are coming true, we must accept that what we are warned about will all come true. Can't you see that everything the Bible says that will happen before the end has already happened? Man is doing exactly what the Bible said he would.

You cannot be a very knowledgeable person. You cannot read or listen to what is going on in the world or read one book of the

New Testament without seeing its fulfillment and the final coming of our Lord quickly coming to pass. I ask you, do not let Satan pull the wool over your eyes. Look beyond and through his smoke screen of lies. You do not have much time to waste.

Are you ready? I mean really ready to look up and see Jesus? If there is a judgment, are you ready to be judged and to receive your just reward according to God's Word? If not, why not? It is entirely up to you. No one can believe it or do it for you. You must decide where you want to fin into God's plan and where your soul will spend its eternity. Yes, you must make the choice while you have the chance to choose.

I know there is a lot running through your mind right now. I know it is tough to accept God's Word over what Satan wants you to believe. I also know you do not believe that it is Satan causing you to believe or disbelieve. Then who is it? Who are you listening to instead of God. Ask yourself.

Who is it that is pressuring you not to accept the power or authority of God? Did he or she die for you? Does he or she love you more than you can love yourself? Then can he or she, they or it, do anything for your soul after death? If there is a hell of fire, can it, they, he or she, keep you out of it? Can anything or anyone stand before God in your place? Now you know if God's Word is true, the answers are NO.

That is why the Word beckons to come. Come try the ways of the Lord. Let Him speak heavenly peace to your soul. Let Him bestow on you the many joys and blessings of worshipping a most loving God. It says to try Him to see if He is good. Jesus wants you on His team, but He will not make you a prisoner. Look, it is His game, His rules, and we are playing on His field. Don't you want to be on the winning team?

It will be the best thing you have ever done. If not, you can always fall back into the same pit He brought you out of. If your first thoughts are not "why did I wait so long?" If the first thing you want to do is NOT to tell somebody about the love and mercy of the Lord, then you can say, "No, God is not for me. I am going to think, believe, and live the way I want." That would be your choice. But not to give God a chance would be foolish.

Food for thought: even after you are saved, God does not make you, His puppet. Yes, He does give you His love and mercy. He shares with you the joys of His blessings. He also sends you the Holy Spirit to guide and inspire you. But you still have the choice to obey His Words and ways, or do things the way you choose. God will not make you love and honor Him. He gives you the chance and the choice to do so on your own. Is that fair enough? Will sin and Satan give you that same option? Are you being fair to yourself? Are you even giving God a chance?

He has so much to offer and so great a love for you, just for the asking. What more can you expect? How much more does God have to show you? How many times does He have to call and touch your soul? Just how much more can God do and still leave the decision up to you?

Why would you shut Him out without ever knowing the goodness and mercy of His love? Why would you deprive your heart and soul of His wonders? That would be so unfair when living and serving Christ would be an improvement in every aspect of your life. It would unbind you from the ways of man and Satan, while allowing you to enjoy the many blessings of the Lord.

You owe it to yourself. You need to give God a chance to prove the truth of His Word. If not, at judgment, you have given God no choice as He proves the power and torments of His wrath. Please do not be cheated out of Paradise. Do not allow your soul to miss out on salvation from eternal damnation.

You can put your faith and trust in the Word of God, for it tells all and will stand through all. It gives you the benefits of a life with Christ, and it gives you the outcome. In it, you will find the joys and blessings of Paradise and the pain and anger of the wrath. It is all up to you. You get to pick your eternity.

You need to choose while you still have time, for this life is almost over. God is about to call for His people. Eternity is about to begin. His Kingdom and His judgment are at hand. While Jesus waits as He calls for your soul to prepare to face God or to be left behind, where mercy and grace does not abound, will you stand and praise God at the final coming of Christ? Or will you run and try to hide your face from Him? You must realize by now that it does not matter what you think or believe. You will do one or the other, so make your decision. No one else can answer for you. It is your soul that will have to pay the price, so take the time to give it some thought.

And then think again. Won't you at least give God a chance? Please ask the Holy Spirit to guide and inspire you to make the right decision. Remember, you cannot blame God if you choose to deny or to reject His Holy Word. Therefore, you cannot blame Him if you go to hell. That was your decision. Hell is real. Are you in or out?

In that great day of our Lord, in that day of no disbelief, it is the day when there is no doubt. Christ will appear in all His power and glory. Then He will call and take the born-again children of God home to forever be with Him in His heavenly Paradise.

Do not be left out and left behind. Do not let your soul face the damnation of God's wrath. Do not think there is another way. Please, for the sake of your very soul, do not let your disbelief of God's Holy Word cause that same Holy Word to condemn your soul to its eternal place of torment and torture. Do not wait until your doubts and disbeliefs are removed by the coming of the Lord and the passing of judgment. Call out for His mercy and be saved today.

As with everything I do for the Lord, let us close in prayer.

Oh, precious heavenly Father, I come to you this moment in prayer. I give thanks and praise unto thee. Lord, it is so wonderful to be able to call upon thy throne of mercy and grace. God, I pray for the lost souls of man. I pray for those who are reading this book. Lord, I ask you to touch them in a special way. Please draw them to you, O Lord.

Help them to be free from the bonds of sin and Satan. Help them to see what lies ahead if they will trust Jesus as their Savior and the result of denying to become born again. Lord, bless us all and give us the divine wisdom and strength to overcome the deception of sin and man. O God, send Jesus to knock at their heart's door one more time. Help them defeat Satan and overcome the ways of man. Lord, whatever it takes, just have your way in their lives.

Lord Jesus, I pray for all those who do not know you as their Lord and Savior. I ask for the drawing power of the Holy Spirit to be ever so strong. I hope they are never left alone. I pray that you trouble their heart and soul. God, help them to take heed to the call of Jesus. As He reaches out to their souls, do not let them have a restful moment until they answer yes to the sweet Savior. Lord God, I humbly pray that you take my efforts and this book, Lord. Use it for thy will. I could not have written it, and I did not write it, except it be through you. Therefore, Lord, I give it unto you for the up building of your Kingdom. Father, I pray that someone be touched and blessed by this book. I hope it speaks to just one lost soul. I hope it inspires someone to seek Jesus and the salvation of their soul.

Dear Jesus, bless this book in such a way that it can be used to draw souls closer to you. Let it help someone from being misled or deceived by false doctrines or hand-me-down traditions or the mere knowledge of man.

Dear God, I know this book is just a book. It is not the Bible. Man should not use it as such or muse it against the Holy Word. I did not write this book to be used instead of the Bible, nor is it to be considered as a revelation to a new word. Lord, you know I wrote this book under the inspiration and help of the Holy Spirit. Its sole purpose is to help someone find Jesus as their Savior.

O Lord, I know who and what I am, and I know that I am WHAT I am because of who you are. I am just a man saved by grace and called to preach, a man with a burden for the lost and a hunger to reach them. O God, help me. Help me to help someone along my way. There are so many, and such a need to find Christ. There is not a lot of time left. I know the end is near. Help me, O Lord, to reach as many as I can. Help me to preach and teach the

Words and ways of the gospel. I need to tell them about Jesus before it is too late.

Lord, I need your grace and mercy. Take me, O Lord. Help me to be just what you would have me to be. I want to be a better Christian and a better witness. My only prayer is to serve, honor, and worship the Lord. Give me wisdom and understanding of thy Word. Help me; show me how to rightly divine your Words of truth.

God, empower me with the Holy Ghost but keep me humble and use me for your glory. Have your way in my life that I may forever be in your grace. O Lord, bless my family and me. Keep us in the center of your will. Have your way in our lives Lord. O God, enable us to inherit that which is in heaven.

Heavenly Father, use whatever it takes to help and awake those who have grown cold. Lord, they need to realize that their fire is either weak or gone out. They need to get back on mark and rekindle the spark. Lord, without Jesus being a light in our life, without being fired up by the Holy Spirit, our souls will be forever lost and condemned. God, help us put on the whole armor of God. Oh, my Lord, help us to be better soldiers in this battle of sin.

Oh, how my heart mourns for my loved ones and friends who are lost and refuse to let Jesus come into their hearts. My heart also cries out to those who will read this book and still turn a deaf ear to the call of the Savior as He reaches out to their souls. Oh, how it must hurt Him as He watches a soul reject Him as Lord and Savior and slip over the jagged walls of death into the fiery pits of hell.

O God, help us to see your mercy and grace. Help us receive the love of Christ that caused Him to come and give His life to save our souls. Praise His holy name. We do not have to face the flames and torture of God's wrath, for we can call upon Jesus and be saved by grace. Thank you, Lord. Thank you. I just want to thank you for hearing my prayers for always being there.

Oh my god! Yes, my heart mourns for the lost. My life is sometimes troubled, but I yearn and await the call of my Lord. I want to be called up to meet Him. I want to look upon His face. I long to kneel at my Savior's feet and thank Him for His saving grace. I want to hold the nailed-scarred hand that reached down and picked me up out of my damnation. O God, I want nothing more than to meet Jesus in the air.

Lord, I give my all to you. Use it as you see fit. O Lord, I know I cannot repay all the things you have done for me. I can never praise you enough, but Lord, I do love you, and I will serve you until the day I die. Then Lord, allow me to praise and worship you throughout the ages of eternity.

God, please bless the moms and dads. Lord, show them the way and words of thee. God, help us bring up our children knowing the love and teachings of Christ. O God, do not let our children drift away from God and into the snares of Satan. Oh, precious Lord, touch mommy's and daddy's, even if they choose the path of sin and hellfire. At least let them tell their children about a man called Jesus. O God, do not let moms and dads be blamed as the souls of their own children burn in hell.

Lord, touch us all. Help us see the errors of our ways. Dear Lord, we are nothing without you. We can do nothing on our own. We need the grace of God, the salvation of Christ Jesus, the Son and the Holy Ghost to overcome the lure, temptation, and entrapment of sin. Oh my God, help us to be saved.

Father, I pray for all Christians to be blessed and led by the spirit. I pray for every lost soul to be drawn and saved by the same spirit. I also pray for all preachers who are called and are anointed by this same spirit. And God, I pray that we as mankind realize there is only one spirit that comes from God, and you must be born again of His Son to receive it. Father, help us to be saved.

Lord, I pray that my every deed and endeavor be done to glorify your holy name, so I give unto you my heart, body, soul, and mind. I want all I have and all I do to be for your honor. Therefore, I dedicate this book unto you for your use. I want no honor or fame. I want no wealth. I want only to please you.

God, I thank you for all you mean to me. I praise you for me salvation. I am truly grateful for each and every blessing you have given. Oh, my Holy Lord, I am delighted to worship and to serve and take great pride in being a child of God. But God, thank you for Jesus. And Jesus, thank you for loving me.

That is why this book means so much to me. Lord, it was your spirit that inspired and enabled me to write it, and I thank you for the opportunity and blessings it has given me. Lord God, use our Words and your book to touch and to bless. Let it serve as my witness and testimony to love, grace, and ways of my Lord.

O God, I praise your holy name. Dear God, it is an honor and a privilege to be a child of the king, just to be able to kneel and call upon your name and the throne of Jesus, for I know that you hear my prayers, and my answers are forthcoming. So, Lord, touch and save the lost. Seal and sanctify your children. Help us watch and pray and blessed by day until our Lord comes again. In His precious and holy name, I pray. Amen. Thank you, Jesus. Amen and praise God forever.

The End

Dear Readers, I truly hope you have taken the time to ask God to save you. I pray we will be able to meet in God's Holy Kingdom. If not, please do so now. Ask God to help you. Ask Jesus to come into your life. Do not deprive yourself. Do not cheat your soul out of the wonders and glories of God. You deserve better.

If you feel that you cannot find it in your heart to call upon God for the salvation of your soul, I hope that this book causes you to think about your way of life and how it fits into God's plan. At least let it spark an interest in you for the Words and will of God. Either way, I really hope that it has been an inspiring or enlightening endeavor.

I gracefully thank you for taking the time to read this book. Now I ask you to use it to help yourself get closer to the true Word of God. Let it show you how much God wants to do for you. Let it cause you to go into God's Word as you look for answers, as you look for the truth. As you seek help and wisdom, let it cause you to meet Jesus. Then let Jesus redeem you from sin and the torments of God's wrath.

If you have accepted Christ, while or after you read this book, then I rejoice with you and thank God for you. We will then be able to shout and sing the praises of victory throughout the endless ages of eternity. But until then, study the Word of God. Get into a true gospel-preaching, Bible-believing church. Let God use you as you grow in His grace.

I then ask you to hold me up in your prayers. Pray that I ever be found earnestly at the Father's Business. Ask God to help me always to be in His will, always going and doing where and what He wants and needs done. Then I will pray for you as we pray for others. May God bless and keep us in His love and grace. May He always be in our hearts, and may our souls be found in His presence. Praise God!

If you feel led to support this ministry or any of our outreach ministries, which include our jail ministry, nursing home ministry, hospital ministry, our Celebrate Recovery, or our aid to the homeless, your gift will be used to bless others, and the Lord will bless you for your offerings. We also stand in need of your prayer support. Please help us pray for the ill and down trodden or those just needing a touch from God for whatever reason. If you have a need, just let us know, and we will add you to our prayer chain that reaches across America.

Please, if this book has been a blessing to you in any way, I would love to hear from you. If I could be of help to you or someone else in living a good Christian life, you may also feel free to write. If you need answers from God's Word to questions you have about life, doctrines, traditions, or the church, I would love to help you look at what God has to say.

I will even go one step further. If you dislike or disagree with my witness and testimony of the true gospel, I want you to write to me also. I will read what you have to say, and then we will both look and see what God has to say. I do not know it all, but I am sure if we search His Word and ask His spirit, He will show us what we need to know.

www.ingramcontent.com/pod-product-compliance
Lightning Source LLC
Chambersburg PA
CBHW051529050726
47595CB00002B/422